Class talk

successful learning through
effective communication

Rosemary Sage

Continuing
Professional
Development

University of Leicester
School of Education

The Communication Opportunity Group Scheme (COGS) Manual and Video are published by the University of Leicester, UK, and the scheme is the copyright of Human Communication International, a charity that promotes effective communication. Enquiries about COGS training courses and post-graduate studies to support communication should be made to:

Dr Rosemary Sage
School of Education
University of Leicester
21 University Road
Leicester
United Kingdom
LE1 7RF
Tel: 0116 252 3669
Email: cpdinfo@le.ac.uk

Published by Network Educational Press Ltd
P O Box 635
Stafford
ST16 1BF
© Rosemary Sage 2000
ISBN 1 855 39 061 2

Editor: Gina Walker
Design: Neil Hawkins, n.hawkins@appleonline.net
Illustrations: Barking Dog Art

Printed in Great Britain by
MPG Books Ltd., Bodmin, Cornwall

Contents

"Language is the source of thought."

Alexander Luria

◆ Introduction

Class talk – what does it mean? Does it denote 'talk' uttered by a particular social group? Perhaps it implies quality of talk, or it could refer to talk in a particular place – a class in school. The words themselves are not a good guide to meaning. We need other clues. If *'class'* were uttered with a cut glass accent and given special emphasis, we might decide that quality of talk is being considered. If the phrase were used in conjunction with a classroom picture of teachers and students discussing books and pictures, we would probably have little hesitation in deciding that this 'talk' refers to spoken and written discourse in schools.

Much more than words is needed to transmit meaning. It's estimated that 93% of the effective impact of what we say is through non-verbal elements such as voice tone, facial expressions and body language. The 500 commonly used words in the English language have some 14 000 different definitions, making us totally dependent on the whole context for understanding. Successful talk brings together multiple messages from sources other than the word. These messages include not only *what* is said *where*, *when* and to *whom*, but why and *how* it is conveyed.

A child of three utters around 40 000 words a day – that is *big* talk for a little brain and body! However, once children enter school, big talk becomes small talk because *teacher* talk takes over. Children in school use roughly 20 000 words daily – the number we expect of a two year old! School seemingly spells 'disappearing talk', but word exchanges are *essential* to learning. Talking is the way we try out, select and sort ideas before stringing them together into coherent, whole notions. It is the quickest, easiest, cheapest and most efficient way of transmitting information, and without it effective learning is highly unlikely.

If 'class talk' is indeed the spoken communication that occurs in lessons, how does it compare with 'home talk', 'peer talk', 'shop talk', 'small talk', 'smart talk' or 'serious talk'? Is skill in one sort of talk needed for competence in another? What types of talk must students engage in before being able to cope with class talk? On average, teachers talk for two-thirds of class time in a monologue style that is quite foreign to many students. This could be thought of as similar to Alice's experience of Wonderland – when she fell down the rabbit hole, swam through a pool of tears, received advice from a caterpillar, popped into a mad tea party and met the King and Queen on the croquet lawn, she soon realised that the talk in Wonderland differed significantly from that she

◆ 7

was used to at home. (For example, Alice was told that 'lessons' were so-called because they *lessened* from day to day!) She found herself confused and disorientated, and unable to make any meaningful progress.

Teachers must understand their students' difficulties in stepping out of home talk into class talk and the responsibilities they have to facilitate communication for learning. *Class talk* helps readers to realise the range of issues in communication. It provides practical suggestions to facilitate successful talk between teachers and students, accompanied by discussion of the processes involved. The aim is to give teachers a helping hand on the way to 'smart talk' for themselves and their students. It is time to *talk* about these important issues!

Summary of chapters

Chapter 1 What do we learn from class talk?

This chapter looks at teacher–student communication and reflects on what is happening on the classroom 'stage'. It uses a drama model approach to consider the scenes that take place, and the actors, roles and props involved.

Chapter 2 How do students talk in different classroom situations?

One of the interesting things about talk is that it varies across context. In this chapter we look at a student's performance in five different class groups and evaluate this information for the planning of learning.

Chapter 3 Why is class talk a teacher's greatest challenge?

'Do you know, Rosie, I've spent 45 minutes explaining the Thirty Years War to the Lower Sixth and they are still none the wiser.' What are the problems of transmitting our meaning to others? Matters of self-interest, the person speaking and how information is conveyed are considered in relation to the roles of teacher and learner in the classroom situation.

Chapter 4 How can you become a top talking teacher?

Teachers have three major talk roles: to *control*, *question* and *explain*. This chapter discusses and reflects on strategies that improve the quality of talking, teaching and learning.

Chapter 5 What is non-verbal language?

The voice is a teacher's most important tool and, as such, must be properly serviced and maintained. This chapter looks at how the voice is used, along with facial expression and gesture, to make the greatest effective impact on students.

Chapter 6 How does communication happen?

This chapter looks at how communication and learning happen as a result of the way our brain develops. Systems of education are discussed in relation to this process.

Chapter 7 How can we teach communication?

Most of us grow up with the notion that talk just happens. Certainly we give it less attention than some other cultures, who consider it a subject area in its own right that is taught and developed throughout the education and training system. This final chapter considers the development of talk within a society that has moved away from mechanical and manufacturing industry towards jobs in service industries, which entail, on average, 80% speaking and listening and only 20% reading and writing.

CLASS TALK — successful learning through effective communication

Chapter 1

What do we learn from class talk?

 "The ability to express an idea is well nigh as important as the idea itself."

Bernard Baruch

'Good morning, class 3L. Today we're going to make flapjacks and then write down what happens when we mix and cook ingredients. Please turn to page 6 and find the recipe in the middle of the page.'

Above is a typical lesson introduction. It sets the learning goal and uses verbal instruction and explanation to achieve this. In schools today, we are preoccupied with outcomes, measured on standards tests and then compared in league tables. The product is everything, which draws attention away from the speaking and listening process through which knowledge is largely acquired. Talk, however, lies at the very centre of the learning process [1].

During the 1970s and 1980s there was a strong movement in education to replace the traditional 'learning by listening' with a model of 'learning through talk'. In this active approach, children come together to explore ideas, find out facts and opinions and then relate these to their own experiences. Talk with others encourages them to analyse, criticise, challenge and speculate, rather than passively listen and absorb information. It helps them become aware of what they know and what they need to know.

Interest in talk directs us to the heart of the process, deepening our appreciation of its importance and helping to organise more effective learning experiences. This is vital for teachers and students, who often experience difficulty in communicating with each other. A survey of 100 secondary school students aged between 12 and 15 years [2] put communication at the top of the list of problems they encounter in school. The ten most common themes arising from this survey are placed in rank order here:

❶ Communication with others, especially adults

❷ Being in large classes

3 Coping with a strict timetable

4 Being expected to achieve well in all subjects

5 Having no time to do what you want

6 Coping with school rules and regulations

7 Coping with homework that is not sufficiently explained

8 Coping with crowds about the place at break-times

9 Coping with teachers who have different ways

10 Not having much opportunity to mix with other years.

Although the sample for this study was minute, as only ten students were consulted in each of ten schools, the list suggests that communication is a major issue for this age group.

This chapter highlights communication by considering ways in which talk can be analysed. Ideas are used from Script Theory [3], which springs from the study of artificial intelligence in computer science. A framework is presented for observing actions in sequence to meet a learning goal. Here, the model has been adapted to focus on the context of the classroom. A 'drama' (an event with unity and progression) involves participant roles, props and actions that support and convey the meaning necessary to achieve the goal. The performance on a classroom 'stage' is represented in a script, which formats the thoughts and actions of the participants. The focus is on bringing together teachers, students and events in a time–space framework. A wider range of insights is thus possible than from the more linear, computer programme approach of Script Theory itself. Let us, the audience, sit back then, while the curtain draws to reveal the classroom characters in action!

◆ The drama and script

This school 'drama' is a cooking lesson. Participants are Tom (T) aged 7.2 years, Becca (B) who is 7.1 years, Kevin (K) aged 7.0 years and the teacher (Te). The 'stage' is a corner of a primary classroom, showing the group seated around an empty table. Opposite is the script recording the conversation exchanges.

We can see that within this whole 'act' (which continues after the end of the script shown opposite) there are several 'scenes'. These include consulting the recipe, assembling articles for cooking, weighing ingredients, mixing them, putting the mixture into a baking tin and placing it in the oven for cooking. The drama contains 'roles' – the

ACT 1 'In the classroom'

The teacher and students are at a round table. There is a large box next to the teacher, filled with cooking ingredients. Behind the group is a low shelf on which cooking equipment is stored.

1 **Te**   (*showing recipe book*) Listen everyone, we're going to make flapjacks. What do we need to collect for this?

2 **B**   Oats, flour, butter and sugar ... I think. (*Te signals K to remove the items from the box and place them on the table*)

3 **K**   The other group used syrup ... you showed them the tin. (*K takes the syrup from the box*)

4 **Te**   Yes, syrup makes flapjacks moist and sticky. Tom, what else do we need?

5 **T**   (*pause*) er ... edd. (*does he mean 'eggs'?*)

6 **Te**   You were meant to say 'baking tin' – yes?

7 **T**   Ummmmm. (*Te signals T to take the tin from the box*)

8 **Te**   Now ... what else do we need? (*pause, then ...*)

9 **T**   Ho-ou-dere (*hot out there*)

10 **Te**   Hot out there (*over articulated*). I know ... but we're thinking about cooking now.

11 **B**   We need a bowl. (*B spontaneously removes one from the shelf and places it on the table*)

12 **Te**   We also want a pan to warm the syrup. Tom, get the pan, please? (*T looks out of the window and does not respond*)

13 **Te**   Tom, you must listen. Get the pan off the shelf. Bring it to the table, please? (*T looks puzzled and turns to B, who gets the pan for him*)

14 **Te**   Now, Tom, what goes into the pan?

15 **T**   Sm duff. (*some stuff*)

16 **Te**   Some stuff, yes, yes, we know, but what? (*impatient tone to voice*)

17 **B**   The butter warmed with syrup and then add oats.

18 **K**   Can I do that, Miss?

19 **Te**   What must we do first?

20 **K**   Weigh 'em out. Put 'em in the bowl.

21 **B**   I've got the recipe. I'll read it and Kevin'll weigh. Tom can mix ...

22 **K**   Right, let's get going ...

teacher and students. There are also 'props', which include the table, cooking ingredients and utensils. Essentials of this cooking drama are the:

❶	Goal	teaching the students to cook flapjacks and understand the science involved
❷	Script	representing the activity through ideas expressed in words
❸	Actors	participating students and teacher
❹	Stage	corner of a primary school classroom
❺	Props	table, weighing scales, bowl, two spoons, pan, baking tin, oats, flour, butter, syrup and the recipe
❻	Actions	discussing the cooking, assembling items, weighing goods, mixing ingredients, placing the mixture in the baking tin, putting the tin in the oven to cook.

Let us spotlight some of the essentials in the drama in order to understand the action.

◆ Actors and roles

All events have 'actors', who are individuals taking on roles in the activity. The actor role is independent of the person playing it. This means a 'student' is a role. However, it is only valid within the structure of the event, so when the event is completed an individual is free to leave and take on another role in a new setting. This happens when students leave class and join their peers in the playground, entering a different situation with roles appropriate for what is taking place.

Actor roles are revealed not only by what individuals do but what they wear. In this example, all three students wore aprons for cooking. In a swimming lesson, swimsuits help define the role of 'swimmer'.

Within specific events, verbal expressions go with roles. In the cooking lesson, the teacher reinforces her role as organiser and imparter of knowledge by her initial command, 'Listen everyone', so gaining attention for the task ahead. Furthermore, the parts people play are tied to 'role motives'. If we know an actor is a teacher, suppositions are made about her within other events. We expect her to arrange what goes on and instruct others. A similar assumption is made about Tom, who establishes a sub-role as a poor communicator in the cooking activity. Teacher actions (at points **6**, **10** and **16** in the script above) reinforce his inadequacies by re-stating and rephrasing his responses, and this seems to produce an inhibitory effect. Later in the event, the teacher asks about the next lesson, as described below.

Te	Tom, who is going with you to COGS? (*the Communication Opportunity Group Scheme*)
T	Mark and Anna.
Te	Mark and Anna.

The teacher echoes an utterance which has perfectly clear meaning, so signalling Tom's incompetence, even though his message is explicit in this instance. We see that Tom's subsidiary role as a poor communicator, established in one event, becomes assumed in another.

There are roles set by the event (teacher and learners) and others that arise as a result of the interaction. Tom has a primary role as learner but his actions reveal he is less able at this in comparison with Becca and Kevin. The result is that they assume a controlling role while Tom concedes to a submitting one. Thus, some roles are fixed while others may change.

Although Becca is in the learner role, she adopts an instructor role (**21** in the last scene of the script on page 13), taking on the teacher's task and organising the other students for the task of mixing the flapjacks. Hence, the fixed role may have others mapped onto it, as a result of what happens in events, so making communicative interactions very complex. This indicates that, for a child in class, roles and goals at certain times may move away from the student's primary role as 'seeker of knowledge'. So, motivation to learn may fluctuate because of the social dynamics of the experience.

TEACHING TIP: Give students opportunities to work in different groups, which should encourage them to take on different roles in each task.

◆ Stage

Events are staged in an 'arena', which places the action in time and space. Achievement of the learning goal depends on everyone working together to use the space effectively. The teacher role demands a position in the room where everyone can view him. This means the he must take up a central spot in the group with students around or in front of him, but he needs to move around the whole space at certain times, to connect with everyone and maintain their participation.

Usually, there is some distance between the person in charge of action and the others, so establishing an understanding of the group dynamics. In the classroom context, the teacher is the leader and the students are the followers. To preserve cohesion, there must be acknowledgement that all participants 'own' the space directly around them. If these boundaries are not respected, there will be problems in interacting freely in a relaxed manner. Can you recall students who crowd together, getting on each other's nerves and eventually ending up fighting? The preservation of personal space is vital for ensuring good group behaviour and this aspect needs to be monitored. Some students react badly to being confined in small areas for long periods.

Obviously, in the cooking activity, all participants need space to carry out their tasks easily. They have to be arranged so that each can view what is going on and learn what to do. Students must recognise the space assigned to them. Roles, status and gender will influence their position in the group. With regard to cooking, a girl might see herself as taking charge because food preparation is a 'female task' in her particular home. She will expect to be near the action, therefore, with the boys taking minor roles in a more distant position.

Time, as well as space, boundaries must be defined and monitored to help students act out the drama and achieve the learning goal effectively. It is necessary to gauge how long each action will take to achieve the overall goal. This depends on a concept of time management, with a top-down and bottom-up appraisal that grasps the whole event and understands how it is broken down into component parts within the framework. Participants will come to the activity with greater or lesser understanding of this dimension. In order to gain co-operative action towards the goal, the leading role player (the teacher) has to make the time and space boundaries clear to everyone. In the cooking lesson described on page 13, the teacher attempts this with the students, ensuring they know what is involved before the task begins, by saying *'What do we need to collect for this?'* This could have been clarified further if the teacher had explained that they need to spend 10 minutes mixing ingredients and 20 minutes cooking them, indicating the whole process takes half an hour. Using a clock to demonstrate helps visualise information while reinforcing the spoken words.

TEACHING TIP: Move position within the lesson, to allow all students to have close contact with the teacher at some point.

TEACHING TIP: State the goal, the steps to reach this goal and the timing involved, so the whole task and how it is achieved is understood.

◆ Props

In activity-based dramas, props are essential. It would be impossible to carry out cooking without ingredients and utensils. The relationships between roles and props quickly become established, removing the need to remark on them in normal conversations. The information is known and shared, so there is no reason for Becca (**21** on page 13) to articulate *'recipe'* and *'on the scales'* in her statement: *'I'll read it and Kevin will weigh.'* Thus, the props carry much of the meaning of an event and make words redundant.

Experience suggests that props are crucial for students having problems with language exchanges, as they reduce the information-carrying load of words. As 'here and gone' phenomena, spoken words do not allow people much time for information processing. Props, however, provide solid images, encouraging communication to revolve around them, rather than relying on the abstract ideas of words.

Events reveal that some props belong to certain people. The black- or white-board on the classroom wall is viewed as belonging mainly to the teacher, whereas the books and papers on the desks or tables are the property of particular students. Views about ownership, therefore, constrain how props are used in an activity.

◆ Actions

Actors carry out a series of actions to meet goals within an event. In the cooking activity these involve consulting the recipe, collecting food and utensils, weighing items, mixing ingredients, putting the mixture in a baking tin and placing it in the oven for cooking. Although these operations belong to the actor, they are a series of sequential behaviours determined by the demands of the situation. One cannot cook flapjacks until the ingredients have been mixed and placed in an appropriate tin. Such acts may be viewed as 'plans', which must be executed in strict time sequence to achieve the ultimate goal – those tasty treats!

 TEACHING TIP: Back up words with pictures and objects (props) as much as possible, to reinforce information and enable meaning to be transmitted successfully.

After reviewing the recipe, the first 'plan' is to collect articles for cooking flapjacks. This necessitates knowing where the items are, locating them among others and taking control by extracting them from their present position.

The *use* plan – the transfer of objects, which involves both physical and mental concepts – occurs continually throughout the activity. Many actions require a change of position, so involving a basic plan of how and where to move something. There is a crucial element of transfer. The cooking activity requires an established concept of *physical* transfer, demanding a knowledge and control of objects from one place to another, as well as *abstract* transfer of ownership. This is seen when Becca locates the mixing bowl, places it on the table and then passes it to Tom for the blending task. We can also find examples of *mental* transfer, when the teacher indicates that the children need a pan for warming the butter and syrup and tells them that the pan is on the shelf. At this point, it is the information about the pan, rather than the actual object, that is transferred.

The tasks in the cooking event have an evaluative dimension. Using positive or negative mental judgements, decisions are made as to whether the mixture is adequately combined, correctly pressed into the baking tin and properly cooked for eating. The evaluation is global in relation to the goal but particular to parts of the event as well.

When considering the actions of a particular person in the event, the role they play is crucial. The teacher, for example, has the instructor role and her speech actions confirm this in the range of moves she makes:

- ◆ opening   (*'Listen everyone …'*)
- ◆ focusing   (*'What do we need … ?'*)
- ◆ framing   (*'Now, Tom, what goes into the pan?'*)
- ◆ answering   (*'Syrup makes flapjacks moist …'*)
- ◆ following up   (*'We also want a pan …'*)

In her leadership role, the teacher expects to control action. She asks the questions, nominating turns and tasks with stereotypical expressions: *'Now, Tom, what goes into the pan?'* Within class events, teachers often say things like: *'Take your hands away from your mouth'* (heard later in the activity), which in other contexts might be considered the height of bad manners but is acceptable in an instructional role. This aspect may prove difficult for students who have autistic spectrum disorders, which interfere with learning social conventions. For example, a boy once told a teacher to change her clothes as she looked like a tart! He had heard similar comments from teachers but had not observed the rule that students are not expected to make this sort of utterance!

In class roles, students are usually required to use non-verbal signals (for example, putting up their hand), as well as words, in order to request attention. They often have to ask permission to enter teacher space, but the reverse is unlikely to occur. Language use, therefore, depends entirely on the role or roles played by each participant in an event. This makes communication an extremely complex process to analyse and facilitate. No wonder we make it a side issue in schools!

In bringing these ideas together, we can identify an underlying structure to classroom talk using the essentials described above. Events can be viewed as particular dramas on a class stage, with actors, props and actions to meet the goal. Once teachers and students have experienced such an activity, and seen it repeated, a basic mental schema is developed and stored in memory.

However, moving into other contexts necessitates the development of variants to this model. A change of situation may include a different social dynamic, with a student in charge of the group cooking activity, for example, or perhaps involving another method of making flapjacks. Thus, the form of many events is language and context specific, providing a source of potential shock and confusion for those who have problems making transfers across situations. Tom, in this example, could be at risk, as he clearly has difficulties in responding adequately within the demands of the cooking lesson. He is a student who needs specific monitoring, to clarify whether a lack of language knowledge and communication skill is preventing learning.

TEACHING TIP: Regularly review plans, so that students can begin to grasp the components of a task and the steps towards the goal.

◆ Dramas and memory

Previous observations in this chapter have focused on basic essentials in communication. The conclusion drawn is that our ability to handle a new encounter depends on a memory of past plans for achieving goals. Without this established 'script of events' it would be impossible to interpret many ordinary exchanges. Take the teacher's first move on page 13: *'Listen everyone, we're going to make flapjacks. What do we need to collect for this?'* An appropriate response requires knowing about what is involved in cooking. This means that actors must be able to generalise knowledge from a wide experience of communication situations in order to carry out their roles. Schank and Abelson [3] suggested that activities are hierarchically organised in memory. They call these **memory organisation packets** or MOPs for short. MOPs are a way of grouping individual events into broad categories. Here is a MOP for mixing ingredients.

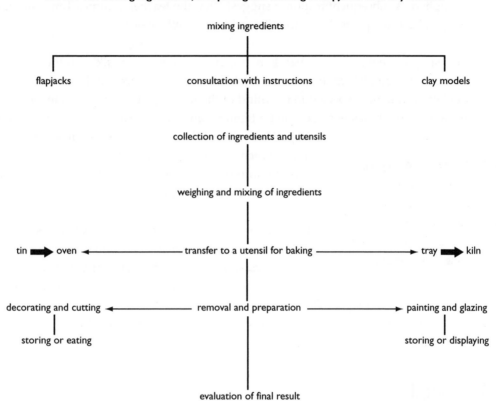

A MOP for mixing ingredients, comparing the making of flapjacks with clay models

This means that any event could inherit aspects from a more general representation. From the cooking task, we might transfer knowledge of weighing and mixing food ingredients to combining clay mixtures for model making. A MOP for mixing ingredients indicates the similarities and differences between the two events. Schank [4] discussed two types of memory, which suggest mapping of one MOP onto another:

◆ general event memory – such as a visit to the hairdressers
◆ situation memory – retaining actions common to many experiences, as in paying the bill.

We have already noted that the roles people play within an event call for them to use stereotypical language. Teachers, in their role of helping children learn, use 'display questions' [5], to check that students have grasped the lesson content, or have the necessary background for understanding new material. This is demonstrated in the first teacher move on page 00: *'What do we need to collect ... ?'* A series of questions erects 'a scaffold', to help the student arrive at solutions and build appropriate spoken responses [6].

Therefore, a learner must not only be able to build scripts from general events and situation memory, but must determine how talk may or may not generalise. For example, consider the incident in the cooking activity when the teacher says *'Tom, get the pan, please?'* Tom does not respond. Perhaps he is unable to generalise from past experience and guess that the word 'get' (obtain) generally carries the message of transfer from one place to another. The meaning is not directly explicit in the word but is implied. A subsequent response suggests that the teacher assumes Tom cannot locate the pan, as she repeats the instruction, adding *'… off the shelf'*.

This simple event shows us that there is a great deal more to talk than the words uttered in the exchanges. When the plan is violated because Tom does nothing, there is a deviation from the expected in the mind of the teacher, triggering an emotional response. She shows her vexation by telling Tom to listen. Her tone of voice reflects impatience. Dyer [7] called this a **thematic affect unit** or TAU, which refers to the emotional responses that are brought into play as a result of events, and triggered by memories of previous experiences of similar situations.

TEACHING TIP: Regularly compare similar experiences, so students can build links between knowledge structures and learn to cope with changes of situation.

Scripts, therefore, representing events, direct us to generic outlines in memory. When a new situation is encountered we understand much of what will happen based on general event memory. We know what props are involved and the roles that will be played. This is the reason why each communicative situation is played in our own style as we know it. It explains how we might respond to events based on our past experiences and helps us understand our own as well as student behaviour.

◆ Comment

This analysis of classroom talk attempts to characterise the knowledge we have of the structure of stereotypical event sequences, such as cooking, and how this is used as the 'hook' on which to 'hang' new learning. Scripts format this knowledge in mental schemas, which may be represented in a verbal transcription of the event to provide evidence of how people process and produce language in ordinary situations. This is a way of letting us view such an activity, emphasising the thinking, language and social issues that underpin communication for learning. However, the analysis does not elucidate the message transactions between participants, which involve aspects of **clarity** (performance), **content** (topic knowledge), **conduct** (behaviour, indicating self-esteem) and **convention** (rules for the exchange). These elements are presented in later chapters, in order to describe the personal and social issues in communication that influence individual and interactive behaviours. A quick glimpse of these factors is all that is allowed at this juncture!

The use of Script Theory, in this drama approach to classroom talk, helps us to focus on the unity and progression of the discourse and the way it influences participants. Children learn not only how to play the student role in class events, but also how to play roles of gender and conduct. The conduct role refers to the behaviour exhibited by participants, by which they are judged. Think about Tom. Responses suggest that he is regarded as a poor communicator (**6, 7, 8, 10, 11, 12, 13, 14, 16, 21** on page 13). The teacher reinforces the notion, unwittingly, by re-stating and re-phrasing his contributions and displaying a natural impatience when he responds inappropriately. Tom augments this view by refusing to answer a question and carry out a request. This may be because he was not paying attention or could not process the information successfully.

A more detailed look at responses in a language and thinking test, described in Chapter 7 and Appendix 5, confirms Tom's problems in bringing together the verbal, visual, spatial and affective information that is necessary to fully understand communicative exchanges. He demonstrates ability to take a turn, but does not show the range of conversational moves expected, such as making requests, asking questions, providing contributions and making maintenance comments. These moves would indicate an ability to thread together the meaning of an event, which is necessary for the development of MOPs. The fact that Tom does not provide this evidence, reinforced by his performance in some other contexts, suggests he is a child at risk of failing academically. His peers, Becca and Kevin, display skills of collaborative talk (**21, 22**) and appear more successful learners.

The cooking lesson, however, involves a mixed ability group with an adult present; when Tom was observed in a pair, with a boy of similar performance, he showed a greater range of communicative conventions and the beginnings of collaborative talk. This emphasises the importance of the ways in which classroom activities are organised. Activities may be carried out in a large class group, with the teacher in control, or in smaller groups of either mixed or similar ability, which encourage more active roles for students. We look at Tom in a number of these situations in Chapter 2.

As children switch groups, they may find themselves changing roles, each requiring a different use of language and behaviour. Primary roles are set in each individual activity and if there is refusal to carry these out appropriately, personal and social esteem is affected, bringing feelings of failure that are remembered by those participating. Experience demonstrates that established views follow students into their new settings. Therefore, a subsidiary role, such as that of poor communicator, could influence the primary role and alter motives and goals. Toms role as learner may be thwarted by his assuming the secondary role of poor communicator. He could come to think that he is unable to carry out his job as learner, because he fails to communicate adequately. This notion can be compounded by others, so that a new role as 'non-learner' develops and changes the original goal of academic success into failure.

Thus, the study of scripts and events leads us to reflect on how social communication is learned and to focus on the importance of a secure knowledge of sequential activities that includes location, space, time, roles, actions, props and the use of stereotyped utterances. What dramas do young children practise? You may see them playing, when given the opportunity, at cleaning the house, shopping, cooking, washing, ironing, going to the doctors, and acting out school. Do they use the correct words, with appropriate voice dynamics of pitch, pace, pause, power and pronunciation to convey their meanings? Do they demonstrate the facial expressions, feelings, postures and gestures

21

CLASS TALK — successful learning through effective communication

that go with the role? Do they show whole or partial knowledge of activities? In a shopping game, for example, Tom ordered a chocolate wagon wheel, accepted it with thanks and began to eat it. Why did he forget to hand over money for payment? Was it because he had not learned the full script for this event?

Such analyses encourage us to think about the teaching approaches for talk that lead to successful learning. They suggest that contextual approaches based on real situations are likely to be effective. It is possible to locate certain basic behaviours – such as greetings, asking for something, expressing feelings and needs – and reflect on how they might be linked at home and at school. Adults are seen to coach, model and specifically teach the language needed for certain activities. We see this when a child is given a toy phone and instructed to 'Say hello to Mummy'. This is generalised in real situations. You may have witnessed teachers in nursery or infant schools asking children to 'Say goodbye to Dad', as parents leave the classroom.

Therefore, it appears natural to prepare children by coaching the right behaviour in their normal activities at home and in school. With those who have difficulties in taking part in the words and actions of normal events, it may be useful to provide grouped scripts so they discover, by comparison, how components are generalised. This can be done in role plays, in which students could consider how to greet their mother, brother, teacher or a stranger, for example. Constantly highlighting similarities and differences between events helps children to become aware of communication structures and how certain elements transfer. They need this direct approach to become competent speakers and writers.

Previous discussions in this chapter reinforce the authenticity of roles, props, actions and language as crucial to successful learning. However, since the conventional roles and relationships of events are 'givens' (for example, the roles of teacher and students) it is easy to ignore them. If the event is about collecting items for school work and the dialogue shows Tom going into *the* class, opening *the* drawer and taking out *the* pencil and *the* paper, we are likely to think that the reason why the definite article 'the' is used is because they are all 'assumed' in this situation. Schools have classes, classes have drawers and drawers have items in them; all these are 'givens'. Hence, a strong link is made between events and grammar, and between events and materials. The drama approach, used in this analysis, provides a system for looking at what can happen to language and action across events. We can then discover which events are more universal and which are context and language specific.

By comparing events and errors made in communicative exchanges, we are better equipped to deal with individual student problems in learning, as the analyses tune into the changing pattern of activities through which a child progresses from home to school.

A number of educators, in the past, have expressed concern about the home–school mismatch of events for teaching and learning [8]. This leads us to consider how home and school styles can be made compatible. Phillips [9, 10] pointed out that children are more relaxed and talkative in school interactions without the teacher, because these more closely match how learning is done at home: by observation, listening, supervised participation and self-testing. The more controlled environment of school, with teachers instructing in a monologue for a large part of the time, encourages passive learning in contrast to the active styles children are used to at home.

In life, we switch roles repeatedly (for example, from student to teacher), and our perception of situations, our roles and the motives of the actors shifts constantly. Education, training and experience of people in different contexts and cultures affects the details and the ways in which they play events. Once we become parents, for example, and participate in the education of our own children, we change our views about instruction. Thus, we evolve a personal style for playing roles in response to our experiences with them. A clash in style between parent and teacher instruction may sabotage successful learning. I remember using a white card under a line of words, to help my daughter develop eye movements across the page while she was reading. The orthoptist advised this to help her overcome her squint, but the teacher was against this limiting approach to text. Reading became fraught and learning suffered!

To summarise the discussion, a drama approach allows us to look inside the communication system of a classroom and understand the way we structure events for the purpose of meeting learning goals. The analyses reveal that goals can become deflected as a result of the personal and context dynamics of the exchange. Understanding what can and does happen encourages us to take measures that will ensure talk is facilitated for successful teaching and learning. For the teacher, this means taking a close look at student conversations and understanding children's needs for smaller group talk. In addition, teachers must talk so that students can listen and understand easily and eagerly. The next chapter continues with this vital exploration towards our goal of successful classroom talk by looking at Tom in a number of different talking situations.

Summary Points

♦ 'Class talk' is a series of events in which the fixed roles of teacher and student have others mapped onto them, which may help or hinder the learning goal.

♦ Aspects of location and time–space, as well as props used in the discourse, are as important as the actual words spoken in defining the action and conveying meaning.

♦ Ideas about memory organisation packets (MOPS) help us to understand how we apply our knowledge of events through the use of general and specific scripts.

♦ Talk helps us to clarify our feelings and thoughts. Students need opportunities to communicate in the classroom so that they can work out what they think before having to organise this knowledge in writing.

Chapter 2

How do students talk in different classroom situations?

"In order to succeed, double your failure rate."

Thomas Watson

Teachers and students dive in and out of various communication situations during the course of a school day. If we look closely at these, it is possible to observe different levels of behaviour among students. Take the case of Tom, mentioned in Chapter 1. He appeared to have some problems with communication in the cooking lesson (page 13). We marked him out as a student who needed careful monitoring. Let us be a 'fly on the wall' and buzz quietly around some of the activities Tom is involved in over a school day. It has been possible to spy silently on five class groups and the conversations are transcribed for us to review. The names are changed and the transcripts have been taken from classroom tape recordings.

Situation A: Tom plus the teacher

The teacher begins the conversation with closed questions, and Tom shows no inclination to expand on 'yes/no' responses (**1, 2** on page 26). As the talk progresses, a 'maintenance move' by the teacher to encourage and facilitate a fuller response has little effect (**7**). It appears that she is asking what happened in the play, from her next response (**5**), but Tom misinterprets the teacher's question at point **3** and responds by stating one of his own activities (**4**). Is this a deliberate withdrawal strategy and an attempt to control autonomy, a problem with the use of the reference term 'you', or an example of inadequate information processing? Tom's later responses (**10, 12**) support the notion of deliberate withdrawal. In terms of Grice's principles of effective communication [1], Tom is violating principles of **quality** (limited ideas), **quantity** (inadequate replies), **relevance** (responses **10** and **12** are not appropriate) and **manner** (unclear messages). This would not present a 'positive face' to others, which is another important issue in interpersonal exchanges. 'Face' is described by Adler and co-workers [2] as the social value claimed by someone in an encounter. Effective communication only occurs when the face of the participants is preserved so that they can appreciate

25

The teacher has been on sick leave and is catching up with Tom on what has been going on.

1 **Te**	Tom, did you do a little play in the Communication Opportunity Group about 'Allies and Aliens'?
2 **T**	Yep.
3 **Te**	What did you do in the play?
4 **T**	Stood behind the Chief Ally.
5 **Te**	Stood behind the chief – but what happened in the play?
6 **T**	Allies won.
7 **Te**	Did they – the Allies won?
8 **T**	Yep.
9 **Te**	Did you show it to the other children?
10 **T**	We lay down dead.
11 **Te**	Did the other children in our class see your 'Allies and Aliens' play?
12 **T**	I shot the Aliens – bang, bang!
13 **Te**	What did the others watching think about your play?
14 **T**	Dunnow.

each other. Constructs of **charity** (acknowledging others' points of view), **rationalisation** (providing good reasons for behaviour) as well as **truth** and **trust** (adjusting views to suit the occasion) are important factors in achieving successful talk. Although these theories provide different frameworks for viewing successful or unsuccessful communication, there is considerable overlap in the components. They provide insight and a possible method of judging talk between people.

◆ Situation B: Tom and Matt (student of similar communication ability)

Tom takes the initiative in this exchange when partnered with a boy of similar communication ability. The conversation goes well with both boys contributing ideas, expressing feelings (**4**, opposite), expanding information (**5, 7, 9**) and picking up on each other's comments. Limitations in grammatical structure are evident. Tom uses the present tense when a past is appropriate (**3**) and does not yet use full verb completions, omitting 'can' and 'will' in response **9**. This demonstrates, however, that explicit grammar is not always necessary for communication. Since Tom and Matt use language forms at a similar level there appears to be no embarrassment or concern over this

Tom and Matt are looking at some photographs of the 'Allies and Aliens' play.

1 T	That's me. I got two guns.
2 M	Mine's big.
3 T	Look! I shoot the Aliens dead. Bang, bang! (*imitates – with a great deal of noise*)
4 M	I like your Ally mask.
5 T	Belongs to Luke, Ms Sage's big boy.
6 M	I like dressing up and acting out.
7 T	Yeah. Ms Sage says we can make a play of 'Cops and Robbers'. We can have a big Chief Cop.
8 M	Mr Barker's (*school caretaker*) got big boots. The Chief Cop borrow 'em.
9 T	Yeah. We ask if he let us. We ask at dinner.
10 M	Pop Brian (*grandfather*) has big, black boots – steel caps. We get 'em Saturday.

aspect. Tom shows ability to follow principles of communication in this context. What he says is relevant and contributes to the development of the ideas. The quality and quantity of talk is appropriate and positive face is displayed in a spirit of charity and trust between speakers.

This example may suggest the utility of grouping students of like ability for certain activities, especially those that target thinking and talking that will lead into writing/recording tasks. Children benefit enormously from having the opportunity to sort out ideas first in words before having to commit these to a written format. Westby [3], among others, alerted us to the importance of narrative (the structuring of spoken or written events) as the primary mode of thinking and makes a strong argument that cognitive development is governed more by this than by the abstract processes described by Piaget [4] and Vygotsky [5].

Verbal exchanges provide the format for narrative and the means by which children learn to string ideas together. In recent years there has been much interest in the shift from talk to text communication. The fact that children are struggling to write coherently is strong evidence of limited ability in narrative discourse. More speaking opportunities would help remedy this problem.

◆ Situation C: Tom with teacher and Richard (student of different ability)

Tom, Richard and the teacher are looking at photographs of the 'Allies and Aliens' play.

1 **Te**	Tell me about these pictures, Tom.
2 **T**	Dunnow.
3 **R**	Our play, 'Allies and Aliens'.
4 **Te**	The play looks really good. Tell me about it, Tom.
5 **T**	Err – yes.
6 **R**	The Aliens stole the Allies' computer. We had to get it back. Look! Dan's dressed up as a computer. We painted the box on his head to look like a screen. Mum got it at Asda.
7 **Te**	Tom, you look very important in your green costume. Who are you guarding?
8 **T**	Ummmm.
9 **R**	He was the chief Alien's bodyguard. He has a laser gun and shot the Aliens. Bang!
10 **T**	K-K-K-f-l-a-s-h dead!
11 **Te**	You all look as though you enjoyed playing 'Allies and Aliens'.
12 **R**	We did, we did. It was good!

The teacher takes the lead in this exchange asking open questions (**1, 4**, above) and inviting Tom to remark on the play photographs. Tom appears unwilling to respond in this context (**2, 5, 8**), although the previous example suggests he is able to do this competently. In this situation, Tom withdraws from the dialogue and allows Richard to answer (**3, 6, 9, 12**). On one occasion, Tom makes a contributory comment (**10**) in response to Richard's statement about shooting the Aliens. Although signalling a willingness to take a turn, the remark does not initiate a new idea. Tom appears to be violating principles of quantity, quality, relevance and manner in this sample. He generally presents a negative face and aspects of charity, rationalisation, truth and trust are not adhered to firmly.

◆ Situation D: Tom with Matt and Dan (two students of similar ability)

The children are sorting out some dressing up clothes.

1 **M**   Look! Here's a Batman mask.

2 **T**   (*takes the mask and puts it on*) Look out, Batman's here.
Wheeeee–whizzzzzz.

3 **D**   Here's a shiny cloak. Put it on. (*turns to Tom*)

4 **T**   (*puts everything on*) Me, Batman, wheeeee – I'm away ...
wheeee–whizzzz–whooosh. Are there things for under?

5 **D**   Here, wait. Red tights.

6 **M**   And a T-shirt and here's a belt.

7 **T**   (*puts everything on*) Me, Batman, wheeeee – I'm away ...
wheeee–whizzzz–whooosh. Who's going to be Robin?

8 **M**   Me, me, meeeeee ... (*very urgent tones*)

9 **T**   Find some clothes. Get going ...
wheeeeee–whizzzzz–whooooosh–woooooooooooooooo.

10 **D**   What about me?

Tom co-operates fully in the dialogue (**2**, above) and takes on the ideas of the others with enthusiasm (**2, 4, 7**). He shows initiative by asking his own questions (**4, 9**). There is a tendency to perseverate responses (**2, 4, 7, 9**), which is a pattern of children showing difficulties with language, demonstrating problems in changing a mental set in response to new stimuli. He is able to take on the comments of others, however, and build on them with suggestions (**4, 9**). Tom is using principles of effective communication in this environment.

◆ Situation E: Tom and the whole class in discussion with the teacher

In the large class group, Tom opts out (**7, 9, 11**, on page 30) showing a persistent non co-operative response even though he has demonstrated an interest in drama activities (the subject under discussion) in other contexts. The teacher's strategy to involve and encourage participation is unsuccessful (**6**) and she resorts to a didactic approach (**8**). In this context Tom could be considered as violating communication principles of quantity, quality, relevance and face. He certainly demonstrates little charity, rationalisation, truth and trust in the way he responds. There is a complete clamp down of his communication here. Does Tom feel under threat in this context?

The class are talking about drama sessions. Lindy, Ben, Kevin and Tom are talking in this episode.

1 **Te**	Ms Sage comes today. Can you remember how she said she was going to arrive?
2 **L**	A cat! A cat!
3 **B**	With an injured paw ... yes ...
4 **Te**	Yes, that's right.
5 **K**	We're going to help her. Can I go?
6 **Te**	We're all going to have a chance to help the cat – some this week, some next. Tom, the cat was your idea. Are you going this week?
7 **T**	*(averts gaze, and says nothing – silence!)*
8 **Te**	Tom you go this week with Matt, Richard, Kevin, Jim, Mark, Ben, Melanie, Frankie, Shula and Lizzie. Tom, collect some props from the dressing up box.
9 **T**	*(sits and does not move – looks out of the window as if he is not listening)*
10 **Te**	What do you think the cat will need?
11 **T**	Dunnow.
12 **B**	A saucer, some milk.
13 **K**	Something to play with ...
14 **L**	A ball, a little squashy ball, I think ...

◆ Communication situations

It is possible to plot the facilitating and inhibiting factors within the five scenes described above, in order to look at the situations in which Tom responds most positively.

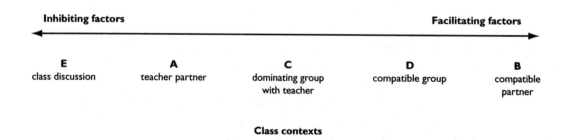

Inhibiting factors   Facilitating factors

E	**A**	**C**	**D**	**B**
class discussion	teacher partner	dominating group with teacher	compatible group	compatible partner

Class contexts

This does not mean that Tom should never be placed in situations A or E. The determining factors for the teacher in deciding which contexts to deploy will depend on objectives for each teaching session. When the aim is to stimulate intellectual development or allow individuals to listen to others exchanging ideas, A and E are entirely appropriate as they give opportunity for students to hear a level of thinking and discourse that is beyond their ability. It provides a goal, a challenge and appropriate models of talk for learning. If, however, the objective is to allow students opportunities to develop spoken language and learn effectively through their own talk, in order to initiate some writing activity, contexts B and D are likely to be the most beneficial to someone like Tom. Here, he is not intimidated by others who are more able at thinking, understanding and expressing themselves and he feels relaxed enough to talk freely.

TEACHING TIP: Think about the teaching *goal* before pairing and grouping students for tasks.

Observation of students has shown that they converse more easily when involved in physical activity, such as sorting photographs and dressing up clothes. It is possible that 'hands on' experience is essential to developing thinking if students have difficulties in processing verbal and/or visual information. Smith [6] quoted from information processing studies suggesting population preferences for learning:

◆ 27% through the visual mode

◆ 24% through the verbal/sound channels

◆ 37% through touch and movement (tactile and kinaesthetic input).

This third mode is less abstract than two-dimensional visual input or transitory verbal/sound information. Unfortunately, school emphasises verbal and visual learning styles and is probably the main reason why some students fail in this context. When they go into jobs, however, they become successful workers because they can process better from real experience.

The five examples discussed above provide information about successful and unsuccessful communication situations. Tom demonstrates violation of the principles of effective communication in some events but not in others. The fact that this did not happen consistently across contexts suggests that it is not always lack of skill that prevents interpersonal exchanges but possibly the fact that partners remember previous difficulties and, therefore, adopt a more didactic stance. Examples of this are shown at points **5** and **11** in situation A (page 26); at **3, 6** and **9** in situation C (page 28); and at **6** and **8** in situation E (page 30). This established perception may be difficult to alter and is liable to restrict communication opportunities.

Tom shows systematic withdrawal strategies in certain communicative contexts and was labelled by his teacher as unco-operative. Such behaviour is not just an individual phenomenon but extends into the social environment, which may keep it from

31

extinction long after any initial cause has been removed. This issue is complex, demonstrating that difficulties in communication are clarified as being both individual and socially interactive. Therefore, students need careful and constant monitoring to observe what happens when the social dynamic changes. Unfortunately, students who withdraw without giving the teacher overt problems tend to be ignored in favour of those who annoy and misbehave. It is very easy for some students to go through school with very little chance to talk. Their learning and self-esteem will be low and we ignore such students at our, and their, peril.

◆ Conversation moves

So what are the important observations a teacher needs to make about students' class talk? The following checklist is a useful guide to the conversational skills that need to be in place before we can expect students to follow the monologues of teacher instruction and narrative text.

Checklist of five conversation moves

Can the student:

1 answer a closed 'what, who, where, when' question demanding a specific response?

2 contribute an idea (even if not entirely appropriate), showing turn-taking ability?

3 listen and demonstrate maintenance moves (such as eye contact for 75% of time, smiling, nodding)?

4 answer an open 'how' or 'why' question demanding an explanation?

5 initiate a new idea in conversation that fits in with the topic under discussion?

If moves 3–5 are in place, this indicates that a student has the basic skills to follow either a spoken or written narrative situation. Attention in listening (move 3), with a forward posture and maintained eye contact suggests concentration and co-operation in information exchanges. If attention wanders it is a sure sign that the listener is bored, or finds the information presented in an unhelpful way or above their level of discourse. Answering open questions (move 4) demands an ability to express cause and effect and link events: '*Shakila, why are you wearing your coat today?*', '*I'm wearing it because it looks as though it might rain shortly.*' This skill in linking events clearly is the base for putting together a narrative discourse structure in a chunk of talk or text. Initiating a new idea (move 5) shows an ability to connect ideas logically within the overall theme. It demands an overview of the situation and an understanding of the parts that fit together to make a whole. This 'top-down' and 'bottom-up' process is necessary in most academic activities.

Think of the reading process. Getting the gist of the story is a 'top-down' process, as is asking students to tell or write a report on a specific topic. The task requires students to narrow the topic through a variety of stages so that eventually they can present general points along with supporting details.

Phonics, however, is primarily a 'bottom-up' process. It requires a focus on details. Students must be able to synthesise sounds (phonemes) into whole words. 'Bottom-up processing' can proceed from the concrete to the abstract (reading a story and retelling it) or vice versa as in building sounds into words. It is analogous to inductive thinking, which gathers information until a general conclusion can be drawn from the accumulated, individual details. 'Top-down processing' equates to deductive thinking, in which the general pattern is sought and the details are only used to check out the general hypothesis formed.

TEACHING TIP: Help students to become aware of conversation. Set up a role play, or show a video of talking, and get them to observe what happens – people taking turns, asking questions, introducing and developing ideas, looking at each other and encouraging with nods and smiles. Older students could discuss a given topic in groups of five (four talkers and one observer). The observer draws a 'talk circle' (see below) with arrows going from talker to talker indicating the directions of speech flow. Encourage students to think about the talk – is it evenly distributed among the group? Do some talk more than others?

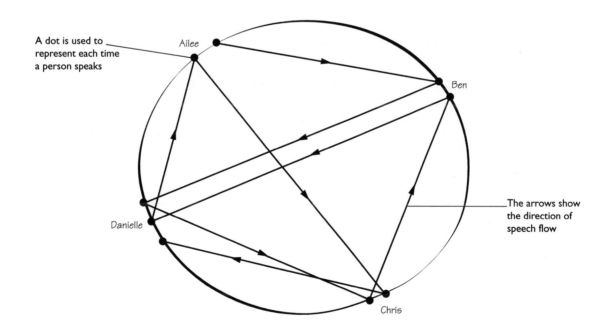

A dot is used to represent each time a person speaks

Ailee

Ben

Danielle

Chris

The arrows show the direction of speech flow

These organising strategies will be considered in more detail in later chapters, when we look at how to present information so that others can grasp it successfully. At this point, we have simply introduced conversation moves that indicate the existence of this mode of thinking. A full range of conversation moves indicates the readiness of students to deal with the formal spoken and written language discourses of the classroom. Many students have not acquired them on school entry and have still not learned them by the time they have reached senior school, with perilous consequences for successful learning, as we shall see later in Chapter 7.

The Carnegie Study in America [7] suggested that 98% of first grade students did not have the full range of essential language abilities for learning, with 51% showing serious problems. Conversation is the vital prerequisite of all spoken and written narrative activity. It is important that teachers organise classroom experiences to give students opportunities to develop their talking skills. We have seen that students vary in their conversational skills across groups and demonstrate better levels of discourse when grouped with others who have similar ability to themselves. This management issue is important to effective teaching and learning.

Summary Points

◆ Students' communicative competence is not static and will vary across context.

◆ Organisation of students for learning is vital for their thinking and language development.

◆ Students need grouping in ways that facilitate their learning. Mixed ability settings are useful for some purposes, but not for others.

◆ Assumptions about student behaviour tend to endure and are not easily shifted.

◆ What works for one student may be disastrous for another.

◆ Talk behaviour of students needs careful monitoring using a descriptive framework, such as talk circles.

Chapter 3

Why is class talk a teacher's greatest challenge?

 "Your listeners won't care what you say until they know that you care."

anon

'Do you know, Rosie, I've spent 45 minutes explaining the Thirty Years War to the Lower Sixth and they are still none the wiser.'

Words frequently go in one ear and out the other. We hear but may not listen; listen but may not understand; understand but may not believe; believe but disregard.

Chapters 1 and 2 focused on some of the factors, 'within' and 'without' the person, which influence classroom talk. We find that communication between teachers and students is governed by personal qualities, individual values, social background and group dynamics. In this chapter, we move on to look at some of the challenges that face teachers in trying to get students to listen. These include matters of self-interest (both the listener's and the speaker's), the listener's perception of the person speaking and how the speaker conveys the message. Each aspect is considered in turn, and the ways in which it influences teaching are illuminated.

◆ Self-interest

As a child, can you remember being told to *'Keep quiet'*, *'Control that temper'* or *'Stop crying'*? These repeated parental commands set up an internal conflict affecting communication. Each of us is born with a strong, sturdy little spirit – *'I need, I want, I demand'* – that ensures our survival. The self-spirit views the world through one pair of eyes – our own. It encourages us to cry when we are hurt, to scream when we feel frustrated, to smack when we are mad and to snatch when we want something very badly.

In order to help us share our world happily with others, adults generally teach us to deny our feelings. The direct line from feeling to action is interrupted and re-routed so we lose touch with our emotional needs. Thus, we fail to learn how to communicate what we really feel and mean. All our true thoughts and emotions undergo a process of being filtered out. How does this experience affect communication exchanges in school?

Think for a moment about class talk. It is often the teacher who does the talking, in a monologue, where he controls the action and speaks from a personal point of view. To persuade, inform or change the listener, the speaker *and* receiver must be actively involved. True communication is always a dialogue – an exchange between teacher and student, actively pursuing a shared meaning. Researchers such as Barnes and co-workers [1], Barr and co-workers [2], Galton and Simon [3], Edwards and Westgate [4] and Hayes [5], among others, have elaborated on this process in the classroom and compared it to normal, social discourse.

So what do teachers do? They tell students to keep quiet and listen to what they have to say. Equal participation is not usually encouraged. On average, teachers talk for two-thirds of the time while students listen [6]. In a class of 30, this means that each student gets roughly half a minute to speak in an hour, which makes a total of three minutes a day! We might ask why should students listen? At home it is normally children who initiate and question while adults listen and respond, but as soon as they step into school this communication pattern is reversed [7]. Evidence of this pattern was reinforced by Wagner [8]. He suggested that children say roughly 40 000 words per day at the age of three, which decreases rapidly when they enter school so that at nine years old only about 20 000 words per day is the norm.

Suddenly, the tables are turned and many children are not prepared for the move from home to school talk. They have not experienced listening to whole chunks of words as in a teacher's monologue. When Alice fell down the rabbit hole and encountered communication in Wonderland, she found it was very different to what she knew. In her own world she knew herself to be a skilled communicator, but here she felt the opposite. Confidence cracked and competence crashed.

When children enter school, they move from centre stage to almost off stage and feel cast from the lime light. It is a tough lesson. Schools are about shutting up and shaping up to adult standards. Some students submit to the regime, but others rebel.

Teaching requirements do not help to ameliorate this situation. Teachers often have so much information to pack into students, to fulfil curriculum and testing requirements, that learning has become like a running race, but with no-one getting too far ahead or behind. Most students are expected to reach the winning tape (assessment targets) at pretty much the same time. There is no time for rest and reflection on the way. It is not surprising, therefore, that *'by comparison with reading and writing, speaking and listening continue to be neglected in coverage, planning for progression and assessment'* (UK Qualifications and Curriculum Authority, 1997). Teachers feel they must control the discourse and allow a restricted range of talking opportunities for their students in order to meet their curriculum deadlines. In turn, the majority of students sense that they cannot stray from the class agenda or they will be thought difficult and deviant.

How can we change this situation and let students participate in class talk? It is vital for their thinking development and must be built into the instructional process. Here's a suggestion! At the end of each section of information given in a lesson, encourage students to talk briefly in pairs about what has been said. This could involve summarising the main points and relating the content to their own experience. It need only take a minute but such talk provides an opportunity to review material and compare it to other knowledge. The expectancy of such a task helps students to engage personal opinions and cultivate further listening.

TEACHING TIP: Divide lesson content into parts. At the end of each section, ask students to discuss a question on the material in pairs, and compare ideas. Allow only a minute for this, to encourage speedy responses.

To create an attentive audience, however, demands much more than involving students, as the speaker needs to direct her own self-interest onto theirs. Discovering the children's needs and motivations, and wrapping the information around these, is a sure way forward. This is not impossible, as everyone in school shares a particular culture, knows the procedures required, interacts with the same cast of characters and spends more daylight hours together than with family and friends. Discovering 'what's in it for students' targets their points of view, before the teacher then tells them about her own. This balances the control and helps motivate students to tune in to what the teacher has to say.

◆ The speaker

"O wad some power the giftie gie us to see oursels as ithers see us."

Robert Burns, 'To a Louse'

The next factor that determines whether students listen is their perception of the teacher as a person. Is he a friend or a foe? The need for this knowledge is built into the very nature of listening. When you listen you give power to the speaker. Although this may be temporary and an active debate is going on inside your head while listening, essentially you are in a passive state. Something is being done to you and you are not in control at that moment. So listening is a 'gift' from the listener to the speaker. Who is getting your gift, therefore, matters a great deal. Trust is vital and this is not easily won or freely given.

Greeting

Think how history has devised tests to determine friend or foe. Remember the origin of the salute – a right hand to the brow. It derives from medieval times when men in armour lifted their visors with their right hand to reveal their faces and signal that they would not use their weapons. Today, we use the handshake and eye contact when we meet to show friendship and trust. Greeting is a very important ritual. It is our symbol of amity. With regard to the classroom context, it is easy to dive into the content of a lesson and forget this little mark of courtesy. Research indicates that it is vital in gaining the attention of an audience and winning them over [9].

Personal qualities

Once we have made contact, our listeners notice and respond to our personal style. How does a speaker strike a listener, person to person? One hundred primary and secondary students were asked to come up with their preferences for personal qualities [10]. The common views are summarised in the table below.

Positive qualities	Negative qualities
Friendly, fair, honest, open, cool (modern)	Stuffy, nervous, talkative, pompous
Organised, enthusiastic, knowledgeable	Talkative, monotonous, lazy, false
Interesting, confident, encouraging	Patronising, remote, vague, uncaring

The positive qualities appear to be a turn-on for students while the negative ones are a quick turn-off. Whatever combination of the positive qualities a person perceives, any one of them will result in a willingness to become an interested listener. The reverse happens in respect of the negative qualities.

Different members of a group, however, are likely to hold opposing views of a speaker. Groups that I teach on the subject of communication are often asked to imagine me as 'the weather' and come up with a descriptive phrase to express their view of me. This is done anonymously on slips of paper, collected in a basket, so no-one feels embarrassed. Always there are opposite views recorded – some perceive me as sunny and warm and others as cold and windy! We strike different people in different ways and it is impossible to appear the same to everyone. Personality differences are a reality of life and add to its spice. We have to accept those that like and dislike us without becoming too upset about it. Every positive has a negative! People's reaction to others is instinctive and without thought – a visceral response. The origin of the response moves from the listener's 'gut' to brain, however, in considering whether the speaker has enough credibility to command attention.

Motivation and personality

People's responses to others are based on a dominant set of motivations that shape how they react. These motivations are established from what is valued and rewarded by their families, peers and society at large. Role models, innate abilities and life experiences give relative and changing emphasis to these influences as people mature. The result is that:

◆ some people are influenced by external forces, and strive toward what others indicate as valuable and successful

◆ some become anti-players in the life game and resist all external expectations

◆ some turn to themselves and respond only to their own internal voices.

People behave, therefore, in ways that feed their dominant motivations and this becomes apparent in the way they relate to others and respond to their demands.

If we look around a class, or any other group of people, at least three main types of personalities can be picked out, which we may call the 'snaps', 'crackles' and 'pops'!

The 'snaps' are the achievers with high standards and goals, who are independent, diligent, disciplined learners. They 'snap into action' without much bidding. They are so strongly orientated that they do not understand concepts of failing. Therefore, some will view them as not having much time for the less able and hard working in the group. However, this may not be true. Snaps are tough task masters for themselves and expect the same standards from others. As learners, they enjoy researching and reflecting on a range of choices about how to achieve something. They prefer individual to group pursuits. Experience suggests that snaps make up about 10% of the population.

Next are the 'crackles'. These are the chatters or yackers who aim to be part of the crowd. They care about how others treat them. Crackles want to co-operate with others but require to be liked in return. Friendships are highly valued by them but their need for approval makes them shy away from unpopular choices. These are generally the smoothers who try to maintain a happy atmosphere in the group. As learners they dislike too many choices and are not so inclined to look at things in any great depth. They make keen team players who might have a hard time beating a friend! Crackles probably make up 80% of the class.

The 'pops' want to be *tops* and are interested in obtaining and exercising power and authority. They will 'pop up' as school captains as well as being leaders of the wild gangs. They take the lead and are not as keen as the achieving snaps in figuring out how to do things, preferring to create impact and influence others. The pops are self-confident and not dependent on the approval of others. They are the movers and shakers of the world. As learners they are less interested in detail and research but are motivated to find out about other successful personalities. Let them loose on some of the characters from history and they are happy! Pops make up about 10% of any group.

It would be wrong to take a rigid view of this personality analysis as no-one fits just one type of description. Many factors shape behaviour and we find doses of all three basic motivations in a person's make-up. It is likely, however, that one aspect dominates in most situations.

TEACHING TIP: Take account of personality differences in class management. Make sure the 'snaps' have opportunity to work alone while the 'crackles' are able to indulge their group learning prefences and the 'pops' have a chance to lead in positive ways.

Personality classifications give us a quick and easy identification process, though we need to be aware of the spill-over effects. An analysis can be useful in identifying both teachers and students and helps us to understand the impact people have on each other in a communicative context. Personality clashes are inevitable between people with differing sets of motivations and we have to survive them somehow!

Being aware is being forewarned and forearmed. It is always possible to minimise problems by judicious management.

The literature suggests that different people will classify personalities differently, depending on their individual frameworks for grouping others. Psychologists have centred on two main issues:

 Does personality consist of permanent characteristics?

 Do general personality factors exist?

Three theoretical trends help to answer these fundamental questions.

Those answering 'yes' to the first question above are known as **type and trait theorists**. These include Eysenck [11], who used 'introvert–extrovert' and 'stable–unstable' continuum dimensions, based on the medieval 'Humours' – melancholic, choleric, phlegmatic and sanguine. Cattell's [12] sixteen source traits, with dimensions such as intelligence and guilt, are also influential. Although both embrace the **nomothetic** approach, which sees behaviour as reflecting enduring personality traits, Cattell, more than Eysenck, recognised the way behaviour fluctuates in response to situation factors.

Those who believe in the uniqueness of the individual represent the **idiographic** approach. Kelly's [13] Construct Theory of bipolar opposites (intelligent/not intelligent, reflective/impulsive) incorporates a person's view of the world and embraces areas of learning, cognition, motivation and emotion when comparing individuals. Maslow's [14] Hierarchy of Needs ('basic survival' to 'full personal potential') attempts to capture individual experience, as does Roger's [15] Self-Theory of self-image and ideal-self.

The psychoanalytic theories of Adler [16], Freud [17], Jung [18] and Erikson [19] arise from clinical studies of personality disturbance and are clearly idiographic. They are concerned with the nature of personality – for example, Freud's pre-conscious, conscious and unconscious mind – and are important because they allow for the possibility of personality change.

This summary of major psychological ideas supports the existence of individual traits, which may be enhanced and tempered by experience. It enables us to reflect on the power of the person and her uniqueness. Personality theory helps us understand our own characteristics and how they might impact on others. This brings a better awareness of the interactions of people and situations. When the circumstance involves a classroom, where people are thrown together in an enclosed space, we need to fully understand the dynamics and the potential for change.

The listener's assessment of the speaker

Whatever a listener's overriding personality type, a series of subconscious questions help determine whether a speaker has the credentials to command attention and sustain listening. At least ten questions are considered by students in relation to their teacher:

- ◆ Does she recognise what I want/need to know?
- ◆ Do I like and respect her?
- ◆ Can I trust her?
- ◆ Can I be comfortable and relaxed with her?
- ◆ Will she affect my life?
- ◆ What does my past experience of her suggest?
- ◆ Is she fair and approachable or unfair and remote?
- ◆ Is she interested in my views as well as her own?
- ◆ Does she show understanding of my specific needs?
- ◆ Is she friendly and flexible?

Look at this list several times. Is there anything else you would add to it? What questions would you ask yourself about someone speaking to you (whether expert, staff colleague, relative or friend)? It is vital to think about these questions; they capture your views and opinions and will shape the outcome of any communication directed at you. They influence the way you listen, as well as whether you listen at all.

The process of deciding your opinions about the person speaking has both body (visceral) and brain (cerebral) components. The 'gut' and the head combine. What you think in your head is filtered through feelings. Most of us feel first. We like, trust, believe, and then follow or flunk, because our senses instruct our thoughts and then our actions. Instincts precede learning. Our survival mechanism ensures that we switch on our defence and danger signals as we enter each situation. We stop, look, listen, think and then act!

Although listening is hardly a life-threatening experience, the 'visceral system' processes what is happening before the mind starts operating. It is the combination of these two responses that produces listening. Returning to the medieval military greeting, we have to lift our battle visor and let the listeners see and feel who we are before our message can be transmitted. This experience has been called the 'Johari window', named after Jo Luft and Harrington Ingram [20], who first alerted us to the importance of disclosing ourselves to others before we attempt to communicate with them. If we fail to do this our listeners are there waiting to dismiss us. We do not want such a negative response, or our message will fly out of the window and never reach the receivers. Those students will never learn from us!

In order to help others listen to us, we need to consider three questions:

1 What style and tone shall I adopt?

2 What sorts of words shall I use?

3 What sentence structure should I employ?

Style and tone

The style of the message should spring directly from the basic aims of the communication, and is vital to its impact upon the recipients. Teachers should seek a particular style that ensures what they say is clearly understood by students and is couched in terms that make the content acceptable, so that students will be motivated to act on the message and retain its information. Choosing a successful style, therefore, depends on the following characteristics of the listeners.

◆ **Age**: outlooks and attitudes vary according to age, which has to be borne in mind when talking to a variety of year groups.

◆ **Background**: everyone is moulded by experience and lifestyle. Those who live in towns and in the country inhabit very different worlds. Examples and approaches used should reflect background interests.

◆ **Interests**: seek out what interests students, as 'hooks' for new knowledge.

Style must also depend on the relationship between speaker and audience. The distance between people is shown by the nature of their communication, whether a formal approach or friendly banter. Students need teachers to be friendly but fairly formal in their style, as befits their instructive role.

Vocabulary and sentence structure

English is rich in synonyms, idiomatic expressions and ways of constructing sentences (syntax). The practised speaker or writer imparts delicate nuances and shades of meaning and selects words aiming at intellect or appealing to emotion that are either sympathetic, cutting, minutely exact or broadly sweeping. For a teacher, specialist and general words need to be used carefully to avoid obscurity or over-simplification. A boy asked by his teacher to 'pull his socks up', did so literally because he was unaware that the expression also meant 'improve your work'!

TEACHING TIP: Become aware of the idioms you use by audio-taping a lesson. Check with students that they understand the meanings of these idioms.

How the information is conveyed

The third factor that affects whether or not students listen is how they are told information. Today, style and technique are important to whether information is told and sold successfully. Although we might instinctively feel that the content itself is the salient issue, we need to understand the techniques that work to get it across.

Information transfer has changed

The ways in which we give and receive information have changed dramatically over the last 50 years. Television and the mass media impart information visually with words as merely an adjunct to the process. Of course, visual images are not new. Prehistoric cave painters, old masters and sculptors told the masses about life and religion long before they could read. A picture has always been worth a thousand words because it is instant, arresting and evocative. It triggers the emotions and imagination of the viewer. The impact is immediate, although it may demand effort to comprehend the message if the picture is abstract in form.

Words always require hard work to achieve their meaning. To listen, to understand, to wait until the end of what someone says, demands attention and concentration. It also requires a willingness to follow someone else's unique style and pace while sorting out and putting together the meanings in, between and behind the words.

Life is lived, however, at an increasing rate and television allows us to receive information in a *pacy* but more passive way, so irrevocably changing the way we communicate. Let's think about what used to happen in order to get our minds around these changes. In general people used to want to listen, talk and read. Words were the major means of interpersonal exchange. Entertainment was telling stories, singing, reading aloud or playing games with one another. People curled up with a book to escape the humdrum aspects of life by spinning a web of fantasy from the written words. The verbal journeys of others were a springboard to wild imagination, before television stepped in with ready-made images of the world.

All this reflected the rhythm of life. Things took place at the gentle pace of a clip clop or a skip and a hop. Time passed, however, and life quickened. The car and the train allow things to be viewed at great speed. Planes distort what used to be our natural view of the world. An hour and a half from London puts you on top of the Austrian Alps! Everything is nearer our doorsteps than we thought. Machines have taken over household chores giving us time to do a greater variety of things. Television has

43

marched into our sitting rooms presenting amazing new sights and insights, changing forever our notions of the world. So, what has it brought? Pleasure without effort? Basic understanding to keep us abreast of global events? Consensus of values and lifestyles? Information that is racy and pacy?

Life has changed, and its rate and rhythm quicken daily. Gone is the opportunity to see it in the longer phase and at a slow pace. A quick image gives a quick fix. That picture, rather than a thousand words, is what we need to keep up and get by in today's world. Now television is the main method of giving and getting hard information and factual data.

Television culture

In autumn 1999, the Learning Support Assistants on Leicester University Numeracy courses surveyed the television habits of 300 students in the senior schools where they worked. The average time spent watching programmes was six hours per day, ranging from nought (one student who happened to be top of the class) to fourteen hours (three students). The higher figure just did not seem possible until it transpired that these three students spent most of the night watching satellite channels and most of the day sleeping it off in their lessons!

Pearce [21] has estimated that by age 13, modern children in the USA will have seen about 18 000 violent murders on TV, so who knows what effect this is having in school. At the very least it may add to stress, which increases fear and strong emotions. Some computer games are also very violent, involving the extermination and demolition of everything that appears on screen. Biederman and co-workers [22] have suggested that playing with computer games can lead to greater hyperactivity in children. They are conditioned to instantly get rid of everything that displeases them.

In order to understand the impact of television on our communication, let us examine the regular news broadcast. The headlines are generally one and a half minutes long, producing short explanations rather than in-depth analyses. They deal entirely with what is new rather than what *is* or *was*, and often do not provide any explanation of how or why a situation has arisen. Technology compresses real time and space. Information comes instantly, and we lose the patience to wait for it.

The message on television is carried mainly by pictures and graphics, with some written and spoken support – it is packaged for easy consumption. We get a strong image and a sound-bite, without having to wade through a welter of words to reach the message. People and the words they speak are no longer the primary message givers. Indeed, the 'talking head' is considered boring and is routinely given only 30 seconds on air. Any words that are heard are faultlessly produced by presenters who have received specialist voice training. They use 'teleprompters' to give an impression of a seamless flow of words. This produces the idea that people speak fluently without stumbles, hesitations or repetitions.

Television has taught us to expect visual proof and not take anybody's word for it. We expect to obtain information easily and effortlessly, without having to work hard to understand. Contrast this situation with the traditional classroom scenario in which the message – which may be highly complex, and explained over a number of lessons – is delivered mainly through the words of the teacher, with some support from pictures and graphics.

Television has also taught us to listen with only 'half an ear'. We frequently have the television on while doing something else – chatting, eating, playing – which encourages us to attend in a dilatory fashion. It takes only 15% of the brain to process and understand language, so we have 85% free attention when someone talks to us [23]. Speakers have always had to fight any possible day dreaming, wool gathering, problem solving and random thinking that takes place in the free brain space – now television challenges even more of this attention base. It teaches us that it is okay to listen a little, from time to time, rather than working to focus and concentrate on achieving a whole meaning from something.

Furthermore, television has taught us that if we don't like what we're watching we can choose something else – if we are bored we just 'channel hop', all from the reclines of an arm chair. This bodes badly for the teacher, who has to work against this now-established norm of information processing behaviour to get a certain message across. How can we motivate students to cast off this conditioned behaviour and perform new tasks, find original solutions and be inspired to move ahead in their learning?

Working with it

This appears to be the current scene: speaking, listening, learning, and information transfer are permanently changed. Pace and passivity are the norm. People expect to be spoon-fed edited, packaged versions of everything, laced with masses of visual titillation. The attention span is shorter, the need to think and understand squashed. However, we cannot just get mad about it. There is no chance that we can change things, so we have to live with the present situation and work with its potential. After all, television is not all bad! At its best, television is our most effective method yet for giving mass information speedily and efficiently. It brings the whole world into our reach, providing endless exposure to complex social, political and environmental issues. It introduces us to a mass of fascinating, different peoples and cultures. When used in an active way, television can be a highly effective teaching and learning tool. All of this is at the touch of a button.

TEACHING TIP: Support what you say with appropriate pictures or objects, as children are often more visually than verbally literate.

Although television may have been damaging to our learning system, as teachers what we must do is adapt and adopt. We have to adapt current technologies and information about visual learning to make communication clear, convincing and persuasive. Presentation software, for example, can be used to project visual images from a computer to accompany what we say. Overhead projector slides provide a cheaper, effective alternative that allows us more flexibility in presenting information as we do not have to follow the sequence of computer images.

Perhaps more importantly, when talking to children steeped in TV culture, we have to adopt speaking skills that are much more efficient and effective, and revisit some of our traditional voice and speech training methods. That is the challenge for our teachers and students today, which we will pursue in Chapter 4.

As preparation for further chapters, do this little quiz to find out whether you learn through what you see, hear or feel.

1 You are out walking – what do you notice first?

   a other people, transport, buildings, animals

   b people talking, cars hooting, music playing

   c the heat, wind or rain

2 When you are annoyed do you ...

   a look someone in the eye defiantly?

   b shout and scream?

   c stamp your feet and make physical gestures?

3 Which of the following do you prefer?

   a reading

   b listening to music

   c making or doing things

4 When learning something new do you prefer to ...

   a memorise from written or drawn information?

   b repeat facts out to yourself?

   c write down what you are trying to learn?

Answers

mostly **a**: visual (seeing)

mostly **b**: auditory (hearing)

mostly **c**: kinaesthetic (feeling – spatially/emotionally)

Did you have a preference for one mode? This may indicate through which pathway you take in information most easily.

SUMMARY POINTS

◆ Information is filtered through feelings, and we need to take these into account when teaching others.

◆ Personality differences in our students mean that some accept what we say more easily than others, so affecting their ability to take on board information. Presenting a positive image helps to counteract any negative responses from learners.

◆ For many people, visual information is more easily processed than verbal information, especially in today's picture-mediated world. Teaching needs to use current technologies, such as presentation software, to enhance the visual message.

◆ Learning competes with leisure in a society in which the latter has increasing emphasis. Teachers have to make learning a pleasant and enjoyable experience, which takes into account their students' points of view.

Chapter 4

How can you become a top talking teacher?

"Perhaps of all the creations of man, language is the most astonishing."

Lytton Strachey

> 'Attention, please. (*sharp note to the teacher's voice*) Simmer down everybody. Open your copies of 'World Transport'. Mark and Tom – take your caps off. Turn to page 5 and find the section on the history of the aeroplane and read paragraph 3. There's too much noise. Please listen quietly. Emma, turn round, and Jack, stop rocking on your chair.'

Can you recall situations when your words glided over the class rabble with no effect. Why did this happen?

This chapter considers the issue of effective teacher talk in the **controlling**, **questioning** and **explaining** roles that are played out in class. Within these three major styles, others can be defined that are constantly used. They are clarified in the table below.

Controlling	Questioning	Explaining
criticising	requesting	informing
disagreeing	suggesting	clarifying
requiring	proposing	helping
directing	confirming	assisting
instructing	involving	co-operating
counselling	motivating	contributing
A teacher in the employee role and the student in the learner role will be involved in: accepting, understanding, executing and effecting		

Let's start with control, because without it nothing is possible. We have to create a co-operative atmosphere, connect with students and know how to communicate in a way that produces positive behaviour and effective learning.

◆ Controlling talk

There is a magic formula for controlling talk:

$$contact + clarity + consistency = control$$

Each of these three elements of contact, clarity and consistency are considered in turn, below.

Contact

Making the connection

In the example of teacher talk at the start of this chapter, no contact or relationship was immediately established with the class, which is vital in gaining group co-operation. An effective strategy is to stand at the classroom door and greet each student as the class enters. This establishes a connection with everyone present as well as signalling interest and value for all students. Before the start of the lesson, an alerting signal is useful to gain immediate group focus. Recently, I lectured on these issues to a large audience of trainee teachers. I blew a whistle to grab attention. They looked at me in disbelief but focus was immediate!

Use your own preferred signal (hand clap or loud tap, for example) – without one you could wait all day for everyone to heed you! When all are settled, a pleasant 'Good morning, everyone, it's good to see you' demonstrates a friendly manner that is positive and enthusiastic. Badger [1] found that teachers were so pressured by curriculum demands that the pleasantries of life were overlooked and treatment of students remained at an impersonal, functional level. Giving time for contact *greatly reduced behaviour problems*. This is a point well worth noting. In Chapter 3, the problem of gaining co-operation for listening was explored – teachers must work at making initial contact, as with this accomplished, half the learning and behaviour battle is won.

TEACHING TIP: Greet students warmly. Express pleasure in meeting them and having an opportunity to learn together.

Eye contact

Eye contact plays the initial role in establishing positive contact with others. It exercises 'power and preference' [2] and it is important that teachers are aware of the role of eyes in interactions with students. When two people look at each other it normally indicates that interaction will take place. Subordinates have been observed to look more frequently at their superiors, although they are often the first to look away. Regarding the person is a sign of attention but if staring occurs there is usually an attempt to dominate the other so it indicates that status differences have yet to be established or are in question. A downward glance is a universal sign of submissive behaviour.

It is particularly important when teachers first meet their classes and are the centre of attention that they make confident eye contact by scanning the whole group with a smile. Eye contact, along with other aspects of behaviour is the way we communicate attitudes. If a student is unable to look back in the face of an accusation it may indicate there is something to hide. Exline [2] compared 'control oriented' subjects, who wished to dominate others, with 'low control oriented' subjects, when confronted with a listener who either looked at them all the time, or never looked directly but swept the air above their heads. He discovered that low control subjects looked more frequently if the listener withheld his gaze whereas the high control subjects looked less frequently. This suggests that those who like to control others may find people whose visual attention is difficult to capture a more powerful force than those whose attention they can maintain. Eye contact or its withdrawal, therefore, acts as an important mechanism in making relationships, as 'high control' teachers may not naturally connect with students who do not make eye contact. Teachers need to establish steady, focused but relaxed eye contact with all students, and be aware of the dilemma 'to look or not to look'.

TEACHING TIP: Work to make regular eye contact with all the class, remembering that we tend to favour our dominant side (right side if left-handed, and left side if right-handed).

Smiling

With eye contact comes the smile. An anonymous verse – 'Smile awhile and while you smile, another smiles and soon there's miles and miles of smiles' – encourages us to use this powerful energiser to spread good will. This is in spite of the book by Ryan [3], *Don't Smile 'til Christmas*, which warned teachers not to be too eager to use this strong social signal! Mehrabian [4] suggested that smiling is associated with a communicator's attempt to relieve tension and placate the audience and, therefore, has submissive connotations. Birdwhistell [5] indicated that the interpretation of smiles is very complex:

"…the presence of a smile in particular contexts indicated pleasure, in another, humour, in others, ridicule and, in still others, friendliness or good manners. Smiles have been seen to indicate doubt and acceptance, equality and superordination or subordination. They occur in situations where insult is intended and in others as a denial of insult."

This implies a wide range of smiles from sneers to pleasing expressions. Lewis [6] classified five types: simple, compressed, upper, lower and broad, with the possibility of each being expressed at low, medium or high intensity. This could certainly account for the range of interpretation suggested by Birdwhistell. Neill [7] and Caswell [8] indicated that teachers who smile when criticising students show they are 'actually enjoying the confrontation' and know they will win. They speak about the 'inner' smile in response to internal thoughts. It is certainly useful for the teacher to be aware of the possibilities of how a smile could be given and received. If a teacher is relaxed, smiling will come naturally in response to the situation. Normal warm, happy smiles, with open body postures (no folded arms) are expressions of solidarity and friendliness and are welcoming behaviours between those who enjoy a positive relationship.

Dr Madan Kataria, a consultant physician in Bombay, would suggest that smiles are to be encouraged well before Christmas. In response to research that suggests smiles and laughter trigger the release of endorphins, engendering a feeling of well-being, he has set up the Laughter Club International and organised a World Laughter Day. In India, hundreds of people gather in the open air, limber up with breathing exercises and progress to smiling, chuckling and chanting. Dr Kataria claims that as well as improving well-being, there are benefits to the immune system with positive effects on our general health.

The intellectual advantages of a good laugh are striking when a problem requires a creative solution. Isen and co-workers [9] found that people who had just watched a video of hilarious television bloomers were better at solving puzzles that tested creative thinking, compared with other subjects who had watched videos on mathematics or exercise routines. Subjects were given a candle, matches and a box of tacks and asked to attach the candle to a cork board wall so it could burn without dripping wax on the floor. Most people given the task fell into 'functional fixedness', thinking in conventional ways and declaring the task insoluble. Those who had watched the funny film were most likely to see alternative solutions. They could visualise the use of the tack box as a candleholder, tacked to the wall. The reason for their superior performance was probably a relaxed body and mind that felt free to move through a variety of possible solutions. We are used to regarding laughter as the best medicine – now it appears to be the best problem-solver! Get the clowns into the classroom quickly!

TEACHING TIP: Try to inject humour into the teaching process, with a funny story or joke, to relax and engage students.

Words

Although the use of eyes, mouth, face, body postures and movements are important non-verbal behaviours that establish contact and authority, words swing into play to either maintain or destroy the connection. Wragg [10] suggested that on average teachers make five negative comments for each positive one, which ruins the good atmosphere of the classroom and reinforces resentment. Maintaining an upbeat atmosphere is the key. Always *reward* and never *punish*.

In the example of teacher talk at the start of the chapter, the following might have been more effective.

'Mark and Tom, nice hats but they are safer in your bags. Emma, I need you to listen so you can do the task easily. Jack, it's four (*chair legs*) on the floor please (*using a hand gesture as reinforcement*).'

In this way, the teacher asserts his needs positively and pleasantly without the negative comment that inevitably antagonises. Transmitting clear information is vital, and the next section expands on this.

TEACHING TIP: Reward rather than punish, to maintain a positive atmosphere and achieve optimum performance.

Clarity

The importance of 'I messages' has long been acknowledged as a powerful verbal trick in asserting control clearly. In the example above, *'Emma, I need you to listen ...'* clearly explains your requirements as well as deflecting blame from the student. It says *'I want you to listen'*, rather than *'You are a pain'*, which is a much more active approach when confronting difficult students. The assertive discipline method does take time to perfect as there are various strategies involved. As one achieves familiarity with the process, it is easy to integrate the skills and respond spontaneously in all situations. Useful skills are listed in the box that follows, to make the process crisp and clear. Although children with specific behaviour problems may be slow to respond to these approaches, experience suggests that perseverance will produce positive effects on all students in time.

---

10 Communication strategies for dealing with difficult behaviour

1 Basic assertion

State your specific need/want, belief or opinion.

'Emma, I need you to listen, so we can cover everything you want for tonight's homework.'

2 Broken record

Repeat your statement, if necessary, with the same voice tone and volume.

'Emma, I know you want to talk, but I need ...'

3 Self-disclosure

State how a behaviour affects you before a request or confrontation.

'I feel anxious about mentioning this, but I want you to know ...'

4 Comprehension check

After a response, paraphrase what the student has said, and ask if she feels you have understood.

'You said the homework was not explained well enough for you to do it. Is that right?'

---

5 Interpretation

State the cause of the difficulty, if indicated.

'You're angry with me but not saying so.'

6 Feedback

Give positive feedback about what you like and if negative criticism has been made, encourage a response.

'Thanks for listening. You've heard what I've had to say so is there anything you wish to add?'

7 Compromise

Prepare to compromise over a genuine clash of needs.

'I accept you didn't understand the homework. Come at 12.30 to the Study Centre and I'll give you some help to get started.'

8 Control and release

Switch attention away from your own strong feelings by counting in your head. Later, find release in physical activity or discussion with a colleague.

9 Conflict resolution

Where conflict has not yet surfaced, first state both positions and then seek compromise.

'I can see you're unhappy about this homework. I need you to have done it by Monday. Can we talk about it and find a solution?'

10 Goal achievement

Clarify behaviour (e.g. chatting in class). State effect (e.g. you feel annoyed). Refer to the incident. Demand change. Allow time and space for a response.

'Emma, chatting in class annoys me. In English this morning, it meant I had less time to explain the homework. Can you listen in silence to help me teach and you learn?'

A very possible reason for the lack of an appropriate response is that listeners are not absolutely clear what is meant by the words, facial expressions and gestures they perceive. There is a need to teach precise awareness. Careful choice of words for instructions is important. For example, *'Listen in silence'* is clearer than *'Listen quietly'* – *'quietly'* implies that some noise is acceptable. Also, as we have seen, positive instructions have more effect. *'Listen silently when others are talking …'* is likely to produce a better response than *'Don't talk while others are talking …'* There is no 'negative vibe' and the word images are more precise.

Get students to devise their own 'Rules for class talk' in groups, which can then be discussed by the whole class before a final selection is agreed. The rules might look something like those in the box below.

Rules for class talk

1   Listen in silence when others are talking and keep yourself still.

2   In pairs or groups – talk quietly so as not to disturb others and control your movements.

3   In class – raise hands to ask questions and when told to speak, talk loudly so everyone can hear.

Control of movement is just as important as control of sound in maintaining calm, relaxed behaviour, so reference to this in the class rules makes everything transparent. Some students are unable to infer from situations, and need things spelled out exactly. So, once students are explicitly aware of the 'talk rules', remind them indirectly using a visual prompt so as not to lose momentum in the lesson. A useful analogy is the 'traffic light warning system', used to adjust noise rather than speed in this context. Put a prepared board in front of the class with a moveable arrow to indicate noise level requirement. A choice of descriptive words caters for different word preferences among students.

Although this might seem pedantic, Robertson and Webb [11] devised a 'Voice Policy' for a primary school that they found effective in raising awareness of noise levels in school. Five coded levels were agreed: 'silence' (blue), 'partner voice' (green), 'table voice' (yellow), 'class voice' (orange), 'playground voice' (red). I have found the idea excellent but a little complex for some students. Keeping concepts in threes (rather than fives) is a good rule to aid memory and the traffic light principle has worked in both primary and secondary settings.

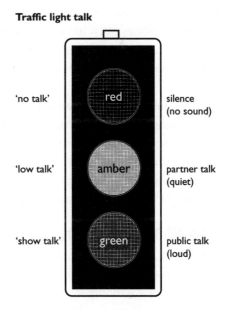

Traffic light talk

'no talk' — red — silence (no sound)

'low talk' — amber — partner talk (quiet)

'show talk' — green — public talk (loud)

Training students to be aware of sound level and its relation to their ability to process input effectively has support from the literature. Kendon [12] stated that the brain is capable of dealing with only limited amounts of information at a time. A speaker often looks away from the listener to organise the next utterance, which suggests that in order to process and organise information effectively, the brain needs to avoid distracting additional input. It seems likely that in the classroom too the brain needs minimum distraction to become absorbed in thinking and solving problems creatively. Rutter and co-workers [13] have supported this from observations in schools:

> "Lessons in the successful schools more frequently included periods of quiet work when the teachers expected the students to work in silence."

Consistency

Devising a school policy

It is all very well thinking up rules and routines and spelling out student responsibilities. That is the easy bit. The

TEACHING TIP: Choose words carefully, with specific rather than general meaning, to ensure your message is clear (e.g. *'Listen silently'*, instead of *'Listen quietly'*).

problem is that their implementation throws us on the mercy of our frail human wills. We can *say* it but can we *do* it? Consistency is one of the hardest aspects of behaviour management to achieve. Keeping up the good work when we are tired, pressured or 'one degree under', needs iron will power.

Many behaviour policies fail in schools not because the principles are wrong but because they are hard to adopt on a consistent basis. Everybody has their own preferred system of ruling their roost and when students move between many different classrooms and come across numerous ways of doing things they feel confused. School behaviour policies must have all teachers and support staff signing up to them otherwise they will be wasted and wearisome. There has to be a system that regularly revisits behaviour and keeps everyone up to scratch.

Attitudes are an essential element of consistent behaviour. There is often much 'norming and storming' necessary to come up with consistent views and smooth implementation of them in school policies. Changing attitudes needs time and commitment. Unfortunately, understanding reasons does not guarantee compliance with rules either on the part of teacher or student. Most persistent offenders can produce a whole gamut of reasons why they should not do something, as they are bound to have heard them recited endlessly.

Dealing with behaviour problems

A student who is bored because the subject is not to their liking may mess around in class because this is easier than participating in the lesson. It is tempting to try reasoning but this is not a winning strategy because the student will never be talked out of the way they feel. The only response is to consistently say *'You find this boring because the topic doesn't interest you, but it's work we all have to do. You may choose to do this now or give up your lunch break.'* The choice gives the ultimate control to the student. This 're-framing' technique provides a consistent solution and re-defines oppositional behaviour in terms that allow teacher and student to view it as a co-operative rather than an antagonistic act. It is devised from the 'ecosystemic approach' described by Upton and Cooper [14] to encourage consistent methods of dealing with conflict.

In a recent teacher course on behaviour management, a participant described his day in a special unit for disruptive students: '*On arrival in the classroom, Mark will normally run around jumping on chairs and making queer animal-like noises.*' It was suggested that the teacher 'mirrored' the boy on the next occasion, calmly watching the behaviour and then copying him before asking what the boy thought of him. Although dubious, Mark's teacher was willing to give it a go, and report on this at the next session. The effect of the mirroring was startling – Mark stopped his inappropriate behaviour instantly and was willing to conform to his teacher's requirements. (The rest of the class were shocked into submission!)

At first sight, it might seem as though this approach is directed at changing behaviour, but it is intended to bring about a change of *attitude* by letting each party act out and defend the other's position. The hope is that they will both begin to appreciate the other's perspective and understand the need for compromise. The object is that they should both agree to behave in ways that are more acceptable to each other and so avoid regular conflicts. The student has to co-operate and understand that the teacher's role is to teach and that students will be required to carry out work that is set to help them learn. The teacher has to acknowledge the problems students have with learning in particular places.

This technique has been used in one-to-one therapy situations, and Rogers [16] described how mirroring can be used with picture material. This starts with a role play something like that described below, to focus on the student, Ben, and the over-loud use of his voice in the classroom.

> **Teacher**: Look Ben, you be your mate, Brian; I'll sit next to you here, OK? Now let me give you a demo.
>
> **Teacher**: (*in the role of 'Ben' – very loudly, and clicking his fingers as if to get the 'teacher's' attention*) GIVE ME A PENCIL!
>
> **Teacher**: (*now winking and grinning at Ben*) Is that right, Ben? That's what I see you doing, Ben.

The session continued with the teacher and Ben making a plan to talk more quietly, by drawing pictures of the bad and then the good situation. The student, therefore, observed himself, as if in a mirror. This therapeutic approach is probably more applicable to a one-to-one session than to a whole-class lesson, but, if used, it can help to change attitudes.

Some advocate that students keep records of inappropriate behaviour, and this approach is worth investigation [16, 17] as it does help reflection. Contracts with students are another common method, and create an awareness of responsibility. There is evidence to suggest that any method used consistently and appropriately in a given context is likely to have a positive effect just because value is placed on correct behaviour and attempts are made to help students understand the effects of their unhelpful actions on themselves and others.

Verbal and non-verbal language play a part in clarifying meaning and achieving consistency in behaviour. The term 'withitness' was coined by Kounin [18] to describe the ability of a teacher to communicate with children by her actual behaviour rather than by simple verbal announcing. The concept is concerned with the teacher being able to spot the student who is instigating the problem behaviour – 'the target of the desist' – at an early stage, before others are influenced. If intervention takes place as a student is about to misbehave, a repetition is less likely. If teachers show this 'withitness' they are proving their alertness. Non-verbal gestures (for example, a hand action to indicate all chair legs should be on the floor) are powerful reminders that convey a willingness to protect the offending student from embarrassment. They make more impact than words and are worth more than a bucketful of hot air.

TEACHING TIP: Consistency in dealing with behaviour is the best policy. Find a strategy that works, and use it fairly and firmly.

Support

Developing a repertoire of useful strategies and using them consistently will reap rewards in dealing with undesirable classroom behaviour, as well as maintaining personal confidences and communicative competence. **Support**, however, is needed to maintain and refine such activity. Teachers need reinforcement from colleagues and from the parents of students they teach, who can back up their actions, help put across a consistent message, and appreciate achievement. Students need assistance from both teachers and parents to keep them on the straight and narrow path to success.

The idea of 'support' can produce contradictory reactions in our society. Some people view support positively, as it enables individuals to do things they might not have achieved alone. Others feel that to admit support is needed is a sign of weakness.

To explore your own attitudes, draw two support maps to connect key words and images – a positive and then a negative one – and show all the people, groups, places, pets, objects and activities that you experience as supportive and unsupportive. Then, try the following word association exercise, either alone or with a colleague. What words do you associate with 'support'? Write a list. Now look at your list – circle the words that have a positive, encouraging tone, and underline those with negative connotations. Pick two positive and two negative words and continue the associations. For example, if you had written down a positive word such as 'determination', you might list further associations such as 'strong', 'able to take set backs', 'confidence in what I am doing'. If you perceive a word such as 'relationships' in a negative light, you might list associations such as 'unfriendly', 'no time to give', and so on. As you focus on these associations, memories of actual experiences will revive and you will find your own pivot point between attitudes.

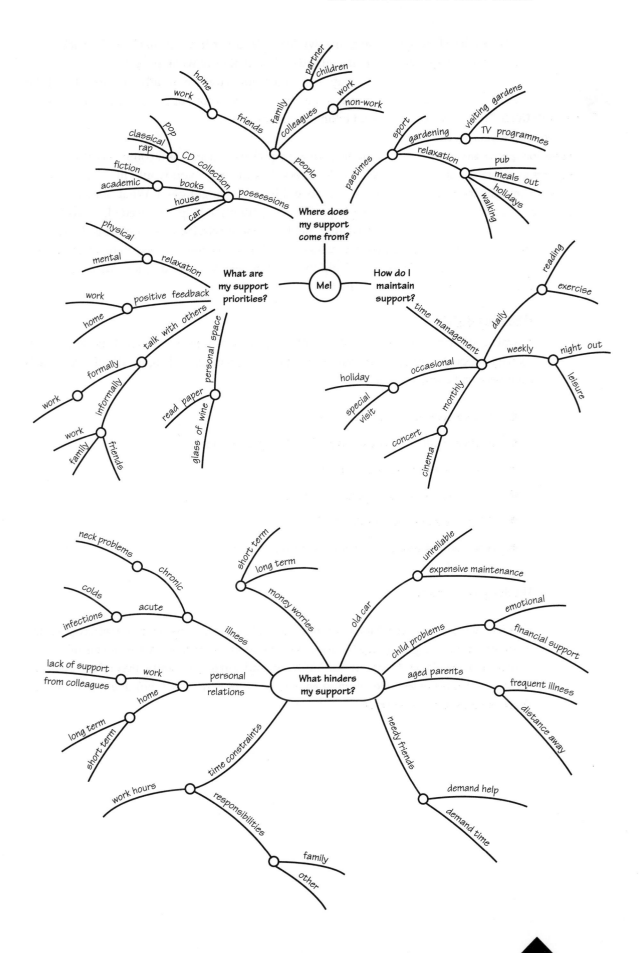

On the one hand, support is *enabling*, while on the other it can be *limiting*. Go back to your support maps and check. If your attitude is that only weak people need support you may find your 'supportive' map rather meagre, but if the reverse is the case your need for support may prevent you from taking decisions alone.

TEACHING TIP: Take time out to look at yourself and your needs for specific and general support in maintaining strong lines of communication with others around you.

Finally, review your current needs as a communicator in relation to school. List the ways you would like support for what you do and how you might get it. What things are stopping you from getting the help you need? It is worth spending time doing these activities, as support is the most important issue if we are going to achieve consistency in our actions. None of us are so perfect that we can dispense with aid that is there when we need it, for classroom control and communicative competence.

Expressing feelings

Learning to express the way we feel is immensely helpful in communicating clearly and gaining support. You could try these exercises with another colleague – think about each statement and complete it honestly.

- ◆ When I go into a new class I feel …

- ◆ When a student refuses to do what they're told I feel …

- ◆ When my teaching is criticised I feel …

- ◆ When the students respond well I feel …

- ◆ When a lesson goes badly I feel …

- ◆ When others don't understand me I feel …

Think up some more!

Keeping in mind any 'roadblocks to communication' [19], as listed in the table opposite, is important in using language for effective classroom control. Distorted forms of communication slip out without our knowing, and can significantly affect the way both speaker and listener feel. Developing an awareness of this, and building a repertoire of alternatives, keeps us on track.

Ten barriers to communication [19]		
1 **Accusing**	e.g. *'You never tidy up.'*	try *'I'd like you to put the rubbish in the bins.'*
2 **Assuming**	e.g. *'You're not looking at me straight so you must be lying.'*	try *'I want you to look at me and tell the truth.'*
3 **Approving**	e.g. *'You're amazing.'*	try *'I'm impressed with your work.'*
4 **Commanding**	e.g. *'Stop whinging.'*	try *'I want you to work without talking.'*
5 **Disapproving**	e.g. *'You're stupid.'*	try *'I want you to settle down to work.'*
6 **Judging**	e.g. *'You're the worst class ever.'*	try *'You're a nice lively lot, but quieten down in class.'*
7 **Interrogating**	e.g. *'Why on earth is this homework not done?'*	try *'I don't want you to miss out on homework.'*
8 **Labelling**	e.g. *'You are a disgrace.'*	try *'I'm disturbed at the way you are disrupting the class.'*
9 **Moralising**	e.g. *'A girl of your age should be better behaved.'*	try *'Let's talk less and work more.'*
10 **Sending up**	e.g. *'So you've honoured us with your presence at last.'*	try *'It's good to see you here.'*

These barriers to communication encourage both teachers and students to behave negatively. If you talk positively to students, they are more likely to respond positively. In the following statements, try changing 'can't' to 'can', and examine how this makes *you* feel.

◆　'I can't control Class 6a.'

◆　'I can't get the books marked.'

◆　'I can't make friends with this class.'

Expressing feeling can help in both *controlling* and *counselling* in the classroom. Acknowledging others' feelings and responses is the first step to solving problems. Getting in to the habit of 'reflecting back' to those you converse with helps to achieve a real rapport with them. Accurate paraphrasing of what people say to you gives you an understanding of their experience and the way they view the world. Try the role play overleaf with a colleague. Take turns in reading the statements so that the other partner can reflect back the content. The following serves as an example. *'I'm fed up with scrimping and saving but still not being able to buy a decent, reliable car'*, might elicit the following paraphrased response: *'You find it difficult to afford the basic essentials on a teacher's salary'*.

A fellow teacher might say to you:

◆ 'I can't control my classes and they have me in tears'

◆ 'I'm tired of being a nobody in this place.'

◆ 'I'm feeling depressed because the head said I wasn't pulling my weight.'

◆ 'It's useless to complain to the management as they never do anything.'

◆ 'It's hopeless organising group work as there aren't enough facilities.'

A student might say to you:

◆ 'I'm always being picked on in class and it's not fair.'

◆ 'I'm really fed up with school and I don't like any of the lessons.'

◆ 'I can't do my homework tonight as I've got to go and look after my Nan.'

◆ 'I just can't understand Maths, it's so frustrating.'

◆ 'School is too much work and the teachers are always getting at you to do more.'

Skilful use of reflecting can be very helpful in difficult, confrontational or discipline situations. Although this is the last thing that comes to mind when you feel angry, threatened or affronted, the paraphrasing technique helps you to start to see another's point of view, and is handy to just whip out and use when needed, so it is certainly worth practising! Johnson and Johnson [20] have pointed out that Sanskrit is reputed to have more than nine hundred words to express feeling states whereas English has less than fifty. What does this suggest? We probably have never gained the habit of expressing how we feel so our vocabulary has not expanded to help us do so!

TEACHING TIP: Learning to express your feelings to both students and colleagues establishes good relationships and clear communication.

Limited communication – limited control

Bandler and Grinder [21] have drawn attention to the way we limit our communications, which may make things difficult for our controlling role in the classroom. These limitations have been identified as **deletions**, **distortions** and **generalisations**.

Deletions

◆ *'You are a nuisance.'* How is the student a nuisance, and to whom?

◆ *'When I take Class 3G, I get very annoyed.'* What is the teacher annoyed about and who causes the annoyance?

Conversation often has missing elements. It is always worth considering whether there is a better way to say things, because clear statements can help to solve discipline problems in class. *'I'm getting annoyed'* is incomplete and troublesome but *'Ann, your pen tapping on the desk is distracting me'*, makes it clear how Ann is contributing to the annoyance. Forms of 'deletion' often involve adverbs, ending in 'ly':

◆ *'Unfortunately, your attitude is not helping.'* To whom is this unfortunate and why is the attitude not helping?

Distortions

◆ *'My choice of Class 3B is making me unhappy.'*

◆ *'The decision to set in French is causing timetable difficulties.'*

Statements are often distorted by changing an actual ongoing process into a fixed event, using a noun instead of a verb. In the examples, 'choice' and 'decision' prevent re-evaluation. Bandler and Grinder suggest an exercise. Nouns such as 'book', 'spoon' and 'picture' can be seen in an imaginary wheelbarrow. Nouns such as 'feeling', 'anger' and 'frustration' cannot be pictured in this way. The inability to imagine these abstract nouns, describing changing behaviour, in a concrete way suggests that they might be better considered as an ongoing process: *'Choosing Class 3B is making me unhappy.'* *'Deciding to set in French is causing timetable difficulties.'*

A subtle form of distortion involves presuppositions, including information that has to be assumed correct for the sentence to make sense. *'If you knew how much work was involved you wouldn't ask me to do this extra lesson.'* The presupposition (*'If you knew how much work was involved ...'*) may be a deliberate distortion to justify the second part of the statement. This form allows the message to be given in a more covert manner and relieves the embarrassment of a direct statement.

Another type of distortion is described as 'cause and effect'. Statements imply that the behaviour of one person causes the state or feeling of the other. *'Your continual bad behaviour upsets me.'* Statements of this kind imply that the other person or event has power over the speaker and can control their life in some way. The use of 'but' may be an excuse for avoidance: *'I would like to teach an extra lesson, but I haven't time to prepare it.'*

Finally, a form of distortion known as 'mind reading' is frequently used. We often make statements that imply that we know what is going on in the listener's head. These can be the root of many misunderstandings, because they are often made regarding a third person who is not present to confirm or deny the thoughts or feelings ascribed to them: *'Tom thinks he can get away with not doing his work.'*

Generalisations

- ◆ *'I find it difficult to teach this class.'*

- ◆ *'It is impossible to trust anyone here.'*

These statements are generalisations, which are limited expressions of the experiences from which they are drawn. They can be challenged: *'Are there no students that are easy to teach?' 'Is there really no-one here that I can trust?'* The generalisation is often an explanation for not behaving in a certain way. It can be used to blame someone, even though the situation suggests the active participation of something or someone else: *'Mark is always talking in class.'* Perhaps Mark doesn't understand the lesson or maybe someone is constantly asking him for explanations. There are always alternative ways of viewing what is said.

TEACHING TIP: Giving full, straightforward and specific information to others avoids the deletions, distortions and generalisations that limit our communication.

These forms of speaking happen repeatedly in the classroom talk of both teachers and students. If we attempted to reduce them, even slightly, it would lead to a more open and honest way of interacting with others and help the discipline and control of classroom behaviour.

◆ Questioning talk

Teachers shoot questions at students as if they were firing on the enemy. Susskind [22, 23] estimated that in American elementary schools, teachers ask questions at the rate of two per minute, while in most classes students ask questions at the rate of two per hour. Wragg [24], in the Leverhulme study, found that in 20 observed lessons there were less than 20 questions from students, and these were procedural (*'What time are we going home?'*) rather than cognitive (*'Why is the sky blue?'*). He tells the story of a five year old girl returning from her first day at school and announcing to her parents that the teacher was no good because she *'just kept asking us things'*. Delamont [25] suggested that *'Cross questioning, checking up and interrogation are rude in everyday life, but the staple of classroom life.'* Perls [26] reminded us that questions often cover up implied statements and are a way of defending us against the feelings that might be revealed. For example, *'Would you get out your books please?'* means *'I want you to get out your books.'*

Why ask questions?

The rules of talk in the classroom are very different from those outside it. We ask students questions not to find out knowledge for ourselves but to discover what they know in order to teach them accordingly. Other reasons for asking questions are to help recall, deepen understanding, develop imagination and encourage problem-solving. Turney and co-workers [27] listed 12 reasons for teachers' questions, which are summarised and simplified opposite, but Bremer's [28] research into the reasons for teachers' questions suggested the reasons are limited to four (in that study, 69% of questions were to check knowledge, 54% to diagnose difficulties, 47% to recall facts, and 10% to assist thinking). There were no suggestions in Bremer's work that questions could be used for students to learn from each other, which has been discussed by Dunne and Bennett [29] as being important for learning.

Reasons for teachers' questions [27]

1 To arouse interest in a topic.

2 To focus attention on an issue.

3 To foster active learning.

4 To stimulate students to use questions.

5 To structure a task.

6 To diagnose difficulties in learning.

7 To communicate that participation is expected and valued.

8 To help students reflect.

9 To assist thinking.

10 To develop comment.

11 To give opportunity to learn from others.

12 To express interest in student ideas and feelings.

Throughout the 1980s and 1990s there was a shift in the perception of the value of using questions in class (precipitated by the writings of Barnes [30, 31], Westgate and Edwards [32], Brown and Wragg [33] as well as Government reports such as those by Kingman [34]). It was suggested that teachers need to consider the *purposes* as well as the *practices* of questioning to encourage students to think, talk and then write.

Approaches to questioning

Nuthall and Lawrence [35] described the typical class in terms of a pattern of teacher action and student reaction. Observation suggests a 'closed' or 'open' approach to questioning by the teacher, which initiates different types of student response. These approaches are clarified below.

The **closed approach** suggests the teacher has decided on an appropriate response. There are four forms:

◆ **Defining** – students are asked to define a word or concept and the accuracy of the definition is evaluated by the teacher.

◆ **Describing** – students are asked to describe an object, event or location and the content is evaluated in terms of accuracy and conciseness.

◆ **Designating** – students are asked to give a single word answer to a question about something or someone and this is evaluated in terms of correctness.

◆ **Displacing** – students are asked to manipulate information (mathematical calculation) and this is evaluated according to correctness.

Such questions place power entirely with the teacher and the only reward for the student is if the answer is correct. Many students' hatred of questions is based on their knowledge of this format and they are very unwilling to respond if they do not know the exact answer.

The **open approach** allows students to answer in the way they choose and they are able to contribute ideas without fear of failure. There are again four recognised forms:

◆ **Stating** – students are invited to give their views on a proposal and the teacher encourages with affirming comments and body language.

◆ **Evaluating** – students offer opinions about the appropriateness of an action, situation or event and the teacher encourages support with evidence.

◆ **Inferring/predicting** – students make inferences from evidence or information and predict future possibilities, with the teacher encouraging the justification of views.

◆ **Comparing and contrasting** – students explain similarities and differences between things and the teacher encourages their perceptions.

The closed approach is more suitable for 'what', 'who', 'where' and 'when' questions, as these tend to produce facts and information. The open approach, on the other hand, demands more explanation, and is likely to involve 'how' or 'why' questions, which generate ideas about processes, feelings and motives. 'Could' or 'would' questions ask the listener to explore their potential.

TEACHING TIP: Understanding which type of question to ask each student is the key to obtaining successful responses. Use closed questions with students who have limited language and open questions to encourage narrative thinking.

Discourse levels

Blank's [36] work on discourse levels suggested when the 'open' and 'closed' questioning approaches can be most usefully used. She encouraged us to assess first the level of reasoning required by questions and then the teacher–student interactions themselves. According to Blank, there are four levels of discourse:

 matching here and now

 selective analysis

3 re-ordering of perception

 4 reasoning about perception.

These have been extended following my own research, as described in the box below.

Levels of discourse

1 Matching perception (target immediate situation)

Example: *'What is this?'* Point to the car.

2 Selecting aspects of perception (target specific aspects of the situation)

Example: *'What colour is the car?' 'What is the shape of this brick?'*

3 Re-ordering perception (think beyond the immediate situation)

Example: *'Show me the cars that aren't red.' 'What do I put in the bowl before the eggs?'*

4 Reasoning about perception (express cause and effect – here/now)

Example: *'Why are you wearing a coat?' 'Why did you pick that apple?'*

5 Relating a familiar sequence (re-tell a familiar sequence of events)

Example: *'How do you cross the road?' 'How do you make a cup of tea?'*

6 Explaining an unfamiliar situation (predict what might happen)

Example: *'How would you spend the money if you won the lottery?' 'How would you make a trip to outer space?'*

By analysing discourse along levels of difficulty, a teacher can determine the cognitive and linguistic structures that lead to understanding rather than frustration. Blank [36] argued that we must expose children to complex language if we want them to acquire it for their learning. Presenting language that is above students' level is different from making unreasonable question demands on them. Blank and Marquis [37] discussed the 'oblige/comment' distinction in relation to exposure versus demand. 'Obliges' require a response from the student. *'Why are you wearing a coat?'* is a level 4 oblige, in the above discourse hierarchy. *'You're wearing a coat in case it rains,'* is a comment that exposes a student to more sophisticated language at level 4 but avoids putting him into a possible failing situation by having to respond. A level 3 question might be *'What do you wear when it rains?'*; a level 2 example is *'What colour is your coat?'*

TEACHING TIP: To limit demands on students but encourage their thinking and language, balance straightforward questions with comments that use complex linguistic structures.

Blank's [36] work highlighted the importance of keeping a balance between questions and comments while in instructional mode. Most problems stem from students being required to answer at a discourse level that is beyond them.

Structuring lessons

Using key questions – *'what ...?'*, *'who ...?'*, *'when ...?'*, *where ...?'*, *'how ...?'*, *'why ...?'* – is the way most teachers structure and summarise their lessons. The issue of what sort of questions to ask is vital and students must be able to make an explanation before 'how' and 'why' questions can be answered. Although 'what', 'who', 'when' and 'where' questions produce limited responses, it is their content in relation to the children, not the form, that determines successful answers. Brown and Wragg [33] suggested a useful mnemonic IDEA for key questions:

I   Identify the key questions in relation to the lesson objectives

D   Decide on the level and order of questions

E   Extend the activity by using supplementary and subsidiary questions

A   Analyse answers that are given and decide on follow-up responses

A 'mind map' provides another way into using questions, which structures and summarises the lesson content [38]. To use a map in this way, write down the theme of the lesson on the centre of a paper or wall board and draw lines radiating away from the theme. On the lines, write questions related to the theme. At the end of each question line, further lines and related questions may be drawn, supplying the basis for collecting thoughts about the topic. Tasks and opportunities to learn can then be built into this structure (see opposite).

An alternative way of planning lesson structure using questioning, is the GAITO approach:

G   Goals

A   Activities

I   Input

T   Timing

O   Order

Here, you consider the goals for learning and the activities to be undertaken. The balance of exposition and questions is decided together with the timing of the lesson segments (allowing for slippage in the programme!). Finally, the order of what is to be done is determined. This order may not follow the sequence in which your thoughts occur, but develops from the needs of the students in relation to the lesson content.

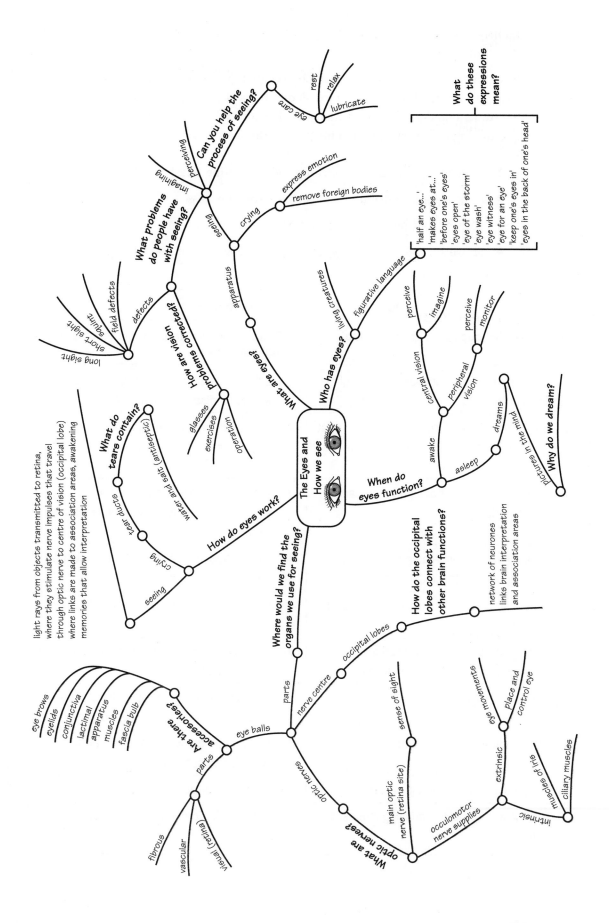

What do these expressions mean?

"half an eye..."
'makes eyes at...'
'before one's eyes'
'eyes open'
'eye of the storm'
'eye wash'
'eye witness'
'eye for an eye'
'keep one's eyes in'
'eyes in the back of one's head'

Can you help the process of seeing?

eye care — rest, relax, lubricate

perceiving

imagining

What problems do people have with seeing?

specific — crying — express emotion, remove foreign bodies

apparatus

How are vision corrected?

defects — field defects, short sight, long sight

Problems with vision — glasses, exercises, operation

What do tears contain? — water and salt (antiseptic)

tear ducts

crying

seeing

How do eyes work?

light rays from objects transmitted to retina, where they stimulate nerve impulses that travel through optic nerve to centre of vision (occipital lobe) where links are made to association areas, awakening memories that allow interpretation

What are eyes?

Who has eyes? living creatures

figurative language

central vision — perceive, imagine

peripheral vision — perceive, monitor

Why do we dream? — pictures in the mind

dreams

awake / asleep

When do eyes function?

The Eyes and How we see

Where would we find the organs we use for seeing?

How do the occipital lobes connect with other brain functions? — network of neurones links brain interpretation and association areas

parts — nerve centre — occipital lobes

eye balls — sense of sight

eye movements — place and control eye

extrinsic — occulomotor nerve supplies

intrinsic — muscles of iris, ciliary muscles

optic nerves — main optic nerve (retina site)

What are optic nerves?

Are there accessories? — eye brows, eyelids, conjunctiva, lactimal, apparatus, muscles, fascia bulb

parts — fibrous, vascular, visual (retina)

Tactics

In summarising this section, we can observe that questions are only as good as the answers they get. It is important to ask questions at the appropriate discourse levels of the students and to achieve a balance of questions with comments. Some key questioning tactics emerge from the present discussion:

◆ structuring, sequencing, pitching and presenting questions clearly

◆ directing and distributing questions across the class

◆ pausing, pacing, prompting and probing

◆ above all, listening and responding with reflection and sensitivity.

'Dos' and 'Don'ts' of questioning	
Dos – effective questions are those that:	**Don'ts – ten common errors that we all make at times:**
1 extend and lift the discussion to a higher level of thinking	1 asking questions that are above the student's discourse level
2 start with a narrow focus and broaden out – recall first and then encourage new thinking	2 asking too many questions and not making enough comments
3 start with a broad focus and then narrow down to detail	3 asking a question and answering it yourself before the student has a chance to think
4 take a circular path – a series of questions leading back to the initial idea	4 asking questions only of the brightest or most eager students
5 take a straight path using questions of a similar type	5 asking the same types of questions repeatedly
6 provide a backbone as a scaffold on which to hang the main ideas	6 asking questions in a manner that students find threatening
7 are balanced with comments using more complex language	7 failing to acknowledge positively students' responses, and putting them down
8 differentiate student discourse levels	8 ignoring an answer and repeating the question to someone else
9 signal that participation is valued	9 failing to correct an answer sensitively
10 arouse and sustain continuing interest in a topic	10 failing to build and extend answers

Knowing what question tactics to employ for each child is vital. Some students could answer a narrowly focused question, such as *'What's the name of the water droplets that fall from clouds?'* requiring the specific answer *'rain'*, but be unable to cope with a broader question requiring an explanatory answer, such as *'Why do we need rainfall?'*

All question strategies depend on good lesson planning and organisation and a knowledge of where you want the topic to go. Examples of questions that probe are given below:

◆ *'Can you give me an example?'*

◆ *'Is that always the case or are there exceptions?'*

◆ *'What are the exceptions?'*

◆ *'How does that fit in with what we have said?'*

◆ *'Why do you think it is true?'*

◆ *'Are there any other views you can think of?'*

◆ *'What is the difference between the two?'*

◆ *'What are the similarities between them?'*

◆ *'You say that it is Y (for example, rain). What kind of Y (rainfall) do you think they have in India?'*

◆ Explaining talk

Explaining something clearly to a student is the art of good teaching. It is not a single activity, however, and the verb 'explain' and its noun form 'explanation' are used in different ways.

Consider these class scenarios:

1 *'Sir, can you explain what this word means?'*

2 *'You have just been told it is raining, which explains why you can't go out to play.'*

3 *'Why are you hanging around the toilets? I want an explanation.'*

4 *'Can you give an explanation of what happens when we have a period of low rainfall?'*

In the first situation, the teacher is being asked for the meaning of an unfamiliar word. A straightforward definition, in relation to the context, is required. In the second scenario the identification of a simple relationship between cause and effect is being clarified. The third case poses a request for an explanation, which is probably a prelude to a reprimand. Finally, we have an example of an explanation that could vary in complexity according to the age and understanding of the person asked. The dictionary definition presents 'explaining' as giving understanding to another, which allows for the many contexts in which this activity might occur. The above examples suggest that an explanation can help someone to understand:

◆ **concepts** – including new ideas as well as the development of established ones (for example, different types of rainfall patterns)

◆ **cause and effect** – the consequences of one thing on another (for example, rain falling on the Earth's surface)

◆ **procedures** – rules and/or requirements (for example, the water cycle)

◆ **processes** – how things happen, behave or work (for example, how liquid water becomes vapour)

◆ **purposes** – why someone is doing something (for example, why a person might boil water)

◆ **relationships** – between people, things and events (for example, between rainfall, sun and wind).

Some explanations might include all the above features. For example, explaining World War II to a class could involve concepts (aggression, defence), cause and effect (what led to the outbreak of hostilities), processes and procedures (how the war was conducted), purposes (why the war happened) and relationships (Hitler and the Jews).

Explanations involve two parties: the 'explainer' and 'explainee'. It is often a reciprocal experience, which in a class involves students explaining to the teachers what they do not understand. Thus, the student's perspective is especially important and to avoid confusion teachers need to:

◆ find out what children already know and understand about the topic

◆ use appropriate language with words and phrases chosen for clear understanding

◆ discover misconceptions that need clarifying.

Analysis suggests that an explanation generally has three phases: an opening or preview, an exposition phase and an ending or review. This overall process helps to shape the presentation and avoid rambling talk.

Opening (preview)

The opening phase sets the scene and prepares for what is to follow. The opening stage is referred to as an 'advance organiser', but there is debate about how effective this is [39].

TEACHING TIP: An old tip is to 'tell them what you're going to tell them, tell them, then tell them what you've told them'.

Although there is some evidence to suggest that children achieve better understanding and higher test scores if given advance organisers, it could be argued that telling them what is going to happen spoils the mystery and reduces motivation. Miller's [40] work on top-down and bottom-up processing is relevant here, suggesting that half of us have a preferred bottom-up deductive organising strategy whereas the rest have a top-down inductive approach.

Those with the preferred top-down style need to have the overall view before they can slot in the detail, whereas others with a preference for a bottom-up strategy are able to process in an on-going way. In Miller's puzzle picture below, the bottom-up learners might find an animal's leg in one of the black portions, leading to a search on the more general level for the rest of the animal. The top-down processor, however, looks for a general outline of a figure. (See Appendix 1 for the answer to this puzzle.)

Experience with countless students has suggested that those with a top-down preferred strategy depend on advance organisers for effective processing while the bottom-up group are not so concerned about a preview. This knowledge demonstrates the complexity of teaching groups. There is evidence to suggest we learn better with teachers who have the same preferred learning style as ourselves and we may be able to draw on our own experiences to substantiate this.

Such information is useful in planning our approach.
Work by Smith [41] highlighted the issue of preferred mode of sensory processing, which suggests the wisdom of producing presentations that have experiential, visual and auditory components so that every member of the audience has a chance to hook in to what is happening. Work by Watson and Jones [42] on the Harlow On-line Learning Initiative (HOLLI), reported at the Human Communication International Conference, indicated that it is possible to set up individual learning projects using information technology that cater for very different styles of information processing. This is the future. Meanwhile we have to tackle the present! Taking account of personal differences in learning style is an important issue in developing successful teaching. Openings can have several purposes, therefore:

◆ to overview briefly what is to come

◆ to arouse curiosity

◆ to tune in to individual learning through experiential, visual and auditory input

◆ to discover what children already know about the topic

◆ to refresh memories of previous learning before new material is introduced.

Exposition (the structure)

The structure of an explanation should determine the strategies used to deliver it, but it can be argued that the strategies determine the structure. This paradox is dependent on the teacher's preferred learning style as well as the subject matter of the lesson. In mathematics, for example, unless you are able to add and multiply you cannot find the area of a playing field. In explanations where there is a logical, linear sequence, it is important to tackle A before B.

Not all subjects follow this mode. In history, one might sequence something like World War II in chronological order, but there is an argument for something different. It might be sensible to start off with a review of what students know about the topic and then move back from present time to explain the outbreak of world hostilities. Teacher's personal preferences are important as some will favour a planned method while others like to 'feel' the group and use an intuitive approach that improvises in response to student needs.

Ending (review and reflection)

The ending is a very important part of the explanation as it brings all the previous information together, re-states it and stamps a personal view on the proceedings. People tend to remember what they hear first and last and many children seem to demonstrate a **recency effect** when they can only recall what they have just immediately heard! Therefore, a careful summary that repeats the main ideas is vital, using anecdotes to personalise and illustrate the meanings.

Use this plan to IMPRESS!

If you use the following plan it may help you to produce clear explanations that are generally well received.

Idea	Decide on the principle aims of the lesson.
Method	Structure the main points in a plan – use anecdotes.
Presentation	Think about posture and voice pitch, pace, pause and power.
Recipients	Remember the receivers and adjust information level to suit.
Emphasis	Review points at intervals to emphasise the main ideas.
Style	Employ a style that is appropriate for the audience and situation.
Safety	Be safe rather than sorry and check the listeners understand.

Analysing explanations

There are several ways to analyse explanations. Looking back at the transcript of the lesson on making flapjacks (page 13), it is possible to make a quantitative evaluation of the number of teacher and student utterances, percentage of talk and non-talk, question types, length of utterances and so on. However, a transcript alone cannot give the full atmosphere of the occasion, as non-verbal aspects of communication such as tone of voice and body language are difficult to quantify. Qualitative analysis provides comments about the teacher's and students' interest and enthusiasm. It is sometimes useful to select an event when an explanation is taking place (for example, making flapjacks) and clarify what is happening:

◆ What preceded the event? (talk about cakes)

◆ What happened during the event? (children consulted recipe, gathered ingredients, mixed, packed mixture in tin, cooked, wrote reports)

◆ What was the result? (tray of flapjacks, short written explanations of the procedures)

◆ What comparisons can be made between the views of those present (teacher and students)? (Tom – *'boring'*; Becca – *'it was exciting'*; Kevin – *'I liked the eating bit'*; teacher – *'all except Tom were interested and keen'*)

A useful way of analysing explanations is to look at the thinking level with which students are asked to engage. Taba [43] believed that once teachers knew how to analyse the relevant classroom processes, they could move children up to higher levels of thinking. She targeted the explanation of concepts, making inferences and applying principles. We can apply her ideas to the cooking activity:

1. **Specific items of data** (*'What are these things called that we are going to mix and make into flapjacks?'*)

2. **Relating, comparing, contrasting data items** (*'Can you tell me some differences between butter and oats?'*)

3. **Factual explanation** (*'What are the things we need to do before we can eat the flapjacks we see in this picture from the recipe book?'*)

4. **Inferences from data units, predictions** (*'What happens when we heat butter?'*)

5. **Inferential logic** (*'What happens when we mix all the items together?'*)

6. **Generalisation from inferences** (*'Can you think of other things we have made by mixing certain items together?'*)

There is no clear research to indicate that this approach to raising thinking levels leads to improved learning or higher scoring on tests [44], but such an analysis helps us to reflect on what takes place. Teachers generally hold the view that it is desirable for children to be stimulated to think in different ways and it is possible to rank these ways according to levels. Bloom's Taxonomy of Educational Objectives [45] describes a six-level hierarchy, which is useful when considering work differentiation for students in classes:

1 **Knowledge** – facts, figures, information, observed situations, recalled situations

2 **Comprehension** – understanding, perceiving, interpreting, comparing, contrasting, ordering

3 **Application** – using knowledge, information, concepts, problem-solving strategies, techniques

4 **Analysis** – perceiving patterns, relationships, components, hidden meanings

5 **Synthesis** – relating, combining, inferring, predicting, generalising, concluding

6 **Evaluation** – comparing, contrasting, discriminating, assessing, prioritising, verifying

Those who learn slowly may benefit from activities targeted at levels 1 and 2 in this hierarchy, whereas the very able students will be stimulated by tasks that concentrate on application, analysis, synthesis and evaluation, thus allowing their own creativity and ideas to be fully harnessed.

Students' explanations

Explaining should not be just the province of the teacher as children need the opportunity to share information with each other, so they can clarify their thinking. Set up an activity where students explain something to others (for example, a game) and develop a report sheet for feedback along the following lines:

◆ **Clarity** – is the explanation clear to others?

◆ **Language** – is the language (verbal and non-verbal) relevant for the task?

◆ **Structure** – is the information well organised?

◆ **Examples** – are demonstrations or examples used?

◆ **Learning** – is something learned from the exercise for both 'explainer' and 'explainee'?

Using feedback sheets helps to monitor aspects of the process. It is from this type of exercise that teachers and students learn to structure the essential features of explaining ideas, such as names, attributes (colour, shape, size, weight, parts and so on), examples and rules that apply. If students are allowed opportunity to 'show and tell' to others, their follow-on written tasks will be more fluent and organised. Some students will never write well unless they have the chance to talk over ideas first. Thinking must take place before the mechanics of expression are brought into play. Nate Gage [46] got to the root of things in his book, by explaining:

"Some people explain aptly, getting to the heart of the matter with just the right terminology, examples and organization of ideas. Other explainers, on the contrary, get us and themselves all mixed up, use terms beyond our level of comprehension …"

It makes sense, therefore, that both teachers and students have opportunities to practise the skill of explaining.

◆ Comment

Three aspects of talk – controlling, questioning and explaining – have been considered in this chapter. Underpinning each of these is the issue of making what you say clear and comprehensible to whoever is listening. We have found in the discussion and examples, that certain features have emerged to indicate good practice:

◆ **Clear language**, with words and sentence structures that can be understood by the whole audience

◆ **Clear structure**, with coherence, links, shape and fluency to the ideas

◆ **Clear match** between the verbal and non-verbal information so that the message is not ambiguous or confusing.

In Chapter 5, we focus on the last of these three elements – the **non-verbal language** that accompanies the words we say. This marks out a role for teachers and students as performers, giving emphasis to the fact that we say words with our mouths but make meaning with our whole bodies. Before moving on to the next chapter, have a look at the following checklist for effective communication. It has been compiled from areas that research has indicated are particularly important to classroom practice.

Checklist for effective communication

Establishing trust:
◆ Do you express your feelings easily and clearly?
◆ Do you allow your students to know what sort of person you are?
◆ Do you let your students know you respect them?
◆ Do you give students routine, roles and responsibilities in the class?

Presenting a positive model:

◆ Do you generally come over as cheerful and confident?

◆ Do you treat all students firmly but fairly and reward rather than punish them?

◆ Do you use positive rather than negative commands?

◆ Do you make clear behaviour and learning expectations, praising when these are met?

Developing learning:

◆ Do you cultivate students' self-esteem and self-confidence?

◆ Do you differentiate tasks to extend all students?

◆ Do you encourage students to set their own goals and plan work towards them?

◆ Do you vary your communication style to suit different types of learning?

Verbal behaviour:

◆ Do you address students in a friendly, polite manner?

◆ Do you adjust questions to the student's language level?

◆ Do you give clear, straightforward instructions and explanations?

◆ Do you use words and sentence structures that students understand?

Non-verbal behaviour:

◆ Do you use regular eye contact with all students?

◆ Do you use your voice with variety and volume so all can hear and attend?

◆ Do you smile, look relaxed and appear pleasant?

◆ Do you support words with useful gestures and facial expressions?

Try the communication profile in Appendix 2 to see what you think about your communication.

SUMMARY POINTS

◆ Contact + clarity + consistency = classroom control

◆ Effective controlling talk depends on an assertive style that uses non-verbal support.

◆ Effective questioning talk depends on understanding the discourse levels of students.

◆ Questions and comments must balance if students are to learn higher levels of language.

◆ Learning styles of the audience need to be considered when presenting information.

◆ Thinking levels help to reflect on what takes place in teaching and learning.

◆ Explaining talk benefits from a structured 'preview, exposition and review' strategy.

Chapter 5

What is non-verbal language?

"An eye can threaten like a loaded and levelled gun; or can insult like hissing and kicking; or in its altered mood by beams of kindness, make the heart dance with joy."

Ralph Waldo Emerson

> *Emma looks the teacher in the eye and takes a deep breath. Then she shrugs her shoulders and tries to look anxious. The teacher smiles, looks on with interest and then points suddenly to the book on her desk. It is Emma's homework.*

The above incident demonstrates communication without words – a non-verbal 'discussion' about the late arrival of some homework. The contact between Emma and her teacher was entirely through facial expression and gesture. We make and receive these non-verbal signs all the time when we are with others but we seldom think about their significance or importance. They are produced by the way we dress ourselves, the movements of our bodies and how we use our voices to convey the meanings of words.

These non-verbal signs reveal our feelings and attitudes more accurately than words and, as we see in the above example, can be used apart from speech. In school, we become aware of non-verbal signs when a teacher puts up his hand to stop noise or beckons someone to come to the front of the class. Such signals can be placed under three main headings: **appearance, body language** (**kinesics** and **proxemics**) and **paralanguage**. Awareness of their place in communication is important for classroom interactions.

◆ Appearance

How someone looks makes immediate impact on us. It reveals a great deal about their personality, role, job and status. Extrovert people tend to wear bright rather than dark, sombre colours and solicitors do not generally dress up like hippies in beads and flowers (at least, not for the office!). In our society, important people are usually seen to dress well. In teaching, a smart appearance is deemed appropriate to show authority, and in some schools both male and female teachers are expected to wear suits.

Students' uniforms signal unity and equality and help to establish group conformity. A well-turned-out appearance indicates positive self-esteem and value. The teacher's appearance is important in providing a good example to students of an attractive personal presentation. It also demonstrates his attitude to the job. By dressing well, we show our commitment and respect.

Thourlby [1] suggested our appearance conveys at least ten types of message to others:

1. economic level
2. educational level
3. trustworthiness
4. social position
5. level of sophistication
6. economic background
7. social background
8. educational background
9. level of success
10. moral character.

Fortenberry and co-workers [2] presented evidence that we are more likely to obey people dressed in a high-status manner. The move towards 'power-dressing' in schools is obviously on the right lines!

Recently, colour analysts have made an impact on workplace dressing, using psychology to match people to spectrums of autumn, winter, spring or summer hues. Many people firmly believe that wearing the right colour for our particular skin tone enhances appearance and adds to self-image. If we look good we feel good. Many aspects of personal appearance are under voluntary control, such as hair and clothes, while others – such as physique and body condition – are only partially so.

Appearance is meaningful only within a particular setting where the significance of details of dress, hair or cosmetics is generally understood. Within modern cultures fashions change extremely fast, so that being up-to-date becomes itself a main dimension of appearance, and is important to some but not to others.

◆ Body language

"… let your discretion be your tutor: suit the action to the word, the word to the action."

Shakespeare

During communication, as a listener you rely more on the message contained in the body language of the speaker than on what is actually said, especially if the two contradict each other. Our bodies are constantly sending messages to others to make powerful statements about who we are, how we are feeling and what we are thinking.

Body language can reinforce our verbal messages, or it can discount them. Can you recall saying a student's painting or design looked nice when your voice and facial expression indicated quite the opposite? (In fact you thought it was a mess!) We can be economical with the truth when using words but our gestures are mostly involuntary and seldom lie. All of us are guilty of a mismatch between our verbal and non-verbal language in certain circumstances.

There are six main elements that we need to consider in respect of the body language we use. The first group of these is known as 'kinesics' and includes facial expressions, gestures and body movements. The second is called 'proxemics' and involves touch, proximity, positioning and posture. We will look at these in turn.

Kinesics

Facial expression: the way we signal with our faces

The eyes and mouth dominate expression signs and are what people look for when trying to weigh someone up. We are able to distinguish subtle variations in smile or look – for example, the raised eyebrow of surprise, fear or acknowledgement. If someone gazes at us constantly then it means they are interested. Much facial expression in humans appears to be culturally universal and largely independent of learning [3]. There are constraints on the expression of negative attitudes and emotions and spontaneous expressions are sometimes concealed. Some aspects, however, such as expansion of the pupils during arousal, perspiration in anxiety and fleeting expressions of hidden feelings, are very difficult to control.

Facial expression is used in close combination with speech. A listener provides a continuous reaction to what is said by small movements of eyebrows and mouth to indicate surprise, disagreement, pleasure or puzzlement. A speaker accompanies utterances with relevant facial expressions that 'frame' what is said showing whether it is funny, sad, serious or important [4].

The table opposite indicates that the face provides a moving picture with fleeting images that have to be registered and read for full understanding of the communication. It is the most communicative part of the body and the eyes are the most expressive part as they speak volumes:

"Our eye beams twisted and did thread our eyes upon one double string."

John Donne

We can think of the face communicating information on three time-scales. There is the 'permanent' face: we tend to think of those with high foreheads as intelligent, thin lips as prim and careful, protruding eyes as excitable (though such interpretations are not necessarily accurate). Secondly, the face expresses emotions that take time to develop, as in anger when the muscle tension increases, the blood flows to the head and eyes bulge. Finally, the face flashes signals rapidly to provide feedback such as smiles, frowns, nods and eyebrows movements, which influence the course of the conversation or presentation. The chart presented below gives a list of common facial expressions and what they might mean.

Gesture: the way we use our arms, hands, fingers, legs and feet as signs

Primary school teachers constantly use specific **gestures** to express the size, height and width of things they are describing. Relative words like big and small, tall and short are difficult for small children to grasp, so gestures help to give precise meaning to the words. The hands are able to express a great deal. Movements of the head, feet and other body parts may be employed but are less expressive than those of the hands. Some gestures indicate general arousal, which produces diffuse activity in the body, while others appear to reflect emotional states; for example, the clenched fist of anger. Body movements help to co-ordinate speech utterances, and these are known as 'baton' gestures because speakers gesticulate like band leaders to keep their whole communication performance together.

Hand gestures are an aspect of body movement that have been studied in depth. Ekman and Friesen [5] distinguished between three types of hand gestures:

◆ **Emblems** can be directly translated into a word or phrase (for example, gestures meaning 'Stop' or 'Okay'). The meanings of these emblems vary between cultures, which could cause confusion in multi-cultural classrooms. Within a given culture, however, the meanings are clear and understood.

◆ **Illustrators** are hand movements accompanying speech and do not have specific meaning in themselves. Sometimes the hand movement adds to the meaning of what is said; for example, a wide rounded movement when talking about something large and circular. The hand movements enhance what is said and help

Facial expressions		Interpretations
forehead	upward/downward frowns	acceptance/rejection
eyebrow	raising or knitting/furrowing	enjoyment/dislike
eyelids	opening/closing, narrowing	friendship/hostility
eye pupils	dilating	interest
eyes	upwards/downward gazing	disinterest/anger
	holding/avoiding eye contact	love/embarrassment
nose	wrinkling	jealousy
	flaring nostrils	assurance
facial muscles	drawn up	agreement
	down	disagreement
	grinning	pleasure
	grimace	pain/displeasure
	teeth clenching	annoyance/attention
lips	smiling	acceptance
	drawn in	boredom
	pursing	anger/control
mouth	wide open	disbelief
	half open	surprise
	wide open	fear
tongue	licking lips	impatience
	moving inside cheeks	frustration
	sucking teeth	envy/empathy
jaw/chin	thrust forward	ease
	hanging down	discomfort
	relaxed	alertness
head	thrown back	stupor
	inclined to the side	pleasure
	hanging down	pain
	chin drawn in	ecstasy
	tilted	satisfaction
	inclined upwards	displeasure/torment

to gain the listener's attention. They are particularly important for students who have problems in processing words. Sometimes hand movements are inappropriate and distract the listener; for example, someone wringing their hands nervously when talking about something happy and pleasant. My hand movements have been described as 'windmills', fluttering around without being useful!

◆ **Adaptors** are hand movements that are self-orientated; for example, scratching oneself, touching one's face or pulling hair. Again, these movements can be very distracting and cause much amusement among the class.

Gestures may have as much to do with the listener as the speaker. Condon [6] analysed frames of films of two people interacting and showed that both synchronised their movements in subtle ways. When the communication is going badly it is possible that this synchronisation becomes disturbed. If you look at people in conversation you will find that they mirror one another by crossing legs, folding arms, putting their heads to one side, and so on.

Henley [7] related body movements to power relationships. A person in a lesser role, when in conversation, will tilt his head – a similar movement to the gestures of appeasement found in some animal species. The superior person will assume a more relaxed position with head back, and perhaps hands behind the neck. If students took up such a posture, teachers would assume their insolence. When students adopt a highly relaxed posture at the back of the class, this often indicates boredom or disaffection. These gestures, however, have to be understood in context. (There is more about posture on page 89.)

TEACHING TIP: Use gestures to aid expression and give emphasis, but beware of movements that distract the listeners.

Other gestures

Sometimes we replace words with gestures, as in the signing systems used by the deaf community. Sign languages such as Paget Gorman and American Sign Language have a syntax that resembles verbal communication. Students with language difficulties appreciate non-verbal support and effective use of gestures helps to make a message clear. Makaton, a sign language devised for the learning impaired, is used alongside speech (rather than replacing it) because it is more visible than words and allows greater processing time, with reinforcement of important word concepts. Signs act as a trigger for words as well as attention devices that achieve connection and co-operation. Albert Mehrabian [8] calculated that, on average, the total impact of a message owes 7% to the words, 38% to the voice and 55% to gestures. People speak with the vocal organs but communicate with the whole of their bodies.

Movements: to support words and express feeling and emotion

Movements are involved in specific gestures, as in a 'goodbye wave', and can be a substitute for words, as discussed above. More general movements are seen frequently in communication situations, reinforcing the spoken word as well as transmitting feelings such as boredom, impatience and relaxation. The movements described below are all seen in communication situations.

Head:	nodding up and down
	shaking sideways
	nodding sideways (urging someone along)
	inclining briefly
	cradling in one or both hands
Arms and hands:	stretched out
	folded across the chest
	placed open on the chest
	held over the mouth
	brushing something away
	patting a table/desk top
	pressed together as in prayer
	jammed into a pocket
	making chopping movements with the side of the hands
Fingers:	pointing (position or direction)
	laced at the back of the head
	running through the hair
	drumming on a table top
	stroking the chin
	patting together
	stabbing with the forefinger
	clenching a fist
	waving
	rubbing fingers and thumbs together
	clicking
	tapping a rhythm
Legs and feet:	crossing both legs in sitting or sometimes standing
	moving legs up and down while sitting
	kicking movements
	swinging legs
	toe tapping

It is important to be aware of the effects of our movements on others. The following exercise can help to develop such an awareness. Divide a group into pairs of As and Bs. In each pair, give B a topic to talk about while A listens and observes. A should make notes about B's gestures and movements, under these headings:

- ◆ head
- ◆ arms
- ◆ hands
- ◆ trunk
- ◆ legs
- ◆ feet

After five minutes, ask the As to share their observations with the whole group, describing the effects that various movements had on their feelings and attention. Then reverse the roles of A and B and repeat the exercise.

Proxemics

Touch (physical contact): who we touch, when, where and how

The British are one of the least 'touching' nations, which may provide problems in relationships with those from other cultures. There is evidence that more touching – within broad social rules – helps us to get on better with others, including those from our own culture. When touched during an interaction, however briefly, we usually feel more friendly towards that person.

There is nothing unusual in a teacher holding a student lightly by the upper arm as she talks to him. It would seem strange, however, if the student were to do the same to the teacher. This unilateral right to touch is an expression of the status relationship between teachers and students. The relative sex and age of those concerned affects the significance of the act. At primary level it is unusual for a teacher to consider the sex of the student but at secondary school male teachers would not touch girls because of sexual connotations. With the present emphasis on children's rights and accusations of physical abuse being levelled at some teachers, some staff consider it expedient not to touch students under any circumstances. This inhibits expression of warm, reassuring attitudes towards students. Wheldall and co-workers [9] found that 'teacher-touch' was an effective 'reinforcer' of work and positive behaviour when accompanied by praise.

Proximity (positioning): how near to others we sit or stand

Everyone needs a certain space around them to feel comfortable, and they do not like their body space invaded because they feel threatened by a close presence. Crowded classrooms and corridors are just waiting for disruption to happen. Children will lash out if they feel oppressed.

The meaning of body **proximity** varies from culture to culture. Latin Americans and Arabs stand very close to each other whereas the English, Scots and Swedes keep a longer distance. In the UK, people tend to keep their distance from those with higher status. Students would not expect to be too near their teachers. People vary in their preferred proximity and these differences are found to be consistent across different situations [10]. We tend to stand closer to people we like and so proximity is regarded as an indicator of the relations between people.

Changes in proximity communicate a desire to initiate or terminate an encounter. Orientation is an important aspect of proximity; for example, in confrontation a head-on position is adopted, whereas in co-operation a side-to-side orientation is used.

TEACHING TIP: Think about your position in relation to students when arranging class furniture. Curved rather than straight desk formations encourage closer proximity with all students.

Proximity is important as it signals the nature of relationships, setting the boundaries that are required by particular situations. It is also a sign of attentiveness. Desks grouped in a circle rather than rows help teachers to keep in close proximity with all students. If desks are arranged in lines with a central corridor, the teacher is inclined to keep in contact with only the central band of students and ignore those on the outsides. This is a useful and important point about facilitating proximity and helping to sustain the attention of the whole class.

Posture: the way we hold our bodies

Posture is the way you unconsciously arrange your body when you sit, stand, walk or lie down. Gestures are related to body postures: the differences are that we make a gesture but adopt a posture; the gesture is a signal confined to a specific body part (pointing finger), but postures involve the whole body; gestures are momentary whereas postures tend to be held for longer periods. In practice gestures, movements and postures merge. Think of a child in a class trying to get the teacher's attention. First she raises her hand only. However, the teacher is busy and does not notice this small gesture, so she starts to move her head and shoulders vigorously. Getting excited, she finally moves to her feet, adopting a posture of urgency.

Posture gives you away completely. If your body is relaxed, others will approach with confidence. However, if you are tense, with shoulders hunched, arms tightly folded and fists clenched, people will be wary. A slumped, foetal posture, indicates your intention to find sympathy. The body shapes into signs for others to read. Look at the stick drawings overleaf. What do they suggest?

Have you noticed that people adopt similar postures when they meet? At a table, if one rests on their elbows and leans forward, the other will probably do so. This unconscious imitation is known as **postural echo** and this ability to mirror someone else is an important social skill as it cements a relationship. Postural behaviour, however, will differ in people of different status. Superiority is shown by a relaxed posture with open leg and arm positions. Inferiority, however, is demonstrated by the exact opposite with

Posture

the body upright, legs together and hands folded as if protecting oneself. When a person is under threat, a whole gamut of submissive postures are exhibited from crouching and grovelling to bowing the head. Reducing height is a stylised form of submission.

In a confrontation, bodies positioned front to front, together with closeness and direct gaze, signal aggression. It is not surprising that in the western culture people stand with bodies slightly averted from one another when in communication. This is considered polite as it shows that intentions are friendly or neutral.

An open posture with legs a little apart and arms relaxed is welcoming but as soon as you fold them and stiffen your body a message of fear and aggression is transmitted. I once had a student teacher who had difficulty controlling the class. She used to enter the room and stand in a stiff position with arms tightly folded. After she softened her posture, her demeanour was much less threatening and the class settled down without disruption.

Fenton [11] suggested that a large number of children in schools have such bad posture that they are permanently damaging their bodies. A person's posture may be a metaphor for their inner emotional turmoil. Someone with hunched shoulders and clenched fists may be working through traumatic events in the mind. Try the exercise described below, to practise analysing posture and emotional state.

In groups of three, examine the posture of each group member in turn. Each person should stand in a relaxed position against a wall, while the others look at the body alignment from the front, side and back. The observers should give feedback on the head position in relation to the spine. Are the hips swung backwards or forwards? Is there drooping of the shoulder or hip? The observers should then adjust the person's body to a better position and ask how this feels.

◆ Paralanguage

Paralanguage comprises the non-verbal sounds accompanying speech, which are separate from the words themselves. They are often about immediate reactions and emotions. We may gasp in surprise or utter 'er' or 'um' during conversing, which signals, *'hold on, I'm thinking out the next bit!'* Sometimes we scream in fright, squeal in delight or groan with pain.

The most important elements of paralanguage are the prosodics known as 'verbal dynamics' – the **pitch, pace, pause, power** and **pronunciation** – that create the melody and meaning of the words. I can shout *'Tom'* to show anger, or trill the name softly to indicate pleasure. There are 101 ways of performing words and sentences to create 101 different meanings.

The rising and falling tones (intonation) of our voices are a crucial factor in comprehension. During the utterance of a sentence the voice goes up and down musically, as the diagram below indicates.

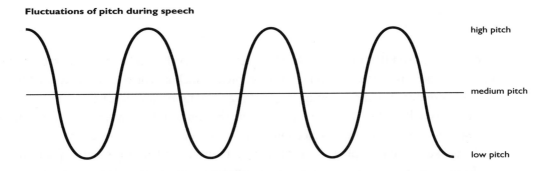

Fluctuations of pitch during speech

high pitch

medium pitch

low pitch

According to Crystal [11], intonation is the most important means we have of organising our speech into units of communication. Think of the phrase *'Meet me in the staff room at 4 o'clock.'* If performed with a rise at the end of the sentence, a question is indicated, whereas a fall in the voice signals a command statement. English is a stress-timed language, as every word of more than one syllable has one segment emphasised more than the others. Think of 'communicate' where the power is on the second syllable. We can vary meaning, however, by shifting the stress of one word to another in a sentence. Consider the effect of this in the sentence 'Luke ate his breakfast'.

	1	2	3	4
	Luke	**ate**	**his**	**breakfast.**

Stress at 1 – Luke, and nobody else, ate his breakfast.

Stress at 2 – He ate it – he didn't give it away or put it in the bin.

Stress at 3 – Luke didn't eat his sister's breakfast, or anyone else's.

Stress at 4 – Luke didn't eat his lunch, or any other meal.

91

My own research into children's language and learning difficulties in the classroom, indicates that they find it difficult to monitor the verbal dynamics of speech, which are the major markers for meaning [13]. Introducing students to performance techniques in poetry and drama activities had a positive effect on their comprehension abilities as it helped them to become aware of how a message is understood.

Being able to vary the tune of our voices and use pitch, pace, pause, power and pronunciation changes to create meaning and hold attention is an important skill for both teacher and students. As we get older, our vocal range reduces, but we can retain our youthful vibrant tunes if we commit ourselves to a little exercising, which also helps to prevent problems with our voices. The next section shows us how to do this easily.

◆ Keeping the voice tuned

"The devil hath not, in all his quiver's choice, an arrow for the heart like a sweet voice."

Byron

Are you surprised that one in ten teachers receives speech and language therapy during her career, because of troublesome vocal problems, such as voice loss, husky quality, chronic sore throat or discomfiture in speaking for long periods? Teachers are professional talkers but do not have, as a rule, the communication training necessary to change a *private* conversation voice into a *public* audience one. Actors are coached for each speaking role they play, working to keep their voices trim for reliable, pleasing performances. Surely then, teachers, who perform on their 'class stage' every day, should receive regular maintenance of their vocal skills. Ideally, they should have a diagnostic consultation with a communication specialist and receive training in public speaking. However, this is the real world and not Utopia, so self-help is perhaps the most realistic answer! Spend a few minutes each day following the steps below, for a top teacher's voice!

Steps to a powerful voice and pleasing talk: Balance, Breathing and Bounce

Step 1: Balance

Public voices need power and this begins with aligned posture for body balance. Listen to your voice as you change position. Repeat a phrase during this exercise, such as *'Top talkers' training tips'*. What happens when you say this phrase with:

- ◆ your weight on one leg?
- ◆ your chin tucked into your chest?

◆ your chin lifted to the ceiling?

◆ your chin pushed forward?

◆ your head bent on one side?

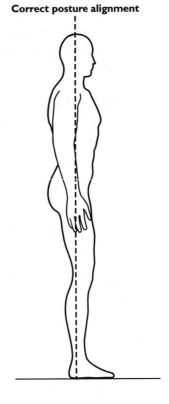

Correct posture alignment

The sound changes in each position, because your body lacks alignment and balance. It deviates from the line of gravity, so muscles become tense as they keep you upright. The result is a tight, strained voice! Check for posture alignment in a long mirror, to achieve correct body balance.

We are schooled to sit and stand straight, throwing head and shoulders back and putting bodies into extension. Correct posture, with weight slightly forward, seems strange. The body is in flexion and we are not used to it. Practice makes perfect. Posture is the key to a confident appearance and pleasing talk, so persevere!

Step 2: Breathing

Now the body is in balance, are you ready for a 'breath check'? Stand in front of a mirror.

Take a *big* breath. Does your chest leap up? Does your head look as if it is sinking into your shoulders? Do your neck muscles start to show? If the answer is 'Yes', you are normal! What a relief! However, you are taking in only *half* of your breath capacity, and public speaking needs *full* lungs for power and energy to produce a bigger voice. You can achieve this using the following progressive stages.

1 Start on your back to eliminate upright tension. Lie on the floor, knees bent, feet flat, using books to support the head. Breathe in and out six times to become aware of the breathing pattern. Relax. Put one hand on your abdomen (stomach area) and the other on the chest. Breathe in, letting your abdomen, lower ribs and back expand. Breathe out. Allow your *stomach* rather than your chest to do the work. Use your hand positions to check this. Repeat this sequence until you happily have the hang of it.

2 Sit on a chair, in correct alignment, with feet flat on the floor. Blow out all the air you can by pulling your abdomen in towards the spine. Blow out more air (there is more than you think). Now, keep your chest still and release the abdomen. Air rushes into the lower rib area. Repeat this until the action co-ordinates and breathing moves down.

❸ Sit on the chair *edge* with feet flat on the floor. Let your body fold over your legs with head and arms hanging freely. Breathe in, feeling the movement of your abdomen, lower ribs and back. Practise to become aware of this deep breathing sensation.

❹ Stand aligned. Clasp your hands and with palms facing the ceiling, and stretch your arms above your head. Check that your head is straight. Follow the directions for stage 2. With arms fixed, you are forced to use your abdominal muscles! When confident about the correct action, release your arms and repeat in both standing and sitting positions. With practice, you will be perfect!

People often react to tense situations by holding their breath. Relax, keep breathing and shake off the 'holding habit'. You don't need it! Talking is pleasant!

Step 3: Bounce

Powerful public speaking requires a big, bouncy voice. You need to 'throw' it up and down, and toss it around quickly or slowly to the farthest boundaries of the space you are in. Are you ready to start bouncing?

❶ First, relax and control your body by pulling every part of you tight and then letting go like a piece of elastic.

♦ Imagine you're a puppet with strings that are stretched. Stand in aligned posture. Move forward slowly onto the tips of your toes. Stretch through your feet to your ankles, ankles to knees, knees to hips, hips to chest, chest to shoulders, shoulders to elbows, elbows to wrists, wrists to fingers. Now stretch the neck upwards. Fold down from the waist with your head and arms limp like a rag doll. Repeat this 30-second exercise three times. Persevere to develop control of your body. Hold and let go as if those puppet strings are being cut with a large pair of scissors – your body should flop!

♦ Relax and control your head and neck by slowly dropping your head onto your chest. Bring it back and repeat, dropping your head to each shoulder and to the back. Roll your head in a circle to the right and then left.

♦ With your hands at your sides and fists clenched, breathe in lifting your shoulders to your ears. Drop your shoulders and release your fists, sighing as you breathe out.

♦ Keep the jaw loose and do six, slow, shoulder rolls to the back. Feel your chest expand and sigh as you breath out.

♦ Screw your face up as if it were a paper bag, then slowly smooth it out. Breathe in and pucker your lips, forcing air through these as you breathe out (making a 'brrrrr' sound).

2 Try the 'King Kong trick'. Drop your jaw and let it hang loose. Breathe in through the nose and out saying *'King Kong, ting tong, ding dong, ping pong, bing bong'*, lowering tone each time so the final *'bong'* eases down to the bottom range. Bounce the voice slowly. Your voice has high, medium and low pitch, so start the *'King'* as high as you can.

3 Now choose a sentence such as *'I want a big, beautiful, bouncy voice,'* and say it:

- ◆ happily
- ◆ sadly
- ◆ excitedly
- ◆ aggressively
- ◆ angrily
- ◆ as if in a huge hall.

Try to express the images of 'big', 'beautiful' and 'bouncy' by moving the vowel sounds. Say the sentence slowly, then quickly. Give emphasis to each word in turn to produce a very different meaning from the message. Change the pitch of the first word for a very different effect. Pause in front of different words. How does this alter your performance? Experimenting with your voice and audio taping the results will help you become much more aware of the power of your speech and the effects that can be produced.

4 After these warm-ups take a piece of text, such as the description from *James and the Giant Peach* below, and read it for different audiences – for children, for young adults and then for older people. What were the differences in these performances?

> The skin of the peach was very beautiful – a rich buttery yellow with patches of brilliant pink and red. Aunt Sponge advanced cautiously and touched it with the tip of one finger. 'It's ripe!' she cried. 'It's just perfect! Now, look here, Spiker. Why don't we go and get a shovel right away and dig out a great big chunk of it for you and me to eat?'
>
> *from 'James and the Giant Peach' by Roald Dahl (1971) Penguin*

You probably found, to your surprise, that you did these routines without sweat. Hopefully, you are now more aware of what is happening in your body and to your voice. Some exercises were harder. Why? Is it because of tensions in certain muscles? Learn to observe yourself and others for better awareness. Try examining television newscasters. Can you see them tighten their jaws, mouths and lips? Often, they furrow their brows as they read and this tension makes their warm and charming voices disappear!

Jaws, particularly, become tight and stiff with the tensions of life. Practise yawning and rubbing the sockets under your ears. This will work magic for your talk! Speaking involves more muscles in your body than any other physical activity. If you talk you must train. Would you find professional footballers running onto the field without pre-match practice? Of course not! They know that physical damage occurs without proper preparation of the body. Take their tip and crack on with the tone and talk routine!

To summarise this section, it helps to get into the habit of exercising the mind as well as the body at odd moments in the day. Remember, correct posture and breathing keep the whole body toned. Try to read poems or pieces of text out loud on a regular basis. This makes you work to express meaning and – like a sing-song – leaves you exhilarated, because it allows feeling to be released. Above all, remember to keep *drinking water*. It lubricates the vocal cords, and – in our dry, centrally heated atmosphere – it is essential for speech and body health.

Relaxation and visualisation

Relaxation lies at the bottom of improved performances, but is not usually encouraged in school. Hall and Hall [14], however, reported the use of imagery exercises with children in school settings that were helpful in encouraging them to relax, create ideas and develop self awareness. I used the following script, one day, when I had a difficult class that would not settle. The writing that emerged from the experience was truly amazing in its description and feeling.

The teacher settles the group, using a slow relaxed voice that is comfortable and pleasant to listen to. She asks them to get as comfortable as they can in their chairs and relax, imagining their bodies are butter melting into warm toast...

'As you relax you will become aware of your breathing – feel the rhythm as you breathe in and out through your nose. Feel the movement in and out, with your hands on the soft part of your stomach. Imagine you are breathing in light, brightness and happiness and as you breathe out all the dark, dreary and troubled thoughts of your minds disappear. Let your eyes close if you want (you can peep) as this helps you to concentrate and become calm.

Think of each part of your body in turn. Start with your head – as you think about it all dark thoughts disappear. Now your body – as you breathe out all the tightness in your muscles goes. Think about your right arm, from your shoulder to the finger tips. Imagine all the tightness in your arm flowing out through your finger tips. Now your left arm – the tightness flows away. Now think where your right leg is – imagine the tightness in your leg disappearing as you think downwards from your thigh to your toes. Then the left leg – tightness flowing out through your leg and foot. With every thought, you feel more and more relaxed and more and more at ease with yourself.

Now imagine you are at the top of some steps and at the bottom is the sea. There is a beautiful bay with water lapping on the sand. The air is warm and scented with sweet smells. You hear birds and the gentle sound of the waves below. Have a look around what can you see? (*pause*) Are you alone? (*pause*) What can you hear? (*pause*) You walk slowly down and down the ten steps, feeling more and more relaxed with each step – ten (*pause*) nine (*pause*) eight (*pause*) seven (*pause*) six (*pause*) five (*pause*) four (*pause*) three (*pause*) two (*pause*) one. You feel a soft breeze on your cheeks. The air is very, very warm. You take off your shoes and walk down to the edge of the water, where there is a large flat stone. (*pause*) You feel very content and in control, very confident that all is well with you. Someone is walking to meet you. They have a smile on their face. What happens? (*pause*)

When it is right, move up the beach and put on your shoes, take the steps up – one, two, three, four – higher and higher – five, six, seven, eight – higher and higher – nine and ten. Open your eyes and come back to this room when you are ready.

Share your thoughts with a neighbour. How do you feel? Can you re-tell the experience? What was the best bit?

A journey in the mind, such as this one, alters the state of consciousness and can be used to project feelings and thoughts. Some children could come together and imagine they were a tree at the top of the steps to the bay. The others can be invited to ask questions: 'What sort of tree?', 'How old?', 'What shape are your leaves?' Encourage the drawing of a tree and a discussion of each other's representations.

Following this, try putting the group in pairs and taking them through these instructions.

1. Face your partner and relax – empty your head and think about the other person.

2. Complete the following sentences using the images you have of your partner:
   - 'When you were little you used to…'
   - 'Right now you…'
   - 'In five years' time you will be…'

3. Share the projections made.

Teachers who believe in these relaxation approaches report better behaved students and more imaginative writing. Try starting off in a small way and ask the students to close their eyes and imagine they have a picture screen in their heads. Tell them to concentrate for 30 seconds and make a picture pop onto this. After this, ask the students to describe what was there. Reassure the group that sometimes pictures do not come and it is quite all right to say they have a dark, blank screen.

You may feel cynical regarding the appropriateness of this approach to your classes. However, these visualisation exercises are extremely valuable in developing the imagination that is necessary to listen, speak, read or write fluently. Hall and Kirkland [15] reported on such activities and suggested a combination of tree drawing (asking students to draw a tree in any way they like, on paper) and visualisation has a powerful impact for improvement in the quality of writing and in the use of statements, explanations and story telling. Stevens [16] suggested that teachers should avoid the following four responses if they want to use imagery in their teaching.

1. **Judgment**: discourage any judgmental comments from anybody about what is reported.

2. **Help**: avoid rushing in to suppress anyone who is expressing negative feelings, as these should be allowed to emerge and be accepted calmly and in a matter-of-fact way.

3. **Expectation**: there are no prescribed outcomes from visualisation and images do not have to be happy or what the teacher intended.

4. **Explanation**: it is tempting to explain someone else's experience but this should be avoided.

The Positive, Active, Clear and Energetic learning system (PACE)

The PACE (positive, active, clear and energetic) learning system, is a popular routine with actors, singers and public speakers who see the value in getting their mind and body in close synchronisation for communicating. It has developed from a realisation of the need to achieve harmonious function of both left and right halves of the brain. The routine – which is described below – is fun, as well as relaxing, and neuroscientists attest to its benefits [17].

The PACE system has been around for a long time. When I was at school, our Latin teacher made us do this series of exercises before each lesson. We were made aware that body and mind exercises were the secret of success. These old ideas, which were practised by the Greeks and Romans to increase their learning power, have developed into a sophisticated repertoire of exercises known as 'Brain Gym' [18]. The routines have become universal but not widespread, probably because of the strongly held view in our society that mind and body are separate. People find it hard to believe that a simple series of physical activities can help us to think and communicate more effectively. Nevertheless, we do communicate with our whole bodies so warm-ups should include all of us and attempt the integration and synchronisation of our many parts.

Have a go yourself and then try it on your students. I have always found it popular with all age groups. It sets them thinking, discussing and evaluating – just the sorts of activities we want to encourage for communicating and learning!

Positive

Are you ready to learn? Try this calming exercise, which balances the right and left parts of the brain. It can be done standing or sitting.

Hook-ups: Cross one ankle over the other, whichever feels most comfortable. Then cross, clasp and invert the hands by stretching out your arms in front of you with the backs of the hands together and thumbs pointing down. Lift one hand over the other, so that your palms are facing, and interlock the fingers. Roll the locked hands down and in toward your body so they rest on your chest, with your elbows down. This activates the input and output areas of each side of the brain.

In this position, rest your tongue on the roof of your mouth behind the top teeth. This brings attention to the mid-brain, lying above the hard palate of the roof of the mouth and releases a tongue thrust caused by postural imbalance. Dennison [18] suggested this configuration connects emotions in the limbic system with reason in the frontal lobes of the brain providing an integrative perspective from which to learn and respond effectively. When done for two minutes with disruptive students, Hannaford [17] reported that the exercise was found to improve behaviour. Teachers often use it when stress levels rise and also to refocus students after changes such as break or lunch time.

Active

Do you want to get your brain moving? Try this cross-lateral walking to activate and co-ordinate large areas of both sides of the brain.

Cross crawl: In a standing or sitting position, touch the right hand to the left raised knee and then the left hand to the right raised knee. Alternate one arm and opposite leg for 25 repetitions. The cross crawl movements should be performed very slowly to involve more fine motor movement and activate the vestibular system (balance), frontal brain lobe in conjunction with the basal ganglion of the limbic brain and the cerebellum of the brain stem. Neuroscientists such as Hannaford [17] suggest this is an effective exercise to free the mind; for example, from 'writer's block'.

Clear

Are you thinking clearly? Try rubbing 'acupressure points' to bring energy to the brain for increased mental and visual clarity.

Brain buttons: Place one hand over the navel and with the other gently rub the indentations between the first and second ribs directly under the collar bone (clavicle) to the right and left of the breastbone (sternum). Rubbing the navel brings attention to the gravitational centre of the body and alerts the vestibular system (balance) so waking up the brain to incoming sensory stimuli. The blood flow through the carotid arteries is stimulated by rubbing the two higher points. Many comment that this rubbing technique brings them back to focus when attention wanders.

Energetic

Do you have the energy to learn? Try the energy yawn and drink some water.

Energy yawn: This is done by massaging the muscles round the jaw joint (temporal-mandibular), which lies at the front of the ear opening. Across this joint run trunks from five major cranial nerves that gain sensory information from all over the face, eye muscles, tongue and mouth and activate all the muscles for eating and speaking. The energy yawn relaxes the whole facial area so that sensory intake can occur more efficiently. It facilitates communication and verbalisation.

Water: This is the most important and abundant inorganic body substance making up from 45–75% of total body weight. It is recommended that we drink about 10 ml of water per 0.5 kg of body weight (0.3 fl oz per lb) daily, and this should be tripled in times of stress. Water, as the universal solvent, is essential for the electrical transmissions within the nervous system that make us sensing, learning, thinking, acting beings. The smooth functioning of this system depends on water, oxygen and nutrients, with water being the most necessary ingredient. Central heating plus many of the chemicals present in modern processed foods dehydrate the body. Interestingly, when we are at our most dehydrated we do not feel thirsty. Many of us lack enough water to function well. There is anecdotal evidence to suggest that schools and firms who install water fountains and encourage their use reap the benefits in lower levels of stress and improved behaviour and productivity.

◆ Comment

This section on **non-verbal communication** (NVC) describes the body signals that we deliberately or inadvertently make when we are with other people. Since our clothes, hairstyle, grooming, face and body decoration are just as much part of us as our postures, gestures and voice tone, they too come under the heading of non-verbal communication. These behaviours happen all the time in interaction. As I look round a classroom, one student is making jabbing movements at his watch with his right index finger and pointing to the door. Another nods her head furiously and beams. A serious-looking lad is frowning. His neighbour is slumped over a desk with head buried in his hands. Further along the row is another young man tweaking the hair of the girl in front. Many signals are passing to and fro during the last few minutes of the lesson even though no words are spoken by these students.

We have seen that non-verbal communication has at least five important functions:

1 It accompanies our words, underlining and reinforcing verbal signals, as well as carrying information about feelings and attitudes.

2 It replaces talk, as when a teacher indicates with a hand movement to keep the voice level down because speech would interfere with the flow of the lesson.

3 It contradicts, as in the comment *'Nice picture'* accompanied by a sneer, frown and sarcastic voice tone with facial expression that betrays a lack of enthusiasm.

4 It helps our self-presentation. As social beings, we have to present ourselves to others. Everything about us – our physical appearance, the sorts of clothes we wear, our regional accent – combines to create a personal image. We can determine the impression we make on others with our clothes, grooming, and personal decorations. Argyle [19] suggested that we do this to overcome the taboo against boasting, as it is not the 'done thing' to brag about ourselves. Therefore, we attempt to do this indirectly through the way we present ourselves. Our students do it all the time with their designer trainers and sportswear!

5 It plays an important part in social rituals. Students must put their hands up if they want to speak. Teachers have their own opening and closing ceremonies to start and end a lesson. These ritual acts in school often serve to reinforce existing differences in status. When I was a student we always rose from our seats when a teacher entered the classroom. This rarely happens nowadays but in other contexts, such as a court of law, the public rises when magistrates or judges enter, recognising them as figures of power. Maybe if we revived the ritual of standing for teachers it would signal their authority in the class and endorse their right to establish good behaviour and work routines.

Focusing on our non-verbal behaviour is important, as it is likely that some of our students will find our words difficult to comprehend but our actions more easily interpretable. Synchronising verbal and non-verbal performance is the key to clear communication. The following check helps us to achieve this for our students.

Check before you speak!

1 Plan beforehand – have notes and documents to hand and in order.

2 Explore alternative points of view – look at what you say from others' viewpoints (visualisation exercises help here).

3 Check out the space – arrange seating so that you can easily make contact with everybody.

4 Eliminate interruptions and distractions – make sure class routines are known and obeyed.

5 Consider the audience – find out what makes them tick and what interests them.

6 Select a style that is appropriate – friendly, firm but fairly formal.

7 Ensure that verbal and non-verbal information matches – become self aware! (Try video taping a class lesson or get a colleague to give you feedback.)

SUMMARY POINTS

◆ Non-verbal communication supports words, with feeling and meaning.

◆ Non-verbal communication makes 93% of the impact of a message.

◆ Verbal and non-verbal communication must match for the message to be understood and believed.

◆ Aspects of non-verbal language need regular practice for maximum performance.

◆ Non-verbal cues may be involuntary or intentional.

◆ Non-verbal communication is specific to countries and cultures and has conventions that just relate to classroom practice (e.g. students putting up their hands to speak).

◆ Non-verbal communication relates to our perception of others and helps to build and maintain relationships.

◆ Non-verbal communication is our most important channel for receiving feedback on our own communication performance.

◆ We need to practise the co-ordination of verbal and non-verbal messages using visualisation and PACE activities to synchronise activities of mind and body.

Chapter 6

How does communication happen?

"Our educational system and modern society generally discriminate against one whole half of the brain. The attention given to the right hemisphere is minimal, compared to the training lavished on the left side."

Roger Sperry, Nobel Laureate in Physiology and Medicine

It may seem strange to wait until Chapter 6 to ask the question *'How does communication happen?'* The reason we have done so is that communication is such a pervasive and complex activity that it takes time to get our heads round the subject and appreciate its many facets. A look at its origins would be meaningless at an earlier stage of the discussion. This chapter considers some of the developmental features of communication and comments on how they might affect learning.

◆ Development of learning

"Nothing is in the mind that is not already in the senses."

Aristotle

Sensation as a prerequisite of learning

Think of a mountain of spaghetti and meatballs! The way the spaghetti and the meatballs weave around is not unlike what is happening inside our brains – the **nerve fibres** (which carry electrical impulses) can be thought of as 'spaghetti', while the **nerve cell bodies** (where the nerve cell nucleus is found) are like tiny 'meatballs'. Communication depends on the growth and interconnection of body and mind capacities based in sensation, emotion and thought. Sensations from eyes, ears, nose, tongue, skin and proprioceptors (sense organs in muscles, tendons and inner ear relaying information about position) are the foundation of knowledge about ourselves and the world.

This growth and interconnection starts in the fetus, within the mother's womb, when the vestibular system of the inner ear, which gives a sense of balance, is very active. The fetus develops a sense of gravity and knowledge of the physical world through movement. Tomatis [1] found, using fibre-optic cameras, that the fetus responds to a particular word sound (phoneme) always using the same muscle. This connection of a muscle response to a particular sound reinforces the significance of anchoring sensory input with physical action when developing learning. It is amazing to discover that the unborn child starts the language learning process inside Mum!

The sense of smell is acute at birth and plays an important role in learning throughout life. Think of a time when you inhaled a strong smell and memories flooded back about a previous occasion when you experienced something very similar. Stiller and Wennekes [2] claimed that memory can be assisted by rubbing the nose prior to learning, since this action stimulates the nerve nets (associations, or contact points) for all known smells.

Touch is just as vital. Physical contact increases the production of the brain hormone Nerve Growth Factor, which activates nerve net development. When touch is lacking, children and probably adults demonstrate depressed motor and mental functioning. Proprioceptive Neuromuscular Facilitation (PNF) has been a successful method of waking up the touch receptors of children with learning disorders. Light touch, brushing, rubbing the skin with ice cubes, and rolling balls across the skin surface of the arms, legs and back, have been found to help integrate movement. Touch and proprioception (which allows the body to remain in balance) are vital to the development of vision. A visual picture starts to emerge at around eight months of age, when a child reaches out and touches something that catches his eye. A little later, sight links with sound when an infant sees something, hears its name, and realises that this sound symbolises the specific object or event that is occurring.

The story of communication, therefore, begins with physical movements and sensations that activate the nerve wiring throughout the body. Modern life makes it hard for us all to benefit from this insight as many of us spend large amounts of time with television, computers or video games which take us away from exercising our bodies and minds, and from conversing with one another.

How we learn

We are born with almost a full complement of nerve cells (**neurones**), though our brains are organised initially to respond only to *position* and *sound*. As we receive sensory stimuli and initiate movements, our neurones develop extensions to others through highly branched **dendrites**. Together with the **axon**, which carries the nerve impulse towards the next connection, the dendrites and cell body form a **nerve unit**, as shown in the diagram opposite. Patterns of communication become established through these expanding cell connections. When we learn something new, new connections are made and nerve impulses pass along new pathways. The formation of these pathways is associated with the development of memory. At first, it is slow beating a path through the nerve jungle. With repetition of the newly learned action, a protective coat called a **myelin sheath** is formed around the nerve fibres, allowing electrical impulses to travel at 100 metres per second through the axons [3].

Simplified diagram of a neurone

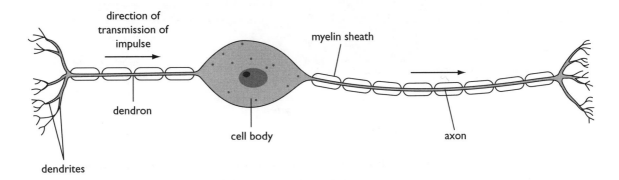

There are three types of neurone: sensory, intermediate and motor neurones. The **sensory** neurones bring in information from the whole body – skin, eyes, ears, tongue, nose and proprioceptors. **Intermediate** neurones make up the 'central command' with a networking function in the spinal cord and brain (which comprise the **central nervous system**) accounting for 99.98% of the cells there. They gather together all sensory information and send messages on to the **motor** neurones to activate body muscles and glands. Swinging your arm will cause simultaneous contraction of up to 2000 muscle fibres. No wonder one feels exhausted after a game of tennis!

At the end of the nerve axons are 'feet', or **synaptic knobs**, containing chemical **neurotransmitters** in little sacs called **synaptic vesicles**. These feet butt up against the membrane of adjacent neurones. Upon activation, neurotransmitters cross the gap (**synapse**) between the two neurones and have an effect that is either **excitatory** (increasing the rate of electrical impulses in the recipient cell), or **inhibitory** (when the reverse occurs). Messages, therefore, are transmitted *chemically* across the cell gaps (synapses) and *electrically* down the nerve fibre in one direction only. Neurones may have up to 10 000 synapses and receive impulses from 1000 other neurones. Many synaptic junctions are made as new learning occurs but become pared down later to increase thinking efficiency [4].

Synapses are the action sites for most drugs that affect the nervous system. For students receiving medication for conditions such as epilepsy or Attention Deficit Disorder the effect is to slow down the transmission process and therefore affect the speed of learning.

The nervous system is, therefore, very complex, both because of the number of connections within it and the fact that some synapses inhibit while others excite the target neurone. The specific balance of information, and of excitatory and inhibitory

Diagram of a synapse

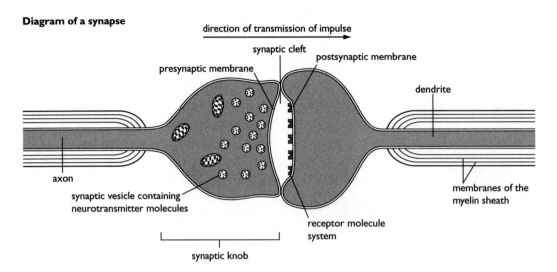

forces, determines how this community of neurones operates. With an estimated one quadrillion (a million billions) brain nerve connections, there are more possible pathways for an impulse to take than there are atoms in the universe [5]. Neural pathways develop from stimulation and experience. As Merzenich [6] observed, *'Whenever we engage in new behaviour, the brain remodels itself'*, retaining this capacity into old age as long as the body and mind remain physically and mentally active. Even after brain damage, rewiring is possible to compensate for lost pathways. The harder we use the brain the more nerve connections are created.

Sensory experience and images

'Images', in the form of movements, feelings, emotions, tones, spoken words, shapes and colours, arise from sensory experience and the resultant nerve networks in various parts of the brain. Movement patterns and emotional experiences are stored in the **limbic system**, tones and words in the **temporal** and **frontal brain**, whereas shape and colour are in the **occipital lobes** (see diagrams opposite).

When we hear the word *'bus'* all our experiences of buses are immediately available as images – we might picture a large, heavy vehicle with big wheels, which is usually brightly coloured, noisy, dangerous and smelly, and recall memories of riding in buses, feelings of fright or fervour as they pass on a road and even love or hate emotions about them. Do you remember that popular nursery song *'The wheels on the bus go round and round …'*, which children generally accompany with circular arm movements? Does this conjure up pictures in your mind? Using these stored images we make sense of new learning and come up with fresh ideas.

Broad-based knowledge depends on the integration of separate multi-sensory images that have been remodelled from each new experience. Think about how we learn a new word. Each sound, word and phrase is supported by an internal image display such as the one described for *'bus'* above. When we read something, the brain actively puts the words into existing sensory images for comprehension. When you are unable to achieve images of something you have read, it is difficult to determine the meaning. Imagery is vital to thinking and understanding and is strengthened through drama and imaginary play. Getting children to close their eyes for 30 seconds and make a picture on the imaginary screen above their eyes is an excellent way of encouraging visualisation. If they are then asked to describe their picture, thinking and language are both stimulated.

TEACHING TIP: Use every opportunity to help students visualise ideas, to help thinking and communication. For example, if you are studying a book, get students to visualise a person, place or object from it, and describe it to their neighbour.

◆ Brain structures

Three parts of the brain have evolved, and develop at different times during growth: the diagram below illustrates these, and the chart that follows summarises the major growth stages before considering some of the detail involved. Unfamiliar technical terms are explained in the text.

Regions of the brain

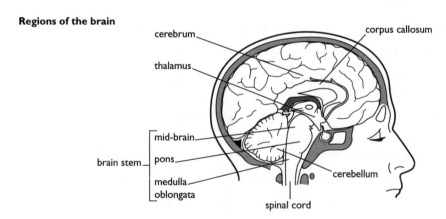

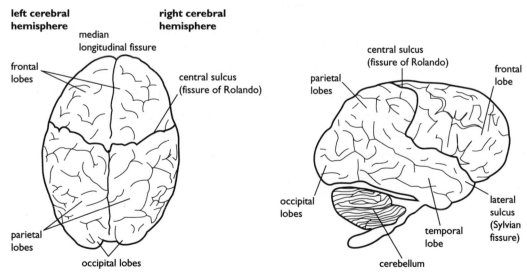

107

Approximate stages and ages of brain growth [7]

Conception–15 months: cerebellum development

◆ Basic survival needs – food, shelter, warmth, security and safety

◆ Sensory development – starts with balance (vestibular system) then hearing, touch, smell, and finally seeing

◆ Motor development – reflexes integrate into movements of neck, arms and legs, leading to neck and trunk posture, rolling, sitting, crawling, walking and exploring

15 months–4.5 years: limbic system development

◆ Understands relationships – self–others; memory and social development

◆ Emotional exploration – own feelings and emotions; language, communication and imagination

◆ Gross motor proficiency – walking, running, jumping, climbing and so on.

4.5–7 years: global hemisphere development (usually right brain)

◆ Whole picture processing – deductive thinking (forms a hypothesis and tests it)

◆ Movement, rhythm, emotion, intuition – builds images from movement and feeling

◆ Outer speech – talks to integrate and develop thoughts

7–9 years: linear hemisphere development (usually left brain)

◆ Detail and linear processing – inductive thinking accumulating information and drawing a conclusion

◆ Refinement of language – speech clearer, syntax more complex

◆ Writing and reading – understands the parts that make up written text: sounds, letters, words

◆ Technique – progresses in music, dance, sport and manual pursuits

◆ Logic – uses linear processing to solve maths problems

8–9 years: frontal lobe development

◆ Fine motor proficiency – manual dexterity and writing refined; foveal eye focus for two-dimensional processing and eye tracking

◆ Inner speech – internal language formed to regulate tasks and behaviour

9–12 years: increased corpus callosum development and nerve myelination

◆ Integrative function of right and left brain – top-down and bottom-up processing proficient

12–16 years: hormonal changes in puberty

◆ Body conscious – learns about body functions, self, others, the community and social interactions

16–21 years: thinking skills extend

◆ Future planning – considers ideas and possibilities

◆ Emotional and social maturity – increasing independence leads to development of coping skills

20–30 years: frontal lobes refine

◆ Formal reasoning – high level of thinking and reflection

◆ Emotional refinement – altruism, love, understanding, compassion

◆ Insight – understands situations at a deeper level and with a wider perspective

◆ Fine motor skills – intricate and complex manual activities are developed and sustained

30 years onwards: further refinement of muscle movements

◆ Hands and face – greater finger and face agility for improved expressive powers

The cerebellum (hind brain)

The **cerebellum** includes the brain stem (**pons, medulla** and **midbrain** – see diagrams on page 107). In evolutionary terms, the cerebellum is the oldest part of the brain and its important time for development is from conception to 15 months after birth. It monitors the outer world through sensory input and activates the body to respond to survival needs. The Thomas and Chess [8] study discovered that competency in adulthood stemmed from three major factors in the early learning environment: rich sensory outdoors and indoors environments that build strong images for children; freedom to explore anywhere without undue restriction (other than required for safety) and adults that act as consultants when children ask questions. The need for full sensory, hands-on learning continues throughout our lives as this remains the basis for knowledge and understanding about experiences.

Many of our educational practices derive, however, from the assumption that students learn well if given knowledge in spoken monologue or written two-dimensional form. In order to learn they must be encouraged to sit still, keep their eyes forward and take notes. We have only to observe the glazed, locked eyes and vacant stares of students in a classroom or lecture hall to know that this is a belief that needs examining!

Linear perspectives in written words and pictures are encouraged in formal learning environments but these are only artistic inventions. Touch and proprioception are the most important organisers of what is seen. Less than 10% of visual interpretation takes place in the eyes and it is touch that is vital for understanding dimension, texture, line and colour (especially the way colours vary with form and texture). Formal learning relies too much on verbal explanations. What is wrong with this? To answer the question we only need to refer back to Einstein's maxim: *'Learning is experience. Everything else is just information.'* Words are only bits of data and are a poor substitute for real, hands-on learning. Sensory patterns are our reference points and provide the context for proper understanding. Without this input our images are distorted.

The limbic brain

The **limbic brain** – the **thalamus, hypothalamus, basal ganglia, amygdala** and **hippocampus** – plays a key role in processing and expressing emotion. By approximately 15 months of age, the limbic system begins the process of adding emotion to the base patterns for sensory input and learned motor functioning. By five years, a child is able to connect reason (from the cerebrum) with emotions, and by eight adds insight (from the frontal lobes) to refine these thought processes. The responsible expression of emotion requires an integration of all parts of the mind–body system at the time when feeling occurs. This facilitates the link of insight and reasoning with emotion. Between one and eight years is, therefore, a crucial time for learning how to deal with feelings.

TEACHING TIP: Poems, songs, stories and role play help children to express feelings and understand their consequences.

The intricate wiring of the limbic system shows that in order to remember and learn, there must be sensory input, a personal and emotional connection plus movement. This strongly supports an experiential basis to learning. However, we make distinctions between thought and emotion just as we do between mind and body. Gelernter [9] has made the point that *'Emotions are not a form of thought, not an additional way to think, not a special cognitive bonus, but are fundamental to thought.'* Emotions, adding to the pain or pleasure of learning, are tied to bodily states so we think with our brains and bodies. Emotional development is responsible for our ability to absorb rules, values and wisdom and without these intelligences we can do little with our learning.

The implications of these insights are enormous, especially to education. Our mind–body system learns through experiencing life in context, in relationship to everything else. It is our emotions that mediate that situation. In order to learn, think and create, learners must have emotional commitment – otherwise school is just an academic exercise. Curriculum demands encourage us to deliver knowledge in segregated subject areas, in an unemotional and, often to students, an unsociable environment. The connection to their own immediate personal concerns is usually remote. Most lessons demand that students settle down to intellectual pursuits that are devoid of social and emotional content. Teachers complain of being disciplinarians rather than educators as they are continually having to clamp down on student social and emotional interactions. Some educational systems, mentioned later (page 118), recognise this issue by adopting a more natural learning style.

TEACHING TIP: Build 'hands-on' experience into all learning situations so students have the chance to develop the mind–body links that facilitate insight and reasoning.

The cerebrum (higher brain) and cortex

The cerebrum and cortex comprise the largest structure of the brain. To get a sense of its size, put your hands together in loose fists with the thumbs pointing upwards. Covering the **cerebrum**, like the peel of an orange, is the convoluted **cortex**, which is 2–5 mm (0.08 to 0.20 inches) thick and contains up to 20 billion nerve cells for the 'central command' function. The sensory cortex deals with incoming messages, while the motor cortex organises outgoing responses. If spread out, the cortex would cover 0.31 m² (500 square inches) of surface area. It uses 0.85 litres (1.5 pints) of blood every 60 seconds and burns 400 calories per day. Although it comprises only a quarter of the brain's volume, it contains about 85% of the total number of neurones [10].

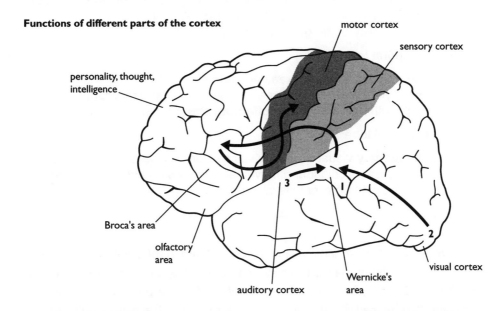

Functions of different parts of the cortex

Labels: motor cortex, sensory cortex, personality, thought, intelligence, Broca's area, olfactory area, auditory cortex, Wernicke's area, visual cortex

1 Speech production (Wernicke's area)
The utterance is thought to be generated in Wernicke's area and sent to Broca's area for putting into motor speech. It is then passed on to the adjacent motor area to be articulated.

2 Reading aloud (visual cortex)
Written forms are received by the visual cortex, and transmitted to Wernicke's area, associated with sound representation. The utterance is then sent to Broca's area.

3 Speech comprehension (auditory cortex)
The ear sends signals to the auditory cortex, from where they are then transmitted to Wernicke's area to be interpreted.

The two squashy left and right cerebral hemispheres, making up the cerebrum and lying over the small cerebellum (hind brain), only developed 100 000 years ago. These upper brain parts could not have evolved without the need for language. The modern human's extra cerebral capacity, acquired since that time, seems to have been involved in word understanding and sentence formation. Positron Emission Tomography (PET brain scanning) now allows us to be more accurate about the cerebral functions that lie in the four lobes of each hemisphere, as it can be used to chart where glucose is used during specific activities [11]. An elementary overview of functions follows in the box overleaf – each lobe subdivides into smaller areas responsible for particular activities.

Functions of cerebral areas

1 **Frontal lobe**

The **primary motor area** controls specific muscles all over the body. The **pre-motor** section is concerned with sequential skilled movements. The **frontal eye field area** controls voluntary scanning movements of the eyes. **Broca's area** translates thoughts into speech and develops inner language.

2 **Parietal lobe**

The **somesthetic association area** integrates and interprets sensations such as shape, texture (without visual input), object orientation and relationships of body parts. Touch, pressure, pain, cold, heat and proprioception are interpreted in the **general sensory area**. Sweet, sour, bitter tastes and past experiences are the responsibility of the **gustatory area**.

3 **Temporal lobe**

The **primary auditory area** interprets characteristics of sound, pitch and rhythm. **Wernicke's area** interprets speech. The **vestibulo area** deals with balance and the **olfactory area** with smell.

4 **Occipital lobe**

The **primary visual area** receives sensory impulses from the eyes and interprets colour and movement. The **visual association area** relates past to present visual experience and evaluates what is seen.

The four lobes of each cerebral hemisphere accept external information from the opposite side of the body, via the brain stem and limbic system. Therefore, information coming into the *left ear* goes to the *right temporal lobe* for interpretation while the *right hand* is controlled by the *left motor cortex* of the cerebrum. All sensory–motor functions on the right side of the body are either realised or controlled by the left hemisphere, and on the left the reverse usually occurs, although some people are transposed, with at least part of the right brain controlling the right side of the body and vice versa. The fact that some people write with their right hand and others with their left is proof of brain differences in the population.

Knowledge is then integrated, organised and reorganised with sensory–motor memory and the gnostic areas of the cortex, through a bridge (called the **corpus callosum**) connecting both hemispheres so that new experiences can be understood in the light of past memories.

◆ The brain's two hemispheres

The functions of the two cerebral hemispheres have become popular lore about the brain and it is now common to hear students described as left- or right-brained because of their learning style preferences. We are, however, likely to be a mixture of styles, with strengths in left- or right-brain activity. Each half of the cerebrum develops and processes information in a specific way. The *linear* hemisphere (normally the left) deals with details, parts and processes of language as well as sequential patterns. In contrast the *global* hemisphere (usually the right) deals with images, rhythm, emotion, intuition and whole processing. It is possible to summarise these characteristics as shown in the table below [7].

Linear (normally left brain)	Global (normally right brain)
sees parts first	sees whole picture first
parts of language	comprehension of language
syntax and semantics	image, emotion and meaning
letters and sentences	rhythm, flow, dialect
numbers	image, intuition
analysis – linear	analysis – estimates, uses intuition
considers differences	considers similarities
controls feelings	free with feelings
structures and plans	spontaneous, fluid responses
sequential, creative thinking	simultaneous, creative thinking
language oriented	experience/feeling oriented
future oriented	present oriented
technique	movement flow
sports – placement of body parts	sports – rhythm and flow
art – media, use of tools	art – image, emotion, flow
music – notes, beat, tempo	music – images, passion, rhythm

In young children, both hemispheres contain all the above functions until specialisation occurs, which is at a different stage of development for each person. This accounts for the fact that some children do not exhibit a 'handedness' preference until quite late. My own son picked up a pencil with either right or left hand to draw or write until he was about thirteen years old. On average, however, the global hemisphere exhibits a growth spurt between four and seven and the linear one between seven and nine years of age. Normally, hemispheric specialisation is in place between nine and twelve years although children who are late developers may establish dominance after this.

TEACHING TIP: Brain development studies suggest that early learning is global rather than linear – so give young children broad outlines, rather than too much detail.

Dominance profiles

Several systems for identifying and analysing learning styles have recently been developed. Among these are Dennison's [12] 'dominance profiles', which assess the laterality of eyes, ears and hands in relation to the dominant brain hemisphere. They give information about a preferred learning style and our responses under stress when we rely on this preferred style. In less stressful situations, when our bodies and minds are relaxed and able to adapt more easily to circumstances, our dominance profiles are likely to fluctuate.

The profile gives information on how we most easily take in and process new learning. Eyes, ears and hands are the primary sense organs through which we see, hear and touch.

The efficiency of sensing depends on whether or not the eye, ear or hand is on the side *opposite* the dominant brain hemisphere. Auditory input, for example, is most efficient when the receiving ear is opposite the dominant brain hemisphere as shown in the following diagram.

The routes between ears and hemispheres as in a listening task

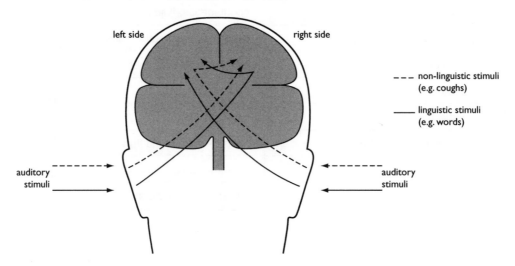

left side   right side

- - - non-linguistic stimuli
(e.g. coughs)

——— linguistic stimuli
(e.g. words)

auditory stimuli   auditory stimuli

Most people show a 'handedness' – a dominance of one hand over the other. In the same way, most people show a dominance of one foot over the other, one ear over the other, and one eye over the other. If both the *left brain* and *right eye* are dominant then vision is facilitated. The *left brain* controls the muscular movements of the *right eye* thus optimising the efficiency of three- and later two-dimensional focus, tracking and peripheral vision. The same would be true for *right-brain/left-eye* dominance. If both the *left eye* and *left brain* are dominant (we would say the person is 'homo-lateral'), the vision is less effective because the dominant brain is not controlling the muscular movements of the dominant eye. People can be 'homo-lateral' in terms of vision, hearing or touch, if the dominant eye, ear or hand is on the same side as the dominant brain, which causes a decrease in the efficiency of perception via these senses, especially under stress. The table below gives basic profiles. Some people have cross-lateral and others homo-lateral patterns. They can also be mixed – a person could be cross-lateral for eyes but homo-lateral for ears.

	Dominant sense	Dominant hemisphere	Preferred learning style
Cross-lateral	right eye	left	visual
	right ear	left	auditory
	right hand	left	verbal
	left eye	right	visual
	left ear	right	auditory
	left hand	right	kinaesthetic
Homo-lateral	right eye	right	limited visual capacity
	right ear	right	limited auditory capacity
	right hand	right	limited communication
	left eye	left	limited visual capacity
	left ear	left	limited auditory capacity
	left hand	left	limited kinaesthetic capacity
The eyes facilitate seeing and visual interpretation			
The ears facilitate hearing, listening and memory			
The hands facilitate oral, written and gesture communication			

The left hemisphere indicates spoken and written language in the right hand. The right hemisphere indicates expressive movement and physical manipulation in the left hand. When both the left hemisphere and hand are dominant, communication becomes more limited. The same is true if the right hemisphere and hand are dominant. These are simplistic explanations, but if you attempt the following tests on a range of people, there will be a considerable range of performance that bears out the theory of brain dominance.

Tests for dominance

1 **Eye**: Look at an object through a paper tube. Which eye do you spontaneously use?

2 **Ear**: Someone behind you shouts your name. Which side do you turn to?

3 **Hand**: Pick up an object from a surface. Which hand do you spontaneously use?

4 **Brain**: Put out your right arm in front of you – level with the shoulder. Either place your other hand on top of your right arm or ask a friend to do this. Change arms and repeat. Which arm is the strongest against the resistance of the pressing hand? (The dominant hemisphere of the brain is on the opposite side to the strongest arm.)

Brain dominance and development, and learning in school

Using similar techniques to those described in the box on page 115, Hannaford [13] collected data on the dominance profiles of a random sample of 218 students attending USA schools in Denver (Colorado) and Kona (Hawaii). The students were identified by their school assessments as being 'talented', 'normal' or 'having special educational needs'. Of those students found to be left-brain dominant, 78% of the had been identified as 'talented', while 78% of the right-brain dominant were students with 'special needs'.

In this small sample, therefore, students with strong verbal abilities and linear processing were more often labelled as 'talented'. Those with weaker verbal skills and global processing were more frequently described as needing special education. As already discussed, linear dominant processors, usually left-brained, focus on details – specifically in language on words, their syntax and sentence structure. They are more adept at using logic in maths problem-solving and employing details in art, music, dance and sport. As music is taught in linear ways, starting with notes, timing and technique, left-brain processing is useful. If left-brained students, however, do not develop their right-brain capacities, they will find it difficult to access images, passion, rhythm and flow to make the music come alive.

Hannaford [13] has suggested that left-brain processes are more positively reinforced in the US educational system. Students with linear capacities are likely, therefore, to have high self-esteem and experience less school stress because work is geared to their competencies. This gives them the confidence to explore right-brain learning.

Global processors, usually called right-brained, are able to take in the big picture, feel the emotional connections, access intuitive understanding and learn kinaesthetically through movement and hands-on experience. In music, art, dance and sport they access the overall view, movement and passion that are essential elements of creativity. They prefer to approach things as a whole, in broad outline, exploring, playing and feeling their responses. If they are not using their left brains adequately, these students will have difficulty in logical processing and dealing with details.

Within our current education system, global processors are more affected by the early push between five and eight years to acquire linear functions in language and maths activities. They learn to judge themselves, therefore, as inadequate. Albert Einstein is believed to have been a global learner. His academic failures are legendary and he referred to his reliance on visual imagery:

"The words of language as they are spoken do not seem to play any role in my mechanism of thought. The psychical entities which seem to serve as elements in thought are certain signs and more or less clear images which can be combined."

Albert Einstein, quoted in Gardner [14]

Mattson [15] has suggested that brain wave activity in 'learning disabled' and 'normal' children displays major differences. Those with learning difficulties show less left hemisphere activation even for verbal tasks and significantly fewer shifts from one brain side to the other for tasks requiring different processing strategies. It is not surprising, therefore, that they become stressed in learning contexts and show increased levels of stress hormones such as adrenaline and cortisol, which Diorio and co-workers [16] have concluded is correlated with decreased learning and memory, and increased attention problems. At the muscular level, during stress the tendon guard reflex comes into play, shortening the leg calf muscles and locking the back of the knees, preparing the body to flee from danger. Hannaford [13] suggested that with the high levels of stress operating in today's society many people end up with their knees, lower back and neck permanently locked. This immobility of the spine decreases the natural flow of cerebrospinal fluid flowing round the brain, depressing the functions of both cerebral hemispheres and their connections. These effects have been noted in children with severe communication difficulties, including autism.

Hannaford believes there is a link between the shortened calf muscle (gastrocnemius) and the inability to speak. She advocates exercises, such as that described in the box below, to stretch and relax these muscles. Hannaford reports great benefits to children with autism and communication impairment after two weeks of these exercises carried out four times a day. Having worked in an international centre for children with severe learning difficulties where we used these exercises daily, I too can vouch for their utility in relaxing the body and energising the brain.

Relaxing the calf muscles

1   Holding on to a chair, keep your body upright and place one foot (heel up) about 20 cm (8 inches) behind the other.

2   Take a deep breath. As you exhale, lower the heel of the back foot to the ground and bend the front knee forward.

3   Repeat several times to relax the muscles and release the tendon guard reflex.

Alternatively, lie on your back with your legs straight in the air. Ask someone to place both hands on the bottoms of your feet and push the ball of each foot forward so that the calf lengthens. At the same time, push with your feet against the applied pressure.

The importance of such exercises is their relevance to the enhanced functioning of both brain hemispheres, and the stimulation of the connecting bundle of fibres (the corpus callosum) that allows right and left parts to be integrated for effective use of the learning processes. When fully developed, the corpus callosum carries four billion messages per second across more than 200 million myelinated nerve fibres connecting the two brain hemispheres. How about that for impressive performance! This quick access allows full operational thinking. Research has found that regions at the front of the corpus callosum are smaller in children with Attention Deficit Disorder [17].

TEACHING TIP: Try the calf muscle exercise along with the PACE routine (page 98) before the start of a lesson to relax and energise the body and brain.

Also, it has been found that in this region females have around 10% more fibres than males [10]. It has been suggested that such differences may not be genetic. People with fewer fibres in this region may have missed out on interactive relationships that include emotion and rich dialogue. Females are less inhibited at expressing feelings and better at language, according to conventional tests. The acceptance of emotional experience and expression in normal learning experiences might allow this discrepancy to disappear.

Brain development and educational planning

This knowledge should feed into educational planning. In the normal course of development, children are accessing global function, which develops and enlarges between four to seven years at the time when they start school at about five. The linear hemisphere does not grow until between seven to nine years old. The most natural way, therefore, is for children to learn initially through sensory experience, rich in feelings, emotion and movement. Children at this stage are very imaginative and love to play, act out their world and mimic adult activity.

Some educational systems, however, including the UK National Curriculum, begin alphabet and number recognition immediately that children enter school, followed quickly by reading. This would not be a problem if a strong experiential programme was followed, but the opposite occurs. Students are encouraged to sit still and learn letters and numbers in a linear fashion. They read books having simple vocabulary and sentence structure with limited images and emotions involved. If you observe children in natural circumstances they love to scribble, draw and mimic grown up writing because of the rhythm and flow of it. This process is global and holistic and should be given prime value in learning. Recognition of such child needs may well prevent a great deal of the behaviour problems that now plague teachers in schools.

Many European countries, such as Denmark, France, Germany and Italy, respect natural brain development and do not start children in school until between six and seven years of age. They teach writing holistically and do not move on to details of spelling and sentence structure until around eight years of age, when the linear hemisphere is enlarging and can cope with these aspects easily. Is it significant that Denmark boasts 100% literacy (Ministry of Education and Research, Copenhagen, 1992)? However, it must be appreciated that Danish schools are less inclusive than those in the UK, for example, so that these statistics hide the fact that they do not involve the range of children now included in the UK National Curriculum Programmes of Study. Nevertheless, their system is worth looking at as it values different aspects in the educational structure.

Danish children are encouraged initially to 'write'. The teacher cannot understand their output, but allows them to read it out to the class. The teacher targets their vocabulary: *'It looks like 'swimming' is one of your favourite words. Would you like to see how I write it?'* Since children enjoy making adult words, the teacher produces a cursive script so that next time the students write 'swimming' they will have learned the spelling easily without effort.

Reading is approached through songs or rhymes. The teacher asks for the verse of a favourite song and then writes it in cursive script for the children to follow as they sing. This establishes a strong emotional and relational connection, which is vital to memorising as emotion and memory are linked processes in the limbic system. Movement and rhythm orchestrate and organise the singing/reading experience.

To learn something new, it is important to tie into the familiar with concrete images that are already known. Look at some of the reading books in use in school. Do they have strong emotional links for children? Many of them reflect very different styles of living than those of the children who read them. This is positive but there must be opportunities to connect with student's own activities. Writing and reading their own books makes a perfect entrance into the reading experience.

Another unnatural challenge is to do with the present fashion for printing letters as the first step in writing them. Printing is a linear process, that interrupts the continuous flow of language as it is experienced in the mind and expressed through talk or hand. A cursive script is more in keeping with a flow of ideas. Those at school in the 1950s may remember the fashion then for the flowing copperplate style! In the UK today, however, children are taught to print at five years of age and at this stage it is hard to do, as it defies natural brain development. After seven, when the linear brain is developed to cope with the discrete operations necessary for word printing, cursive writing is then encouraged. It is no wonder that some children find writing such a chore.

Many European schools do not teach printing and find that students have no problems going from their own cursive writing to reading printed text at the age of about eight years when linear brain development at this stage makes transfer possible. German teachers have switched over to teaching block printing as the first step to written language but are reporting more student difficulties. Seligman [18] talked about *'learned helplessness'*, which results from children being expected to perform tasks that are beyond them. It leads to them opting out, giving up or making much less effort to learn. Excessive testing also creates this situation by promoting habits where students learn for the tests. Those with anxiety about assessments end up in a continual state of worry. It could be that we are sacrificing successful long-term learning for short-term illusory gains. Learning for testing encourages shallow rather than deep understanding of concepts and sets firm agendas for teaching.

It remains to be seen whether students will develop adequate deductive reasoning abilities in the absence of opportunities to talk and discuss issues in depth. Epstein [19] showed in his research in 1979 that formal reasoning had not been an effective outcome of the style of educational process used in the US, as by age eleven only 5% of the population tested had acquired this level of functioning. A quarter reached it by age 14, but only half the adults assessed were fully functional formal thinkers. We are now more than 20 years on, but anecdotal evidence suggests that the levels of thought required to cope successfully in an increasingly complex world are still not being achieved.

Learning is not just in our heads

So what does all this information suggest? Real learning, which establishes meaningful connections for the learner, is not complete until there is some physical and personal expression of thought. Much learning is involved in establishing skills that enable us to show what we know. Speaking, writing, drawing, painting, modelling, computing, singing, making music, dancing and sport are some of the expressive forms that develop to support and demonstrate our knowledge. Building these skills establishes neuromuscular routes that tie into cognitive ones. Learning is not just in our heads but also in our bodies.

Unfortunately, society separates the two and we are encouraged to think of physical development as achieving brawn and mental development as achieving brain. Language, however, is a system that – both in speech and writing – is utterly dependent for its expression on the intricate movement of body *and* mind. It serves to integrate and express knowledge and facilitate thought. Pictorial, symbolic, musical and gestural means of expression also bring together movement and thinking processes to deliver meaning. Sport meshes knowledge about space, time and human dynamics (motivation, teamwork and goals) with skilled muscular co-ordination. Arts and athletics are powerful and important ways of communicating with the world, which must have a central place in the curriculum and equal value with academic subjects.

We are all different

It would appear, however, that schools favour students who process linearly, take in information in an auditory or visual way, look at the teacher and re-state in a logical, coherent way. Hannaford [13], in her study, found students with this full sensory access (as a rule left-brained, right-eyed, right-eared and right-handed people) made up only 15% of the test population. In the same study, 22% of the 'talented' students had a kinaesthetic and 'not verbal' learning preference, in contrast to 89% of the 'special needs' group. Language ability is valued in our educational system. Curriculum tests reflect this by testing linguistic and logical/mathematical intelligences. However, Gardner [14] defined many other kinds, in a 'theory of multiple intelligences':

1. logical/mathematical
2. linguistic
3. visual/spatial
4. bodily kinaesthetic

musical

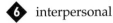 interpersonal

 intrapersonal.

Schools have always valued the linguistic and logical/mathematical intelligences as these are the ones that are publicly examined. By neglecting the other important ways in which we know and learn about the world we often make it impossible for children to be properly included in the curriculum. Many students sitting in our classrooms are kinaesthetic learners, yet the curriculum offers them limited techniques. There seem to be fewer opportunities of doing subjects like practical cookery and science than when I was at school, for example, and a greater proportion of even 'hands-on' types of lessons is now given over to theoretical concerns.

We tend to believe that students can only learn if they look at us. Eye contact is an important aspect in the relationship between speaker and listener, but in Hannaford's [13] study 72% of the 'special needs' group were visually limited, compared to only 27% of the 'talented' group. If concepts are new or difficult to understand, you might find these visually limited students looking away or shutting their eyes in order to take in the topic more easily by their dominant sense. This may be construed as inattention but it does call into question the emphasis on visual learning in our classrooms. Auditory learners, when constantly asked to look at the teacher and the board may lose concentration and optimal ability to learn. The visually limited profile affects the ease of reading, especially under stress. In this situation the eyes move peripherally and the dominant eye muscles will not receive full motor function from the dominant brain. This makes foveal focus and tracking across a page difficult. The 'Lazy eight' exercises, described later in this chapter (page 128), help the eyes work together for maximum visual intake.

The left-eye dominant trait is also interesting in connection with learning. Most of us are not completely binocular because the nose interferes. Therefore, we have one tracking eye and the other follows. The right eye naturally tracks from left to right and the left has a reverse pattern. In the Hannaford study, 81% of the 'special needs' students were left-eyed and right-handed. It is these sorts of children who reverse letters and numbers and who have difficulty starting reading. Vision tracking with 'Lazy Eights' will help this problem considerably.

Another interesting item in Hannaford's study that is worth mentioning is the fact that 75% of the teachers involved were left-hemisphere dominant – right-handed and right-eyed and limited in auditory terms. People with this profile tend to talk about details and not listen. They expect students to look at them.

The most disadvantaged group of learners are those who have limited capacity in all senses (homo-lateral for eyes, ears and hands – see table on page 115), especially when they have right-brain dominance. 5% of the 'talented' students compared with 49% of the 'special needs' group came into this category. These students process through internal images, movement and emotion and find it difficult to express themselves verbally. These students prefer to study alone but can be helped:

◆ if they are able to involve movement in learning as in drama and role play activities

◆ if they can get hold of an overview first so that the details can be slotted in later

◆ if they can start linear processing from 7–8 years of age onwards

◆ if they feel secure in their relationships

◆ if they can take time out for learning alone and expressing themselves in ways other than words.

In most classrooms, most of the time, these students will feel stressed and be in 'survival mode'. Some, especially the emotionally insecure, may end up on support programmes.

Hannaford describes a teacher in the USA who took dominance information very seriously. She had all the students test themselves at the beginning of the school year and then organised them accordingly. Visual learners were at the front, auditory learners behind, with right-ear dominants on the left of the class and left-ear dominants on the right. The right-brained fully-limited students were at the back with clay or wax to play with during lessons to key into their touch and kinaesthetic learning pathways.

In the UK, some of these ideas are just beginning to be slotted into teaching methods and many teachers value this information as it helps to explain the wide variety of responses one is likely to encounter in every class group. We need to consider, also, some of the other intelligences and promote these as the way for better inclusion. Particularly, we ignore the interpersonal and intrapersonal skills that are expressed in language and social behaviour. Who would think these are worthy of certification? It is assumed they develop naturally. However, the Carnegie Study [20] suggested that 98% of children lack these very skills on school entry and 51% have very serious problems in this respect. They are the foundation of formal learning and are considered in more depth in the next section as the key to personal and academic success.

TEACHING TIP: Try the dominance tests (page 115) and the learning style questionnaire (page 46) with your class. Accommodate the groupings uncovered in the way you organise lessons.

◆ Language and learning

Language is the source of thought. When a child masters language he gains the potentiality to organise anew his perception, his memory; he masters more complex forms of reflection of objects in the external world; he gains the capacity to draw conclusions from his observations, to make deductions, the potentiality of thinking.

Alexander Luria [21]

Language powerfully combines the processes of body, mind and emotion, and through it we develop our capacity to think. Understanding how language develops can help us determine how it can be helped or hindered in its expansion.

How language develops

We have seen how language is one of the earliest processes to evolve. Its progression occurs as a child moves from a sense of vibration and rhythm in the mother's womb, to hearing and tone as a small toddler. The child mimics the intonation of others, babbling and playing with sounds, which develops the nerve fibres in the voice box (larynx) and enables a variety of tones to be made. Almost half of the motor cortex deals with vocalisation (page 111); it stimulates muscular movements of the larynx, tongue, mouth, jaw, facial muscles and eyes that form and express words.

Muscular memory resides in the basal ganglion of the limbic system, which links with the frontal lobe to control thought and vocalisation. This area is actively involved in movement, thought and speech. The nerve connections between the motor cortex and the formal reasoning area of the frontal lobe suggest the importance of movement to thought processing. Most people like to talk and share ideas, write or draw pictures of them, because these skills tie directly into thinking.

The acquisition of language takes place in stages.

1 Sensory/motor (0–15 months)

The young child is learning to discriminate rhythm and tone and co-ordinate the movements of breathing and sound-making in readiness to express with word symbols the link between objects and events. This awareness of sound contours allows the child to be sensitive to dialect and accent. In order to perform words, we need a grasp of voice dynamics. If these abilities are not developed, language acquisition suffers. Healy [22] suggested that *'Children are not speaking properly because they're not hearing words pronounced slowly.'* She suggested that a fondness for watching television means they are used to hearing words at a fast pace, which does not allow them time to focus and link the words with their picture referents.

If this is the case, it is difficult for children to gain meaning from what they hear. Also, at this early stage, many youngsters suffer frequently from ear infections because the tiny Eustachian tubes from the ears to the throat are too small to allow proper draining when upper respiratory infections occur. Levinson [23] discovered that over 90% of children with learning difficulties had ear infections as infants. It is believed that babies exhibit elevated adrenaline levels due to the stresses in their environment and are more vulnerable to ear infections. This means that children miss hearing complex tones and are at risk for speech and language difficulties.

2 Functional use of words (15 months–4 years)

Children between one and four years of age gain a functional sense of objects, people and events and begin to categorise and name them. The language modelling of carers plays a vital part in this process and movement is the way to explore the world and learn about things in it before the link can be made with a word referent. Without touch and movement, understanding the attributes of things is impossible. Size, weight, material, colour and component parts of objects are only properly understood if they can be thoroughly investigated. The child and others around engage in a game of vocabulary building: *'What's this? What's that?'* If children are encouraged to think beyond the name to the function, understanding is deepened. *'I wash to keep clean'*, is an expansion of *'This is a flannel'*, so creating a broader view of the relationship of the object to the child. The limbic brain searches out relationships so that this language coaching cashes in on normal brain development.

Before four years of age, a child takes most of his behavioural cues from what he *sees* rather than *hears*. Remember telling a child not to do something but finding that the next moment they are carrying out exactly what they were told to avoid! The sensory fascination and physical stimulation is so compelling that a verbal command does not register. At this stage, children do not understand the consequences of their actions, so that *'Do not touch the hot stove'* means nothing until they have experienced the discomfort of intense heat.

After the age of four years, Wernicke's area in the temporal lobe (page 111) enlarges to assist the link of understanding to higher reasoning. At the same time Broca's area in the frontal lobe expands to enable clear speech to develop. When this happens, children are able to override the enticement of doing something they were asked not to. It is at this stage that adult–child conversations become meaningful exchanges and children are able to co-operate with others successfully.

3 Outer speech (4–7 years)

Once speech is in place, a child processes thought through verbalising what she is presently thinking, until about the age of seven. A child talks continuously as she experiences the world and gains insights. This outer speech is the way a child of this age solves her problems and conscious thinking and speaking is essential to thought and language development. *'How'* and *'Why'* questions that demand an explanation become more interesting than the 'What, 'When', Where' and 'Who' questions that just result in specific information.

In school, however, children are often required to keep quiet and not encouraged to talk. In a recent study of school students in Leicester (UK) [24], an independent evaluator questioned those who participated in the research about talk in class. It emerged that students liked opportunities to speak, feeling that they normally had to be quiet in school. They expressed the view that *'talking makes you better at school'*, saying that *'when you talk ideas come and become real.'* These children noted that *'the clever ones are good at talking'*, *'more talking makes things easier to get help from other people'*, *'help with talking helps with asking questions in class.'* One student said that talking with others *'helps me do more work on my own.'* Such comments are illuminating and support the thinking that children need to have frequent talk experiences in class in order to encourage their own thinking and reasoning. So important is the need for outer speech, to hear one's own voice and thoughts, that silent reading is ineffective before seven years of age. You will notice that in class, children can read aloud to themselves and swap stories without bothering their classmates. These activities must be encouraged and supported if children are to become successful learners.

4 Inner speech and reading (7 years onwards)

Social interaction, with experiences of talking and being talked to, not only structures a child's immediate activities but also helps him form the processes of reasoning and learning. Thus, a child gains knowledge about given tasks and gradually *internalises* the instructional process itself. This allows him to reason and regulate his own physical and mental activities silently so enabling him to complete tasks independently.

Externalising feelings and ideas into a verbal context, which is sequenced in a way that is understandable and expressed clearly in a written mode, is not a simple extension of what is done when participating in talk. Conversations frequently involve incomplete utterances and so context clues are used to grasp meaning. In written mode, though, children must be able to de-centre or de-contextualise their thinking and take on the role of the reader in order to make meaning clearly. The written medium is abstract and demands fuller information and explanation to make up for the fact that the real context is missing and non-verbal clues are absent. Wood [25] discussed the fact that children who are poor at giving information and explanation in a written form are academically weak. These are demanding sorts of narratives and he suggests that skill in understanding and producing coherent and intelligible information predicts levels of literacy. Although there is, at present, no strong evidence to prove Wood's prediction, work by Hunter-Carsch [26] reporting on the Literacy Summer Schools in Leicester, UK, and that by Sage [27] would support a connection between narrative ability and literacy.

Everything written in English can be decomposed into twenty six alphabet letters. Analysing spoken English into its constituent sounds (phonemes) reveals forty four elements with voiced and voiceless equivalents [28]. (There is further information about this in Appendix 3.) Clearly, there can be no simple relationship between spoken and written forms of English. Also, the same phoneme may sound different when produced in different contexts; for example, the 'b' in *'bark'*, *'beetle'*, *'hobble'*, *'tab'* or *'lamb'*. In fact the end letter of *'lamb'* is silent so the last sound heard in the word is the nasal sound 'm'. Speakers with different accents will also produce different sounds, but the corresponding written account will be identical. Literary forms are thus more uniform and neutral, as well as being less sensitive to context, when compared with spoken ones. When we help children to read, we are doing more than teaching a new, more neutral code – we are introducing them to a novel way of thinking about language. Perera [28] has suggested that the neutrality and uniformity of the written word renders it less prejudicial. The same sounds may have different written forms; for example, rows/rose, an ice cream/a nice cream, attacks/a tax. Therefore, the discovery that a word has several functions could be facilitated by reading and writing.

Wood [25] pointed out the problems children have with word meanings. He gave an example of a maths problem: *'Ten sweets are shared between two boys so that one has four more that the other'*. This provoked protest among the children: *'That's wrong, if you share, they must have the same – they'll each have 5, so one can't have four more!'* Similarly, in graphical problems, 'straight' for many children meant a line perpendicular to a page edge, so a slanting line could not be considered straight. A further example was provided: a child was asked what 'volume' means in the course of a maths lesson, and replied that it was a button on the television remote control. Wood suggested that mathematical terms are often 'parasitic' upon everyday words. Their use in mathematical activity has to be negotiated. Such difficulties with word meanings were discovered frequently by the Secondary Mathematics and Science Research at Chelsea College, London [29].

Learning to read and write, therefore, poses challenges, as children have to communicate more clearly outside the shared context of conversation, which demands a well-developed understanding of words and how they are used. Vygotsky [30] argued that literacy leads children to develop more explicit theories of language and helps their self-regulatory abilities as they learn to plan, monitor and evaluate their work. Writing clearly demands the capacity to take on others' perspectives and construct language situations that are 'givens' in conversation. It entails a great deal of hard work!

There are other issues to consider. Written text provides very limited representation of the vocal dynamics of spoken language. Full-stops, commas, and colons provide some guidance on how a sentence should be read. Tactics such as italics and underlining are used to indicate emphasis. The example *'I wasn't talking seriously'* or *'I wasn't talking, seriously'* illustrates the way expert readers process text, as follows. Frazier and Rayner [31] suggested that as each word is read, the tendency of the reader is to attach it to what has gone before if this is grammatically acceptable. So, without the comma, this principle dictates that the word 'seriously' in the example is an adverb that refers to the manner of the talking. With the comma present, it suggests that the word is merely an aside. Thus, what seems a simple piece of punctuation exerts a marked effect on the interpretation.

The fact that many features of tone, voice and manner of speaking cannot be conveyed in print leads to an enlarged vocabulary for writing purposes. When we hear talk we know if someone is shouting, whispering, insinuating or implying. In text, however, words such as 'whispered' are used to accurately convey the meaning. The reader has to infer how text is analysed to reveal its structure and decide where stress and emphasis should be placed. Therefore, children have to interact with text to interpret what the writer means, so acquiring special language and thinking skills.

One of these skills is involved in deciding the meaning of sentences such as this simple one: *'Luke likes fruit.'* Imagine the sentence spoken in different ways. If the stress was on *'Luke'* it would indicate a denial of a previous utterance such as *'Helen likes fruit.'* Now suppose the stress is on 'likes', this might imply another denial such as 'dislikes'. Stress on 'fruit' may serve to negate another suggestion such as *'Luke likes chocolate'.* Repeat the sentence with a rising tune at the end and a question is indicated rather than a statement. It is only by considering the surrounding information that we can hit on the most likely interpretation.

This requires the reader to take in and memorise long stretches of text so that the right stress can be properly applied. It demands an ability to knit together ideas and consider a whole event. This narrative skill is initially learned in conversation when a child has to thread together the ideas that are spoken in order to produce an overall meaning of what is said. Therefore, a knowledge of both verbal and non-verbal elements, such as voice dynamics, is essential to make meaning from written text. As one reads the words they are mapped onto existing knowledge of how they sound in speech.

When skilled readers encounter a difficult passage, they often resort to reading it out aloud so that they can talk themselves through the text. In this way they are able to try out different ways of saying things in order to grasp the meaning. Skilled reading takes place at around 300 words a minute [25], which is twice the speed of normal speech. It would seem unlikely that experts normally read by 'talking' to themselves. It is not clear exactly what happens. Underwood and Batt [32] suggested that expert readers do not convert visual symbols into sub-vocal speech and that understanding is a more direct process passing from the written words straight into meaning construction. That meaning, however, is centrally stored and based on using words in spoken form.

Thus, teachers must prepare children for rapid reading by ensuring that they have acquired excellent levels of spoken language and are able to stress the words correctly for their meaning, to facilitate their comprehension of text. Reading and writing bring the benefits of more explicit, organised language and so help the child to develop further levels of thinking and linguistic structures for expressing this. (Appendix 3 presents a summary of language structure for reference purposes, and Appendix 8 provides a chronological checklist of language skills.)

In addition, reading is dependent on a special development of the eyes to focus on two-dimensional forms. In a three-dimensional environment, such as outdoors, the eye is in constant motion, gathering sensory information to build intricate images necessary for learning. The brain integrates these images with other sensory information, such as touch and proprioception, to develop the visual perception system. The retina (the sensory nerve layer of the eye) contains light receptor cells – 95% rods and 5% cones, so called because of their shape. The rods are distributed around the periphery of the retina and are stimulated by dim light. The cones are grouped in a small area called the **fovea centralis** and require bright light for stimulation.

Lazy eights

Exercises have been developed by therapists to reduce stress and encourage eyes and hands to function efficiently. These are called 'Lazy eights'. Let's start with the writing exercise. Draw a sideways eight on paper as in the diagram below. Start at the middle with a pencil and take an anti-clockwise route – up, over and around, then clockwise, up, over and around back to the mid-point. Do five or more continuous repetitions with each hand and five or more with both hands together. This is best done in a large figure on 20 x 30 cm (8 x 12 inches) paper, to stimulate the large muscles, but within the near visual field. The exercise is very relaxing as a start to writing and freeing up the thinking processes. If students do not have pencils handy, training with fingers on a desk top is just as useful, repeating the same sideways 'eight' pattern.

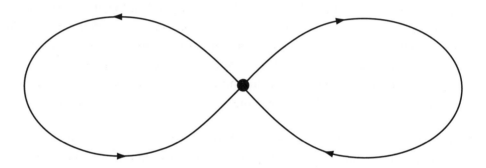

Lazy eights for eyes involve eye movements in a similar pattern, to improve co-ordination. The movements for these exercises should be slow and conscious. Train the eyes on a moving thumb as it describes a sideways 'eight'. Hold the thumb at eye level in the mid-line of the body at an elbow length from the eyes. Hold the head relaxed and still and

move the eyes to follow the thumb. Move the thumb directly up the mid-line centre (nose) to the top of the visual field and anti-clockwise – out, around and down to the left side. As the thumb reaches the lower mid-field, bring it back up the centre and clockwise – out, around and down to the right side. Continue in an even, flowing movement about five times with each hand.

Then clasp your hands together, with the thumbs forming an X. Focus on the centre of this and repeat the Lazy eight pattern of movement. This activity is used for children who have squints and need to strengthen the extrinsic muscles of the eye. It also assists the network development and myelination of the frontal lobe, which is responsible for fine motor tracking. The exercises have been beneficial to children with language problems who often have tracking difficulties when it comes to reading. They are useful, too, when spending long periods in front of a computer screen as they help to relax the eyes and shoulders and allow more productive work. Obviously, regular practice is needed for the benefits to accrue.

Reading requires foveal focus. Before the age of seven years, the ciliary muscles that shape the lens are short, causing the lens to be thin and elongated so that the incoming image is spread across the retina involving both rods and cones. The lens shape easily accommodates three-dimensional, peripheral and distance vision. At around seven years the muscles lengthen, allowing the lens to round out and more easily focus the image on the fovea centralis.

Children are introduced to books earlier than age seven in the UK, and need big letters in order to compensate for their lack of two-dimensional eye focusing capacity. Considering the ratio of cones to rods, it suggests we are *not* designed to spend long periods exclusively engaged in foveal focus activities such as reading, watching television and working at computers. The eyes need to experience the world as a whole for vision to develop the spatial awareness necessary for clear perception, thought and communication. This information on eye development again reinforces the fact that reading and writing are likely to be less stressful and more rewarding after seven years of age when the requisite brain processes are in place.

5 Complex language: the 11–13 shift

By the time children reach 13 years of age, they are using grammatical forms in their writing that are more complex than those found in their everyday speech. For younger children, the opposite is largely true. As children develop and learn, the efficiency and accuracy with which they can absorb information from the written word exceeds what they can take in from listening to speech. Walker [33] found that the written word was superior to the spoken word for all children tested regardless of their reading ability. Shown a video-tape of a discussion between two students and verbatim written accounts of the same events, sixteen year olds recalled more of what they had *read* than what had been *said*.

Studies of spoken language at this stage reveal the emergence of complex grammatical constructions that are involved in creative and effective writing. Speech begins to inherit structures encountered in text. Romaine [34] illustrated four stages:

1. This guy he owns the hotel he went to B.
2. This guy that he owns the hotel he went to B.
3. This guy that owns the hotel he went to B.
4. This guy that owns the hotel went to B.

Children at this stage achieve a greater command of the determiners, 'a', 'the', 'this', 'that' and so on, and go through a process of 'overmarking' [35], such as the redundant use of the pronoun 'he' in the example above. The child who is fortunate enough to achieve fluent literacy has at his disposal a new range of words, language structures and planning skills to create interesting and coherent narratives. Two powerful skills can be exploited. One is the voice, rich in tone, variety and melody, which – along with bodily movements – orchestrates interactions with listeners. The other is command over literary devices that can also be exploited in speech to powerfully express flexible and interesting meanings. Powers of narration, fluent literacy and the ability to use language informatively bring rich rewards both personally and academically. But what of students who do not reach these levels?

TEACHING TIP: When teaching reading, emphasise how meaning is created by using voice pitch, pace, pause and power, as this will help comprehension.

The Bullock Report in the UK [36] estimated that two million people in England and Wales had reading ages below nine years. At the time of writing, schools in the UK are attempting to get 80% of their students to adequate standards of literacy by age 11. Wood [25] suggested that children who fail to reach these levels are likely to face problems in narration and in information-giving situations. However, analysing speech into elements that make possible the creation of a visual code that can be read is an intellectual achievement and not just the natural product of the ability to talk. Speech, for most people, is an automatic affair but reading becomes an object of study. Students have to think objectively about speech and learn how to analyse it and represent this in writing.

Writing

Children use their knowledge about speech to discover the rules of written English. Think of words like 'said', 'slept', 'missed' and 'heaped'. How different are the /d/ and /t/ sounds involved? In writing they are distinct ('ed', 'd', 't') but are difficult to distinguish by ear. How do children come to master these words?

Mastering written rules

At the **pre-phonological stage 1**, words are written with little systematic structure. As children start to learn the correlates of spoken and written language they enter the **phonological stage 2**. At first, they assume rules are regular, which account for words written as 'kist' for 'kissed.' Children think that sound patterns /d/ and /t/ involve the common token /t/. The situation is complicated by the fact that English sounds have voiced /d/ and voiceless /t/ equivalents, which means they are made in the same manner with only the difference of voice. At **phonological stage 3** children discover that 'walked' is written with an 'ed' ending. They are then likely to over-generalise and produce 'sleped' for 'slept.' **Phonological stage 4** is crucial. Here, children stop over-generalising 'ed' for 't' in relation to non-verbs but will still do this for irregular verbs. They are obviously making use of implicit knowledge of the distinction between verbs and non-verbs. Finally, in **phonological stage 5** they clean up their act and move towards conventional, mature use. Good hearing, therefore, is vital for clear sound differentiation.

Bryant, Nunes and Bindman [37] addressed this issue. If children show knowledge of verbs and non-verbs before they master spelling conventions, then one can assume that grammatical awareness provides the foundations for spelling. We should then be able to predict which children will spell easily and those who will struggle. Conversely, if learning how to spell 'ed' and 't' occurs before children show grammatical distinctions then we would expect early spelling success to predict later developments in language structure.

Awareness of sentence structure

In the study by Bryant and co-workers, children were read two sentences, such as *'Tom helps Mary'* followed by *'Tom helped Mary'*, with the tense changed from present to past. Subjects were then given a sentence like *'Tom sees Mary'* and asked to transform it like the example (*'Tom saw Mary'*). Children succeeded in these verb analogy tasks before they achieved stage 4 or 5 in spelling. Therefore, they showed awareness of verb processes in speech *before* learning how to write them down. This suggests that awareness of basic patterns in the structure of speech and knowledge of grammatical categories pre-dates and *makes possible* achievements in writing. This, again, reinforces the importance of adequate spoken language before written forms are introduced.

The importance of inference

However, reading and writing involves more than proficiency in phonology and grammar. A study looking at the demands that reading makes on children was undertaken by Oakhill, Yuill and Parkin [38]. They worked with seven and eight year olds and asked them to listen to stories like the one below.

> 'The car crashed into the bus.
> The bus was near the cross-roads.
> The car skidded on the ice.'

The children were asked if the following 'inferences' were possible from what they had heard:

- ◆ The car was near the cross-roads.

- ◆ The bus skidded on the ice.

There was no link between the bus and the ice in the story so the second inference seems less plausible.

Two groups matched for age and performance on word recognition tests, but differing by two years in reading comprehension ability, took part in the study. The children's reading comprehension abilities were mirrored in their ability to draw inferences from spoken narratives. Those who found it difficult to make the correct inferences in the car and bus story were the ones who were poor at reading comprehension.

Since the groups were matched for age and performance on sight vocabulary it would seem that comprehension involves more than decoding skills and that differences in the ability to draw inferences from spoken narrative influences reading comprehension.

Training that focuses on drawing inferences in poems and prose improves reading comprehension dramatically.

TEACHING TIP: Help children to play detective with words, to build inference skills. Take the poem 'Algy and the Bear':

Algy met the bear.
The bear met Algy.
The bear was bulgy.
The bulge was Algy.

The information that the bear ate Algy is missing, so focus on this. What happened to Algy? What did the bear do?

Reading comprehension

Perera [28] suggested that many children find reading and writing difficult because they lack the relevant experience that helps them understand why various writing genres (types) exist and the way they demand different styles to convey a number of purposes. Although students might understand the reason for writing a letter to a friend and draw on their own experience to make sense of the demands involved, they probably have not listened to a history or geography book being read to them or heard a scientific report, so that there is no understanding of how and why people write about such things.

Home circumstances that allow access to books and the experience of being read to are positive indicators of likely progress [39]. A questionnaire survey of students' home reading habits in 1968 [40] found that 75% of 100 parents said they read to their children at least twice a week. A similar survey of 100 parents in the same school catchment area in 1998 discovered that no parents read to their children as much as twice a week. Such very limited evidence should be viewed cautiously, but at the very least it suggests a shift in child rearing practices.

In the intervening thirty years, between these two small studies, television has taken a stronger grip on people's lives. In addition, it has become more common for both parents to work outside the home, which means there is often less parent–child contact time overall. Obviously, such influences have changed the way we live. In June 1999, a long-established UK television advertisement for a brand of gravy, which focused on a 'typical' family at mealtimes, was abandoned because research indicated that only one-third of UK families ate meals around a dining table in this way, and this was far from a regular occasion even within this group. Trays in front of the television are the norm – the image of a happy family chatting and sharing a meal, as they cluster cosily around a table, is far removed from the reality of our present way of life, it seems.

Because talking about the day's experiences around the family meal table, and elsewhere, is no longer the norm, it is possible that modern children get far fewer opportunities for extended talk at home. Thus, more children are probably entering school lacking the experiences of being read to and talked with, and they come to formal learning with a limited sense of what words sound like and mean. Interaction with text in conjunction with others may be almost unknown for increasing numbers of our children.

A tally method used to help reading

Palincsar and Brown [41] used intervention strategies that made text audible for students. The teacher discussed a story with the children, speculating aloud what might come next and how ambiguities might be resolved. A student would then play the teacher role and use the same techniques with others. Using this talking method resulted in huge progress. At the beginning of the study, these 12–13 year old subjects were in the bottom 7% of their class on standard assessment tasks, but by the end their success rate had risen from 10% to 85%, putting them in the average range for their age group. The important issue to note is that the subjects in the study had word attack skills (sounding out words, or 'decoding') that were average for their age. It was *comprehension* of the whole ideas of the text that was so depressed. Opportunities to talk and explain increased their awareness and understanding dramatically. A case study in Chapter 7 will illuminate this further (page 143).

The argument underpinning these studies is that students who find difficulty in interacting with text can learn to do so if this process is made an explicit part of teaching. They are able to internalise self-regulatory activities so that they eventually become an automatic part of reading. Brown and Campione [42] called this strategy 'reciprocal teaching' and have followed large numbers of students using this approach, reporting not only improved reading comprehension but also improved levels of academic achievement.

At present many researchers and educators are making a plea for teachers to give greater emphasis to self-regulation skills and meta-cognition. These are about developing awareness, and depend on more talk between teachers and students but often place formidable demands on them because of the constraints of a prescriptive curriculum. Evidence suggests, however, that numbers of students come to school without the language awareness to make connections between spoken and written forms.

What children need to read

A knowledge of sound and grammar structures is essential for learning reading and writing. In addition, an ability to draw inferences from spoken narrative (go beyond the information given) enables children to construct models of the situations they come across in stories and elaborate beyond what is explicitly mentioned in the text. Knowledge constructed in the course of understanding and explaining everyday experiences provides the foundation for the interpretative 'scripts' or frameworks that are exploited in reading for meaning [43]. There is enough evidence to reject theories

133

that children learn the structure of language from written representation, suggesting that knowledge of form, content and use is developed in speaking but extended through mastering written words.

Some children fall behind their peers in learning how to read and write and we can surmise that their problems have many origins. Some display limited awareness of the sound patterns of speech, while others perform inadequately on tasks demanding grammatical distinctions. Yet others who can decode print into speech find reading comprehension a huge problem because they are unable to draw inferences from text and interact with what is written to bring together a whole meaning. There are good grounds for optimism, however, as more emphasis on talk between teachers and students, as we have seen, reaps rich rewards for academic progress.

◆ Comment

This chapter has outlined the main stages of brain development and considered this in relation to learning. The translation of thought into speaking and writing is a very complex task. It involves sensory areas, primary auditory, auditory association in conjunction with primary visual, visual association, motor speech and gnostic (knowledge) areas of the cortex. Movement is a vital part of language as integrated thought patterns are transmitted to the vocalisation areas of the motor cortex and basal ganglion of the limbic system to bring thought into word formation. Large areas of the brain cortex are devoted to sensations and motor functions for speech and vocalisation. There are more nerve fibres going across the temporal–mandibular joint (jaw) from the sensory and motor innervation of the face muscles than in any other part of the body. These muscles give us facial expressions that amplify words and show the meaning behind them. They produce expression in the eyes and move the tongue, mouth and jaw to pronounce sounds and words. The concentration of muscles and nerves related to verbalisation and expression in this area suggests it is a prime site for exercises that can enhance communication. We need to focus on this activity because:

◆ Talking is essential to thinking and language development but in our culture television and video games give children fewer opportunities to interact verbally in ways that are meaningful.

◆ The Rankin study carried out in 1928 [44] set daily communication times as 45% listening, 30% speaking, 16% reading and 9% writing. In 1975, almost 50 years later, the Werner study [45] showed a different balance was actually occurring: 55% listening, 23% speaking, 13% reading and 9% writing. The balance needs to be shifted away from listening and further towards talking.

◆ Arbor's American Use of Time Project [46] estimated that 38% of the population's free time is given over to television watching, while less than 10% is spent reading, which amounts to fewer than 3 hours of reading per week. Speaking was not assessed, but since such a large proportion of leisure time is dedicated to watching television, it seems likely that the amount of time spent talking is small.

Preserving conversation

Conversation, it seems, may be a dying art. Yet it is essential to human relationships and the development of intuition and judgement about situations and events. It is the arena in which we test out our ideas with one another and through discussion develop our thinking and evaluations. The importance of talking to children in full sentences is vital as they love to mimic, which exposes them to ideas that have already been developed, giving them a model to follow on which to base their own thinking and language.

Books lay out ideas in complete sentences and thus help to extend linguistic knowledge, but as we have seen, language must be developed to a certain level before text can be understood. Children need experience of words in many contexts to appreciate their subtle and various meanings, as well as having repeated opportunities to thread together a number of ideas to produce a whole notion. Conversation is the activity centre for dealing with ideas. In such events children are able to string together the 'beads' (words) to make a complete 'necklace' (narrative event).

Continual practice is vital so that students come to understand the conventions that deal with the content of what is spoken. For example, one has to pitch the voice tone at a slightly higher level than the previous speaker and catch the eyes of the listeners in order to make an entry in conversation. This grabs attention and shows participants the rules of exchange of information are known and obeyed. The art of conversation is as much about reading the signals of non-verbal behaviour as understanding the content of the talk and being able to contribute ideas to this.

Unfortunately, there are children forced to read, because the curriculum dictates this, who have not developed requisite language and communication conventions. They learn to 'bark at print', decoding the written words into speech but not making very much meaning from what they have read. Children need to be engaged in full, conscious dialogue to assist them to communicate their feelings, values, information, creative ideas and intuitions. If students are able to verbalise and flesh out their ideas with others, by working in pairs or groups, their thoughts become anchored in understanding and meaning. The Quality in Higher Education [49] research on employer satisfaction indicated considerable dissatisfaction with the spoken and written communication skills of graduates, which suggests we should be emphasising these skills not only to improve academic performance, but also for personal and professional success. Unfortunately, the curriculum may not allow students opportunities, in sufficient measure, to develop these necessary skills.

Bennett and co-workers [47] and Galton and Williamson [48] examined how children talk and work in smaller groups and suggested that the outcomes are not as one would hope and expect. They put this down to the ways in which children are selected for tasks and the nature of these. Galton says the main reasons for lack of success are that children are not schooled in the attitudes and skills needed to sustain effective collaboration. The most important of these is the skill of conversation with an ability to turn-take and develop a topic theme. Also, children receive mixed messages: typically,

TEACHING TIP: Considering ways to increase the emphasis on talk in class in a planned way has rich rewards in terms of both student behaviour and work performance.

they are expected to work alone, silently and quickly, so that they find it hard to switch to talk and discussion in groups. To make this an effective way to learn, ground rules for behaviour need to be negotiated and students taught the skills of group talk in an explicit way. Chapter 7 tackles this important subject so that successful learning is a reality and not an uncertainty for all the students that we teach.

SUMMARY POINTS

◆ The brain develops in stages and educational demands do not always concur with these. Reading, for example, requires linear processing and foveal eye focusing which does not develop easily before seven years.

◆ Teaching activities tend to favour those who have left-brain dominance as they are geared to logical, linear learning in two-dimensional forms.

◆ Language also develops in stages and children need opportunities to develop language through speaking before reading and writing are tackled.

◆ Reading helps to extend language patterns as students experience words in full sentences, which may not happen frequently in the speaking patterns to which they are exposed.

◆ Opportunities for students to talk in small groups are necessary to help them lock learning into their minds. Group-talk opportunities need planning, and skills of talking and arguing need to be taught so that children are able to make full use of these experiences.

Chapter 7

How can we teach communication?

"Communication is likely to be one of the top topics of this new Century."

Sylvia Anderson, Director of the Human Communication International Conference, April 2000, 'Communication in the Technological Age'

The above quote, from a conference address, suggests that communication *should* be at the top of all our agendas. There are at least two reasons for this. Firstly, the world population is growing fast, and there will be more and more people communicating around the world as the new century progresses. Secondly, technology is developing novel ways in which we can make contact with one another through e-mail, video conferencing and the Internet Multi-User Dimension (MUD). This latter process connects many thousands of educational, research, commercial and social organisations and has huge potential for sharing information. Our social, educational and work worlds are today therefore vastly increased, and make greater demand on our abilities to communicate effectively across cultures.

◆ Readiness to learn

There is evidence, however, that our communication skills are not what they should be. Boyer [1] reported research on pre-school children's readiness to learn, in the USA: *'When asked to identify the areas in which students are most deficient, teachers (7000 of them) overwhelming cited lack of proficiency in language.'* The statistics are alarming: 98% of children on school entry were regarded as having communication problems and 51% of these were serious. (A chronological checklist of language skills in provided in Appendix 8.) Related skills show a similar pattern, as shown in the table below [1].

Problems in six dimensions of readiness for school		
Readiness skills	**Problems**	**Serious problems**
language proficiency	98%	51%
emotional maturity	98%	43%
general knowledge	98%	38%
social confidence	98%	31%
moral awareness	90%	21%
physical well-being	74%	6%

The table represents information gathered from 50 American states and, although there is no comparable research in the UK, anecdotal evidence suggests that UK children may have similar levels of difficulty when they enter school. This puts a huge burden on teachers who not only have to implement a highly prescriptive curriculum but must develop programmes to help students access it.

The focus in schools is on literacy, which in its fullest sense means learning to communicate verbally and non-verbally, responding to music, dance and the visual arts as well as words. Long before children can speak clearly, they are soothed and stimulated by music rhythms, dance routines and the metre of rhymes, as well as being drawn to interesting, bright, shaped objects around them. A drawing or painting, an action poem, a song's rhythm and a dance's steps are the symbols that enliven and enrich a child's world.

Children, today, live in an environment that is full of sound, visual and movement stimulation. Why is it that they lack a readiness to learn formally in school? There is no evidence that modern parents are less caring or committed to their children's progress. What has changed, however, is the nature of family life, with its increasing fragmentation under conflicting, competing pressures of home and work. Lack of job security and hectic schedules keep families constantly stressed and out of touch with one another. Parents may lack necessary support, living away from close relatives, and become torn between work and family obligations. Some children suffer, and one of the most important outcomes of this situation is *communication and language deficiency*, which dramatically affects learning. Parents simply do not have the time to regularly talk, play and read with their children anymore and television and computer games frequently take the place of person-to-person interaction. This is a downside of modern life – we have more money but less time. Time and attention, however, is just what children need for the development of their full potential.

Natural abilities

The notion of the child as a problem-solver, designer and builder of her own knowledge is entirely compatible with the views of eminent educationalists such as Piaget [2]. Bruner [3] also described the child as a problem-solver and viewed instruction as helping to discover manageable problems. Accepting the child's natural problem-solving and self-instructional abilities does not imply that their interactions and encounters with others are not crucial to what and how they learn. Robinson's [4] work argued that language and intellectual development are progressed by specific social experiences and students can be helped to increase thinking and understanding by becoming more explicitly aware of the processes through which they communicate.

Studies of adolescents, however, portray a grim picture of children's natural language and thinking abilities. They also suggest that the right kind of educational experience can play a vital role in determining to what extent children are able to gain expertise and use language to explain, instruct and self-regulate. In a large study of adolescent communication skills, Brown and co-workers [5] worked with five hundred 14–17 year old students in Scotland. Three hundred of these were judged by their teachers as representing the lower third of their year by virtue of their academic attainments in class. They were considered unlikely to leave school with any formal academic qualifications.

In this Scottish study, students were observed talking informally in pairs and were recorded as being chatty and amusing. In fact, in this activity they appeared to be confident and competent communicators, with no problems. Minor increases in communication demands, however, produced marked impairments in performance. Asking a student to talk to a friend on a tape recorder led to speech that was far less fluent, articulate and coherent than that witnessed in face-to-face communication. The absence of a live partner to supply interactional and non-verbal support had huge impact on the quality of the students' communication. When demands were increased further, by asking the students to give detailed instructions and explanations to others, performance deteriorated even more.

Different styles of talk

Underpinning the research in communication by Brown and co-workers [5] is a distinction between 'chat' and 'informative speech'. The latter was the subject of the investigations. 'Chat' is referred to as informal conversation without a planned outcome to the exchange. It is highly interactive, and participants share responsibility for the topics of talk, and there is mutual understanding of what is expressed. In this informal talk, the discussion can go anywhere: it might start with comments about some ghastly homework and end up with swapping ideas on what to wear for tonight's disco.
In interpreting the responses in the Scottish study, Wardhaugh's [6] work on the social practices and values implicated in conversation is relevant. He pointed out that normal, everyday conversation is typically and literally mundane. It is about common, routine experiences and events, requiring little analytic activity. There are implicit conventions that inhibit us from going too far in probing other people's motives, behaviour and beliefs. The boundaries will change, of course, according to the relationship and intimacy of the participants. These are very obvious observations but are important when considering a child's experiences of talk and the use of talk in school to acquire a specific body of knowledge.

Differences in the underlying purposes of talk in and outside school are reflected in the nature of the relationship between the people involved and their use of language in a particular situation. We have already discussed the fact that it is legitimate for teachers to ask most of the questions in class even though this might be undesirable for students (page 65). Out of school discourse, however, questions will perform various functions, including the search for information. This will be legitimised if the person answering understands the reason for the question. In a shop conversation, for example, a query from a prospective purchaser such as *'Does this cake contain nuts?'* is quite in order if the sales assistant understands that this is vital information for someone allergic to this ingredient in food.

Questions outside the classroom are also used to frame requests for permission or help: for example, *'May I park my car here?'* The answer poses a moral as well as a linguistic issue: does the person have a right to park here? Such a request becomes unreasonable if there are negative consequences for the person questioned. He might, for example, be in trouble for allowing a stranger to park in a place where people have to obtain a licence to do so. In addition to such situations, questions are used to display courtesy and interest: for example, *'How are you?'*, *'Have you had a good journey?'*, and so on.

In school, however, questions often violate established conventions and confuse students. Teachers expect to receive answers to questions such as *'Paul, why are you scratching your bottom?'*, even though these flout the normal conventions of politeness. Questions are often asked by teachers when it is obvious to students that they know the answers: *'What colour is the grass?'* Wells [7] mentioned that parents also address this type of 'display' question to children, designed to elicit known answers, but failure to comply will have very different significance for children when compared to the school experience. Parents are unlikely to admonish an inadequate reply. Teachers, however, frequently ask students to justify or prove what they say: *'What do you mean you haven't done your homework?'* Getting answers *right* (in the teacher's view) is the principle concern in class, which is of little consequence in the informal chat outside those four walls.

The child, therefore, has to discover and comply with a number of conventions and obligations that are part of the roles of students and teachers. These conventions imply differences in language function. Information giving is concerned with providing clear instructions, directions and explanations. In the Scottish study [5], students were found to be incapable of providing comprehensible narratives.

To remedy this, Brown and co-workers designed a range of co-operative tasks of varying levels of complexity to help foster student skills in giving information and instruction. Some were games where one student had to tell another how to perform a task. Other activities involved creating narrative accounts. Assessments were devised to evaluate student performance. These demanded the presence or absence of critical information, and its appropriate sequence as well as the use of reference terms such as determiners ('a', 'an', 'the', 'this', 'that') and pronouns ('his', 'hers', 'their' and so on). Substantial progress was revealed on the assessments and sustained in follow-up reviews. The students who first played 'listener' were significantly more articulate and informative when later they played the 'speaker' role. It appears that the experience of carrying out instructions, when required to act out what is told, is important to talking informatively with others. Coaching in both listener and speaker roles was deemed to be important in developing narrative skills.

Such evidence poses the question *'Why were these students so inarticulate?'* The fact that they could be helped easily proves that they had the capacity to learn, but why had this not happened naturally? The research highlights the problems of understanding and using certain styles (registers) of language. The style of classroom language is very different to that of home. It seems that students do not always naturally acquire new forms of listening and speaking.

We might argue that the schools had not previously presented these students with opportunities to learn new ways of communicating because such skills were not thought to be their major concern. Inability to process large amounts of information, as well as organise, regulate and express what is known in a coherent way, would appear to be a major handicap to any satisfactory school progress. The Scottish research project was not about helping students master different dialects of speech but enabling them to process and express information clearly and logically. If we can accept this as a legitimate goal of education why does it appear so elusive for such a large number of children?

Brown and co-workers suggested that part of the answer lies in classroom discourse styles and the way teachers talk to students and expect them to respond. In face-to-face communication there is synchronisation of behaviour between participants, and conversation is rather like a dance where each must be in step with the other, otherwise the whole activity falls apart. In classroom discourse, however, the cues that enable this to occur may be inhibited or demolished so that the teacher is out of synchrony and sympathy with the students' responses. These will vary from child to child because of the natural differences there are in processing and making meaning from information, making the whole business of transmitting knowledge extremely tricky.

Teachers, for example, leave about a second of silence after a question before resuming talking. Studies on the effects of different teacher 'wait times' on student responses show that when they are asked to hold on for a buzzer allowing a three second interval, the student responses were more frequent, relevant and thoughtful [8, 9]. It appears, therefore, that teachers are so anxious to keep the lesson going and flowing that students just do not have sufficient time to formulate their thinking. When it comes to set tasks based on the information given, many children will produce less than their best.

"Teaching is not only a special form of conversing with others, it is an especially difficult form, if for no other reason than that the teacher must 'converse' with a large heterogeneous group of listeners. Good teaching requires one to be good at a particular kind of conversation. It is a skill not easily acquired because of the special demands it makes and is not a skill one can readily practise outside the classroom, since it is rarely appropriate to any other circumstances."

Wardhaugh [6]

Successful talk in the classroom, therefore, begins with the teacher being aware of the multiplicity of issues that have formed the debate of the previous chapters. Evidence strongly suggests that many of our students are ill-equipped to deal with the monologue language of school, where they are expected to put together a message from large chunks of information provided as talk and text. The narrative structure required demands a new knowledge and skill in communicating. The table overleaf summarises some of the differences between home talk and class talk, as a basis for understanding what we need to do to develop the additional abilities required. To succeed in the classroom, students must be aware of the specific ways to use language and communication in a relevant, appropriate and effective manner. This requires them to judge what they do, and to modify this if indicated on another occasion. Many children do not develop this awareness of the different requirements of language until relatively late.

Characteristics of home and class talk	
Home talk	**Class talk**
Informal, familiar style – many statements	Formal style – many questions and commands
Adult modifies words, sentence length, information to suit the child, signalling turn-taking and a shift of topic clearly	Language adjusted for the mid-ability range so some students are not catered for in terms of discourse level
Language content and context based on shared assumptions about experience. Language is particular and more meaning is available in non-verbal ways	Language demands frequent interpretation of non-shared assumptions. More meaning coded in words. Language is universal
Frequent turn-taking between adult and child according to social and cultural conventions	Teacher monologue dominates. Little turn-taking except within the class conventions
Frequent individual comments by adult and child to clarify what is shared	Children expected to listen in silence. Teacher comments about the world at large
Generally small amounts of information shared, dependent on the context	Large volume of information used to expand content that is not about the present context
On-going checks for understanding. Language is contextualised	Frequent reference to previous information without checks for understanding. Language is decontextualised
Purpose of language is to share topics and terms of reference and take equal turns in the dialogue. The talk normally lacks a tight focus and is unplanned	Purpose of language is to transmit knowledge. Talk is normally goal-directed with emphasis on technical terms and words meanings
Home talk is simple in ideas and usually about personal concerns that involve the here and now	Class talk is mentally complex and remote from individual concerns, referring to a context that is not normally present
Participants' assumptions depend mainly on a specific context and can be taken for granted	Assumptions are based on what is said in a general context and cannot be taken for granted

The findings that have been presented in this discussion would appear to rule out assumptions that narrative skills in explaining and instructing are natural and inevitable. What explaining and instructing demand is a specific type of experience, and the fact that many adolescents are inadequate in these communication skills suggests schools need to do more if they want improved student performances. Communication in the classroom is a challenge for both teachers and students. Teacher-directed questions appear to be the dominant communication register and may be effective in achieving certain managerial and instructional ends but seem unlikely to provide the right conditions for developing students' own powers of informing, narrating and self-regulating.

◆ Teaching talk

The challenges confronting teachers demand considerable expertise in very special forms of communication. This is full justification for the development of a scheme that is designed for the purpose of helping students to achieve the communication skills they need for learning.

The Communication Opportunity Group Scheme (COGS)

The Communication Opportunity Group Scheme (COGS) [10] developed from a UK schools' project in the 1980s and 1990s to investigate why children failed to make progress in class when they tested as normally intelligent. A case study of an 11 year old girl is presented below to illustrate that a child may produce adequate results according to certain assessment criteria but give a false picture of her learning potential.

Katy is 11 years old and in her first year at a comprehensive school of about 2000 students, in a large UK town. She had attended a small village primary school and found the change of context quite alarming. Within a few days of starting 'big school', Katy was playing truant. Specialists were brought in to try to help her cope. She said that she could not get on with the lessons, and certainly her reading level was about two and a half years below her chronological age. One of the tests given to Katy was the *Clinical Evaluation of Language Fundamentals* (CELF) – *revised* [11], as there were queries about her language comprehension. One of the sub-tests involves listening to paragraphs, and the assessment story, with Katy's responses, is presented in the box over the page.

CELF Listening test

The passage

Central School was sponsoring its tenth annual computer science fair and schools from all over the country were entered. Jamie knew that the competition was stiff. He also knew that extreme care had to be taken in category selection. One of his friends had an outstanding entry in last year's fair in the area of computer programming. He might have won if he had chosen a different category. Jamie had already given his own project careful consideration. He had asked several of his teachers and finally decided to enter in a new category called 'artificial intelligence'.

Questions asked in the test, with Katy's responses

'Who was sponsoring the science fair?'	Answer: School.
'What was the boy's name in the story?'	Answer: Jamie.
'Why didn't his friend's project win the year before?'	Answer: Wrong group.
'How did Jamie decide on a category for his project?'	Answer: Ask the teacher.

Katy's answers in the CELF test were spot on, giving her full marks. She was, however, asked to complete an extra task that was not part of this assessment. Katy was asked to re-tell the story in her own words. The story she gave is given in the box below.

Katy's story re-telling

Title given by Katy: **The Big School**

A boy went to school one day. The sun was shining. He did not want to go to school. It was Friday morning. He was going to the football match. He wanted to go. The boy had no money. He asked his friend if he was going. His friend said 'No'.

What is going on here? The story re-telling bears no resemblance to the original one. The ideas are clear and grammar and syntax correct, although the sentences are simple rather than the complex ones expected from an eleven year old student. Clearly, Katy has either not understood the task, or has not been able to bring together the information given to her. She has a language format for narrating the events but the content is haywire. Why? It seems that although she can deal with details, what she lacks is the ability to bring these together in an overall meaning (if it is accepted that she understands how to re-tell a story).

Bell [12] talked about such students and described them as having 'Gestalt imagery weakness'. Gestalt imagery is the ability to create an imaged whole: *'Readers or listeners construct mental models of the situation a writer or speaker is describing.'*

Imaging is a sensory link to language and thought. Gestalt imagery connects us to incoming oral or written language, links us to existing knowledge, accesses experience, establishes vocabulary and creates and stores information in memory.

Clark and Paivio [13] proposed Dual Coding Theory to explain behaviour and experience, in terms of *'dynamic associative processes that operate on a rich network of modality-specific verbal and non-verbal representations'*. This seems complicated but merely illustrates what Einstein meant when he said *'If I can't picture it, I can't understand it.'* To verbalise (in speech or writing) you must be able to visualise. Bell suggested that listening and reading are dependent on making 'movies' in your head. If you cannot picture what you hear or see in print it is difficult to comprehend the meaning.

This brings us back to the left-brain (verbal) and the right-brain (visual) activity. *'The right hemisphere 'thinks' in images and the left hemisphere 'thinks' in words'* [14]. The effects of Gestalt imaging weakness illustrate a lack of integrated right- and left-brain function. The effects are described by many researchers and summarised below:

◆ limited oral language comprehension and expression

◆ limited reading comprehension and written expression

◆ limited sense of humour

◆ limited ability to follow directions

◆ limited understanding and expression of cause and effect (cannot deal with 'how' and 'why' questions).

Such problems are insidious as they are often difficult to detect because students, like Katy, can have clear speech and be able to answer specific questions adequately. The causes are puzzling. There may be hereditary factors. Both Katy's two brothers and her mother were found to have similar profiles and consequent learning difficulties. Research suggests that a specific brain etiology is likely.

Cases such as Katy's do indicate that perhaps comprehension is assumed too readily in schools. Certainly, the focus on reading has been on decoding skills and only recently have researchers been interested in language context effects.

Katy is typical of the students seen on a UK project in Leicester in the 1980s and 1990s, which was set up to examine and explain their inadequate school progress. She is also similar to the students described in the Scottish project earlier in the chapter (page 138), who appeared to have difficulty in processing chunks of information and making coherent responses. To alleviate this problem with Katy and her peers, the COGS teaching scheme was developed to focus on communication for learning. The rationale for COGS is discussed over the page.

COGS rationale

"Practice doesn't make perfect. Perfect practice makes perfect."

Vince Lombardi

Communication can be very simply described as a process that involves source and destination.

sender ➡ message ➡ receiver

Although this linear explanation takes the process back to its bare essentials, the reality is a great deal more complex because both speaker and listener contribute a different set of attributes to the event, which affects the transmission of the message. These are summarised below.

Attitudes of speaker and receiver in communication

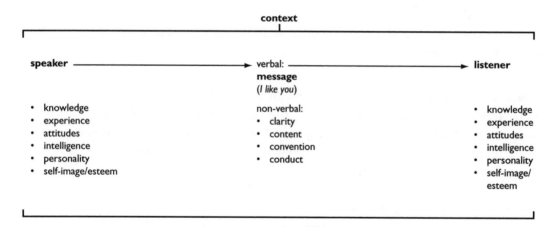

The speaker and listener bring varying qualities and experience to the communication process and these have to be taken into account in the content (*'I like you'*), coding (speech) and treatment (pleasant tone and manner) of the message. The speaker and listener themselves are 'givens' and it is not easy to change who and what they are in a short time. Improving the message component, though, is entirely possible and within this framework we can examine the speaker and listener dimensions. Aspects of clarity, content, convention and conduct are involved in the transmission of information. It is these components of the message that are of primary importance in the exchange, as explained in the diagram opposite.

Components of a communication message

Bounding the communicative process are four main issues:

1 **Opportunity**: chances to listen, speak, read and write depend on personal abilities and inclinations and the roles and status of the participants in an activity

2 **Attitude**: feelings and views affect social contact and the meanings shared between the sender and receiver of the message

3 **Personality**: sociability along introvert (inward-looking) and extrovert (outward-looking) dimensions affects the communication exchange; conversation is the milieu that extroverts thrive in but introverts die in!

4 **Intelligence**: as most thinking is expressed in words, intelligence controls activity; it is the ability to cope with life and its problems, demanding feeling and reasoning approaches to situations.

These four processes place constraints on the communicative operations now defined:

◆ **Clarity** is about making the message clear and depends on skills involving the use of words as well as performance in voice pronunciation, pitch, pace, power, posture, gesture and facial expression.

◆ **Content** is the topic of the message and is organised in different ways according to the purpose of the presentation.

◆ **Convention** is the protocol that governs the giving and receiving of messages in different situations. It is evident in the form of greetings, apologies, explanations, instructions, negotiations and narrations of experiences as well as in the way words are arranged in sentences.

◆ **Conduct** is the image a sender or receiver has of the other and is demonstrated in the confidence shown when communicating and the manner in which the exchange is handled.

147

COGS uses this model for teaching success skills to both children and adults. Reviews of the literature from the 1970s, summarised by Brigman and co-workers [15], have emphasised instruction in communication because of its strong correlation with positive peer relations and academic achievement. Successful strategies for teaching these critical abilities have involved individual, small group and whole class instruction.

Although documented internationally over the last thirty years, the problems of students lacking requisite communication skills for learning persists *at all levels* and may be the main reason for inadequate school, college, work and life performances. COGS attempts to translate what is known about developing personal and academic success skills. It is based on a model of what is involved in giving a message and also on how ideas are developed and expressed verbally and non-verbally.

The diagrams below and opposite illustrate the COGS scheme graphically. The teaching scheme encompasses 14 levels or goals, covering primary, secondary, tertiary education and job training communication requirements. Each of the goals requires 8–10 hours of teaching, after which participants are assessed on target spoken and written competencies. Examples from goals 1 and 10 are available in Appendix 4.

How ideas are developed in COGS

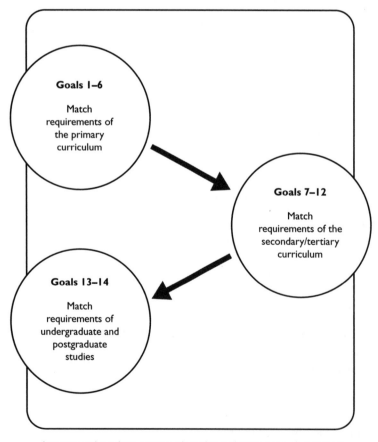

There are five activities for each goal level – one each for clarity, content, convention and conduct in spoken tasks, and the fifth a creative writing activity. This represents the 80% speaking to 20% writing split of everyday activities, commonly agreed as the approximate ratio in the literature. There are three possible frameworks for study: 'Communication' (see Appendix 4), 'Communication through Performance' and 'Communication through Creative Writing'. The first framework provides a general scheme that develops a wide range of communication abilities, while the latter two concentrate on more specific areas.

Listening and speaking equate with reading and writing at each goal level.

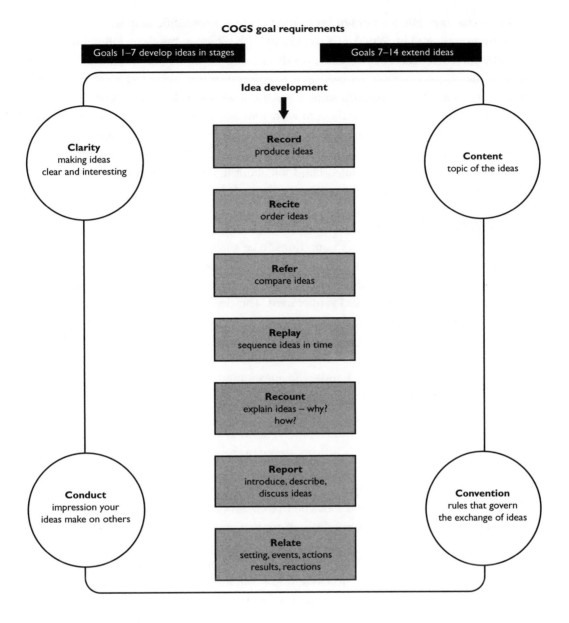

COGS goal requirements

Goals 1–7 develop ideas in stages

Goals 7–14 extend ideas

Idea development

Clarity
making ideas
clear and interesting

Content
topic of the ideas

Record
produce ideas

Recite
order ideas

Refer
compare ideas

Replay
sequence ideas in time

Recount
explain ideas – why?
how?

Report
introduce, describe,
discuss ideas

Conduct
impression your
ideas make on others

Convention
rules that govern
the exchange of ideas

Relate
setting, events, actions
results, reactions

The teaching strategy uses a 'tell, show, do and coach' approach, which includes systematic sequencing of teaching with review, demonstration, guided practice, and corrective and supportive feedback. There is a mixture of group and independent activity, which Wang [16] found to be the most effective mode of instruction after reviewing 50 years of research.

Using COGS for teaching and learning

In thinking how to use the COGS framework, let us go back and visit Tom, a seven year old lad in primary school whom we met in the cooking lesson in Chapter 1 (pages 13 to 14) and then in several events in his classroom in Chapter 2 (pages 25 to 31). Tom, we could see, had problems talking in some groups and in formal situations such as large

149

class discussions. His teacher felt he would benefit from specific help with communication and he joined a COGS group with others in his class, following the 'Communication' framework (see Appendix 4).

Obviously, teaching begins with some base-line assessment. It is easy to spend a long time on the testing process but the aim with Tom was to move straight into the teaching with the minimum of preliminaries. In order to achieve a base-line, his teacher filled in a checklist (see Appendix 5) and Tom underwent a ten-question interview, which was followed by a story re-telling task. This took about ten minutes to complete. The results of the interview are given in Appendix 6.

Comments from the interview

The interview enables answers to questions to be analysed according to the content and conventions demonstrated, as well as the clarity and conduct displayed. The first two dimensions of content and convention are objectively scored in terms of the ideas expressed and the grammar and syntax used. The clarity and conduct evaluation is more subjective but there are criteria for marking that enable the information to be considered in a standard format.

We can see that Tom is able to handle the question-and-answer process but that his responses are consistently limited. His overall score of 50 puts him in the 4–5 year mean range of the pilot norms that have been gathered for the test. Tom's use of conventions is his lowest score. He demonstrates past tenses and links ideas with 'and'. However, his syntax is very basic and there is little evidence of the enlargement of ideas with adjectives, adverbs, noun/verb phrases or the use of relative clauses. His story re-telling task confirms this and his responses in the cooking group activity described in Chapter 1 are of a similar performance level. The five classroom discourse transcriptions in Chapter 2 also demonstrate limited use of content and conventions.

This information points to the fact that Tom is operating at COGS level 1. He is producing ideas but these are limited and not well organised. He needs opportunities to expand his concepts and express these appropriately. If the ideas are there, the form is more likely to develop for delivering them. If you look at the competencies at goal 1 (Appendix 4), they seem entirely appropriate for Tom's ability. Therefore, Tom underwent ten weeks teaching for goal 1 and was re-assessed on the interview test six months following his base-line assessment. The results are compared opposite.

Tom's interview tests 1 and 2		
Questions and answers	**test 1**	**test 2**
1 Who lives with you?	Mum and Pete	Mum and Pete
2 What do you like doing?	Playing	Playing football
3 Where do people keep food?	Cupboards	In the fridge and in cupboards
4 What do people wear on their feet?	Shoes and socks	Socks, shoes, trainers
5 Tell me a drink you like and one you don't like?	Sprite and Cola	I like Sprite not milk
6 What did you do yesterday?	Went football	Went Dans. Played Rampage 2
7 Tell me some things you might do next weekend?	See my mates	See Nana. Go to Dans.
8 Think of a loaf of bread, a pencil and your bed. Which is the lightest and heaviest?	Pen and bed	Pen and bed
9 What do you do when you cross the road?	Look and listen	Look right and left. Listen. Cross and look.
10 Tell me a story that would make me laugh.	Spiff drank beer. He sleep and sleep.	I was asleep. I fell off the bed. There was a lump.
Scores:	content = 13 convention = 8 clarity = 17 conduct = 12 total = 50	content = 20 convention = 14 clarity = 20 conduct = 20 total = 74

The results show considerable progress after the ten hours of teaching. Appendix 6 shows Tom's assessment report. Students are marked for core competencies as detailed below as well as the specific competencies that each activity demands.

Core communication competencies for COGS	
Spoken competencies	**Written competencies**
1 Physical awareness, correct posture and effective use of space	1 Clean, neat appearance
2 Effective use of facial expression and body gestures	2 Well-formed letters and spaced words
3 Regular eye contact	3 Relevant content and quantity
4 Effective use of voice: pitch, pace, pause, power and pronunciation	4 Accurate punctuation
5 Appropriate grammar and syntax	5 Appropriate grammar and syntax
6 Appropriate vocabulary	6 Appropriate vocabulary
7 Awareness of audience and ability to adapt information (relevance/quantity)	7 Clear, concise expression
8 Ability to hold audience interest and convey meaning	8 Imaginative ideas that convey meaning
9 Confident, pleasant manner	9 Appropriate structure and logical order
10 Appropriate time organisation	10 Ability to convey personal views

Tom showed ability to progress quickly with COGS and his second test score of 74 puts him at a 6½ year mean level of performance. Like the students on the Scottish study [5], he was able to learn the necessary skills when they were specifically taught. His reading moved up to a similar level. Other studies with COGS show the same progress. Two groups of fifteen children, between five and eight years old were selected from schools 'N' and 'W' (on the basis they were clients of the speech and language therapy service and performed academically below their peers). There were no significant differences on language and reading on base-line tests but, after School N children had received ten hours of grammar teaching and School W had undergone ten hours of COGS training, the situation was very different [17], as the table shows.

Language test	Mean scores for School W	Mean scores for School N
1 (base-line)	20.13	19.8
2 (after ten hours of teaching)	42.40	23.40

Several studies [10, 18, 19, 20] show the same trend in assessment results after COGS teaching. In the next section we look at how to carry out this method of developing communication.

The learning experience

COGS teaches communication based on five learning principles:

1. Co-operation
2. Empathy
3. Active learning
4. Learner-centred activities
5. Message-orientated communication

The term 'message-orientated communication' was coined by Black and Butzkamm [21] to refer to verbal and non-verbal language used as a means of communication. This includes not only words, but gestures, facial expressions, tone of voice and 'props' (pictures or objects) that might be part of the on going activity. An example is classroom discourse that gets things done in a lesson, as in the cooking activity described in Chapter 1. As we saw in this event, communication situations develop when exchanging comments on what is happening. This facilitates knowledge and understanding.

These principles are in contrast to many teaching situations, which are geared towards 'skill getting' with specific exercises and responses and an emphasis on the product rather than the process of learning. The target in such circumstances may, therefore, be on certain elements of the communication process, such as sound, word or sentence patterns. COGS aims to develop a more holistic approach that centres on a real communication activity and analyses the specific competencies and skills required for this as part of a whole process of understanding and expression.

Two devices are used in the activities to help develop communication:

- **information gap experiences**, which force participants to exchange information to find a solution (solving puzzles, making explanations or writing summaries); these are practised in guessing games and problem-solving tasks

- **opinion gaps** created from controversial ideas, which encourage participants to share feelings, describe experiences and defend views; these are encouraged in discussion activities.

Learning is more effective if participants are involved in the process and activities are relevant to their normal experiences. Thus, the content of COGS arises from the learning needs of the context in which participants are involved and uses information and opinion gap experiences to develop thinking, language and communication.

COGS teaching

Communication activities are best carried out in numbers of 8–12, which give everyone a chance to speak and can provide smaller group possibilities for certain tasks (pairs or threes). Groups across age are possible, as students can work on their individual goal levels within the session. For example, in one after-school group, the youngest was eight and the oldest seventeen years old. However, personalities must gel and the basic requirement is that all must co-operate reasonably well with one another and have chances to work with those of similar ability in the session. It is essential to have good models of behaviour and general performance within the group so that those with difficulties have an idea of what to aim for. The more able students can be put in situations where they have to 'teach' (for example, supporting someone reading) and this allows them to develop a new set of communicating skills, sharing knowledge and strengthening understanding.

Groups should operate at least once a week for an hour. If students are in school, careful consideration has to be given to the timing of the sessions as distress can be caused if they miss favourite lessons. Although time-tabling is a difficult issue, problems can be resolved if there is the will to do this. Anyone working in this way with students will be so sure of the personal and academic benefits to them that they will seek to make this a priority area. In the UK, COGS has been successfully taught within the English and Personal and Social Education curriculum. It slots well within the Citizenship syllabus as personal communication is a core topic within this.

The COGS levels are best taught in an 8–10 week schedule, which focuses energy towards a goal certificate. Interruptions in the weekly programme will diminish progress, so teaching is best delivered at times when trips, visits and examinations do not intervene. The assessment for the certificate is an essential part of the process as it is the product that arises out of the interpersonal teaching process and brings an awareness of the goals that are aimed for at each level. (Teachers who want to use COGS as part of the qualifications process should receive a special training for this: contact details are supplied on page 2).

Organising the group

"He drew a circle that shut me out. Heretic, rebel, a thing to flout. But love and I had the wit to win and we drew a circle that took him in."

anon

A circle is the ideal format for group communication as it encourages easy listening, giving all participants a chance to speak. The facilitator encourages patience and tolerance, modelling acceptance and non-judgement. Take into account the following factors when planning:

- ◆ physical space
- ◆ disturbance of others
- ◆ the size of the group
- ◆ student age
- ◆ level and interest
- ◆ the elements to be studied
- ◆ resources available
- ◆ cultural issues.

Rules may be introduced if required, such as listening while someone else speaks, passing a turn if you want to, not reminding others of what they should do, and no 'put downs'. Try to get the students to decide and agree upon the rules if possible. It is important to establish that all are equal, which is helped if the facilitator joins in with activities.

The session is organised in three sections:

1 **Contact games**, giving opportunities to form the group dynamic. Games bring enjoyment, relaxation and experimentation. They help lose self-consciousness and stimulate interest and motivation.

2 **Communication activities**, practising tasks for the goals. Students may be working at different levels within the group and divide into sub-groups for preparation tasks.

3 **Closing period**, revising the session and orientating students to the next meeting.

The major goal is the spontaneous, creative use of language. To achieve this:

◆ focus on specific elements that need development, such as syntax patterns and sound pronunciation in a games format that is fun

◆ teach the appropriate skills by modelling, reinforcement and review

◆ ensure equal participation of both slow and fast learners

◆ adjust tasks for age, level and interest

◆ promote healthy competition and praise all efforts

◆ encourage students to vary activities, introducing their own ideas.

Important Do's and Don'ts

◆ **Don't** force a student to join in, but let her observe and help.

◆ **Don't** persist with a dud game but encourage the group to come up with an alternative.

◆ **Do** stop while the students are still enjoying it.

◆ **Do** allow a decent interval before re-introducing a popular game, or come up with another version.

◆ **Do** keep the same teams over time to build group spirit.

Example of a session

Form a circle and explain what the group is going to achieve in the next few weeks – a certificate in 'Communication'. Discuss what communication is:

a sender – an idea – a message – a receiver

Play Chinese Whispers to demonstrate (for example, the phrase *'mad cats'* can turn into something like *'bad bats'*. With adults, the phrase *'typically nasty weather'* has been turned into *'tickle your arse with a feather'!*). This introduces the idea of getting over a message clearly, which is the first section (clarity) of each goal.

Small children may like to make megaphones from cardboard and enjoy hearing about how the ancient Persians communicated over distance before the time of the telephone. At an appointed hour each day they would climb on to the roofs of their houses and use megaphones to contact neighbours with essential messages. Such an experiential activity helps to focus on the notion of a *public* voice, which is very different to the private one used in one-to-one conversations. This 'performance' voice must be slower, louder and clearer, with good use of emphasis and pause.

Explain that each session will involve 20 minutes of games to make contact with others in the group, then there will be 30 minutes working on the sections of the 'Communication' certificate (explain the topic for this particular session). In this part of the session, participants may work on their individual tasks in pairs or smaller groups and assemble at the end for sharing what they have done. The last 10 minutes will be closing activities, to talk about what has happened and discuss plans for the next session. Encourage participants to bring in items to talk about.

All sessions follow roughly the same pattern, whatever the level of the groups, using a week (or two) to develop each certificate section theme – clarity, content, convention, conduct and creative writing. Use the contact time to develop the group dynamics using a game activity that will facilitate the particular section theme being practised. The game suggestions in Appendix 7 are grouped according to the particular section skills, although they are generally appropriate for any contact part of each session. Most games can be adapted for any age group, although some are obviously better for young children and others for older students. There is no developmental sequence to the games presented. A lesson plan at the start of Appendix 7 gives guidance as to how to organise activities.

Contact games

Each session should include a greeting activity and games to practise the skills needed for the certificate section that is the focus of the week. If the target for session 1, for example, is 'clarity', introduce games that will emphasise this concept (see Appendix 7).

Communication activities – 'certificate section'

It is useful to take one certificate section (clarity, content, convention, conduct and creative writing) per week or two weeks, depending on the speed of learning in the group. For example, you could spend one session, or two, covering the 'clarity' element of the certificate. The clarity section of goals 1, 4, 6, 9, and so on, includes performing poems. Select poems that tie in with work students are doing in school or college. Give opportunities for pair activity (speaking and listening to each other's choices) and then a chance to perform to the whole group at the end of the session. Other goal levels, such as 2, 3, 5, 7, 8 and so on, involve reading for the clarity task, so use a class book or the student's own current book to base this work on.

Students need to be taught how to stand to speak clearly – with feet about 30 cm (12 inches) apart and weight over the balls of the feet. Encourage open mouths and practise voice exercises (see suggestions in Appendix 7). For performance tasks, students need to be aware of issues such as correct posture, frequent eye contact, voice production over distance, use of vocal dynamics (pitch, pace, pause, power and clear pronunciation) in order to convey meaning.

Closing period
Try to spend a few minutes reviewing what has been achieved and planning for next time.

◆ Comment

When a large number of important phenomena have to be understood and explained to students, they have to be grouped into a smaller number of more general categories. For example, in COGS four general functions of communication are contained within the elements of message clarity, content, convention and conduct. These are:

- ◆ the *informative* function of communication
- ◆ the *control* function of communication
- ◆ the *social* function of communication
- ◆ the *expressive* function of communication.

These various functions of communication relate to elementary 'speech acts' (also known as illocutions), which are identified in the literature of philosophers, psychologists and linguists. A speech act is what you perform when you communicate, regardless of whether you are talking, writing, gesticulating or whatever. There are several lists of speech acts available but a simplified version is as follows:

- ◆ a statement – *'He is reading'*
- ◆ a question – *'Will he read?'*
- ◆ a command – *'Don't read'*
- ◆ a declaration – *'I promise to read'*
- ◆ an exclamation – *'Wow'*

There is, of course, a relationship between functions of communication and speech acts. The informative function corresponds to statements and questions, the control function to commands and the expressive function to exclamations, while declarations may have a number of functions. The social function may be fulfilled by any speech act or a combination of them. These speech acts are evaluated by very basic criteria:

- ◆ they should be true in relation to actual conditions
- ◆ they should be sincere in relation to the speaker
- ◆ they should be correct in relation to accepted norms.

COGS aims to teach these basic functions and criteria in a way that is understandable to both children and adults and relates to daily tasks. Through its various levels, participants in the COGS process become aware of the complex interaction of personal, interpersonal and intrapersonal variables within communication.

The future of communication is closely related to the future of our general means of communication, which is changing rapidly with constant technological innovations. Today we are surrounded by the products of advanced communication science and engineering. Such progress, as we have seen, has both positive and negative impact. Although electronic communication systems of different size and complexity have no doubt increased the rate and amount of communication world wide, they have some negative effects at the individual level: for instance, they lead to less frequent face-to-face communication and perhaps increased feelings of loneliness and isolation.

All innovations, when first introduced, cause increasing knowledge gaps between the 'haves' and 'have nots'. We see it in schools, with some students having easy access to the latest computers at home and using the Internet to help with homework, while others have no such resources. On the other hand, it can be argued that electronic communication may contribute to the maintenance and even expansion of what has been called 'social capital' – the trust between individuals and groups. The World Wide Web brings students into contact with others in schools all over the world and allows them a dialogue that increases their motivation to make contact and communicate.

Technology, however, only provides us with tools for us to use. We shall never be able to dispense with the need to communicate clearly and concisely in both speech and writing with those around us. It is our life blood. The aim of this book has been to engender greater enthusiasm for developing this most precious and extraordinary of human gifts and allow readers to reflect on the multiplicity of factors involved in its progress that must be taken into account in the classroom.

Communication is the web that binds us all together. It should not strangle and stifle us but allow us to grow and create a rich, rewarding pattern of human contact. One thing is certain: where messages travel round the world at the speed of light and sound, all students should have the mastery of their language and communication to keep abreast of this progress.

"Every student is an unknown country, which the teacher approaches like a water diviner, and only when he touches the springs of interest will language flow."

Newsom Report [22]

We are the vital force in promoting effective and successful communication. If we do not use this power our children will be lost in a barren wilderness where they will cease to grow and bloom. Success is only one step away for students. It is you giving value to your own and their communication. 'Class talk' is smart talk for teachers and students.

"He who knows that power is inborn, and so perceiving, throws himself unhesitatingly on his thought, instantly rights himself, stands in the erect position, commands his limbs, works miracles."

Ralph Waldo Emerson

Summary Points

◆ Children do not naturally acquire formal styles of communication needed in school.

◆ Studies show grim pictures of student skills in communicating.

◆ In schools, the communication balance is tipped in favour of reading and writing. In life, the balance is tipped in favour of speaking and listening.

◆ Schools need to consider how to teach communication if they want higher academic standards and improved student behaviour.

◆ Communication teaching is rewarding as there is overwhelming evidence that it works to achieve greater confidence, and improved learning and behaviour.

◆ COGS is a method of teaching communication that is easy to set up and slot in to the learning curriculum.

Appendix 1

Puzzle answer

from L Miller, 'Problem Solving Hypothesis Testing and Language Disorders', in G P Wallach and K G Butler (Eds), Language Learning Disabilities in School-Age Children (Baltimore, Maryland: Williams and Wilkins, 1984)

Sage (2000) Class Talk. NEP Ltd

Appendix 2

Communication questionnaire

How do you feel about yourself and the way you communicate?

Name _____   Date of birth _____   Date _____

The following statements are concerned with aspects of life and communication. If a statement is mostly **true** for you, tick the letter 'T'. If a statement is **false** or not usually true for you, tick the letter 'F'. Try to answer all statements.

1	I am generally satisfied with my life.	❏ T ❏ F
2	I feel I have many good qualities.	❏ T ❏ F
3	I am often lonely.	❏ T ❏ F
4	I am generally upset by criticism.	❏ T ❏ F
5	I set my aspirations low to avoid disappointment.	❏ T ❏ F
6	I delay things rather than deal with them immediately.	❏ T ❏ F
7	I am generally patient with other people.	❏ T ❏ F
8	If someone is rude to me I let it pass by.	❏ T ❏ F
9	I find it difficult to say 'NO' to demands made on me.	❏ T ❏ F
10	I take charge of things if I have a chance.	❏ T ❏ F
11	I do not like change and variety in my life.	❏ T ❏ F
12	I am always well organised and on time for events.	❏ T ❏ F
13	I find it difficult to finish off things I have started.	❏ T ❏ F
14	I worry about making a good impression on other people.	❏ T ❏ F
15	I find it difficult to relax.	❏ T ❏ F
16	I make decisions regardless of other people's opinions.	❏ T ❏ F
17	I like an ordered pattern to life.	❏ T ❏ F
18	I keep an open mind about things.	❏ T ❏ F
19	I like activities that involve mixing with other people.	❏ T ❏ F
20	I do not find it easy to show people I like them.	❏ T ❏ F

21	I make a favourable impression when I talk.	❑ T	❑ F
22	I do not find it easy to look at my audience while speaking to a group.	❑ T	❑ F
23	I enjoy giving a talk in public.	❑ T	❑ F
24	Some words are harder than others for me to say.	❑ T	❑ F
25	People sometimes seem uncomfortable when I am talking to them.	❑ T	❑ F
26	I dislike introducing one person to another.	❑ T	❑ F
27	I often ask questions in group discussions.	❑ T	❑ F
28	I find it easy to control my voice when speaking.	❑ T	❑ F
29	I do not talk well enough to do the kind of work I would really like to do.	❑ T	❑ F
30	I am not embarrassed by the way I talk.	❑ T	❑ F
31	I talk easily with only a few people.	❑ T	❑ F
32	I talk better than I write.	❑ T	❑ F
33	I often feel nervous when talking.	❑ T	❑ F
34	I find it hard to talk when I meet new people.	❑ T	❑ F
35	I feel confident about my speaking ability.	❑ T	❑ F
36	I wish I could say things as clearly as other people do.	❑ T	❑ F
37	Even though I know the right answer I often fail to give it because I am afraid to speak out.	❑ T	❑ F
38	I hesitate when asking information from other people.	❑ T	❑ F
39	I find it easy to talk to people on the telephone.	❑ T	❑ F
40	I forget about myself soon after I begin to speak.	❑ T	❑ F

Appendix 3

Language use

◆ Effective language

Effective use of language depends on the following aspects.

Vocabulary: General and specialist words that transmit spoken and written meaning.

Grammar: Parts of speech used in sentences.

Syntax: Conventions that govern sentence formation.

Style: Words, sentence structure and tone adopted for a specific communication purpose.

Inference: Interpretation of nuances and shades of meaning in, between and behind words.

Judgement: Critical evaluation of what is said/read to reflect on its effect and modify if necessary

Awareness: Rapport with the recipient so the message can be received and understood.

Spelling: Reproduction of words in their accepted written form.

Punctuation: Writing marks that help the meaning and convey the feelings of the writer.

◆ Useful definitions

Sentence: A group of words that conveys a complete meaning. It must have a subject + finite verb. In its written form, it begins with a capital letter and ends with a full stop.

Simple sentence: A sentence with a single subject + finite verb in its predicate.

Complex sentence: A sentence with two or more main or dependent clauses.

Phrase: A group of words that are related in sense and are often introduced by a preposition (for example, *'on his way to work'*, *'at the moment'*, *'in the top drawer'*) or a conjunction (for example, *'after a busy day at work'*, *'as soon as possible'*).

Phrases do not contain finite verbs but can be introduced with participles (for example, *'**Opening the door**, Luke saw a black cat sitting on the window ledge'*).

Clause:	A group of words forming part of a sentence and possessing a subject and finite verb. Clauses are linked by conjunctions (for example, *'He arrived late **because** the train was delayed'*).
Main clause:	Complex sentences may be made by joining main clauses with co-ordinating conjunctions (for example, *'She paused **and** she had a sandwich, **then** she resumed work'*).
Dependent clause:	This clause cannot stand alone and is linked to a main clause by a subordinating conjunction (for example, *'As the weather is bad, we shall come by car, **even though** it means delaying the repair to the cracked windscreen'*).

◆ Grammar

Words are the building blocks of a sentence and carry out specific functions:

- ◆ nouns
- ◆ pronouns
- ◆ articles
- ◆ adjectives
- ◆ verbs
- ◆ adverbs
- ◆ conjunctions
- ◆ prepositions
- ◆ interjections

What is a noun?

These are the naming words, which act as labels for things – objects, people, places, events, ideas and so on. Nouns naming real, physical things such as 'cup' and 'spoon' are **concrete nouns**. Those which express thoughts, ideas, and feelings such as 'affection' and 'communication' are called **abstract nouns**. There are other sub-divisions:

Common nouns:	everyday objects or ideas (for example, *'pen', 'weight', 'library'*)
Proper nouns:	names for people, places, art works (for example, *'Rosemary', 'England', 'Mona Lisa'* – NB proper nouns have capital initial letters)
Collective nouns:	names for groupings or collections (for example, *'class', 'team', 'bench (of magistrates)'*)

What is a pronoun?

These are identifying words that replace nouns:

People:	*'I'*, *'you'*, *'him'*, *'her'*, *'mine'*, *'ours'*
Things:	*'it'*, *'that'*
Question forms:	*'**Who** is going?' '**What** do you think?'*
Completion forms:	*'I hurt **myself**.'*
Further information forms:	*'The girl **who** is blond.' 'The book **that** is about language.'*

What is an article?

Articles define nouns (for example, *'**the** class'*, *'**a** lesson'*, *'**an** idea'*).

What is an adjective?

Adjectives describe and extend the meaning of nouns and pronouns. They usually come before the noun or pronoun in a sentence, but occasionally after. (For example, *'The **exhausted** teacher promptly dismissed **her** class because she was **busy**.'*)

Adjectives may denote possession (for example, *'**my** house'*), identify something (for example, *'**these** ideas'*) or introduce a question (for example, *'**What** time is it?'*)

What is a verb?

Verbs convey actions, identify thought processes or denote states of being. For example:

- ◆ *'He **cooked** a meal and **ate** it.'*
- ◆ *'She **considered** the proposal carefully.'*
- ◆ *'The teacher **was** aware of the difficulty.'*

Verbs are used actively to express the actions of the doer (for example, *'He **read** the report'*). They are also used passively to make the doer the agent of the action (for example, *'The report **was read** by him'*). Passive verbs make the message more distant and impersonal.

What is an adverb?

Adverbs extend the meaning of verbs or adjectives (for example, 'He spoke **slowly** and **clearly**', 'We need an **extremely** fast typist'). Most adverbs are recognised by their '-ly' endings. They indicate 'how', 'when', 'where', 'to what extent', 'how many' and so on.

What is a conjunction?

Conjunctions are linking words to join ideas together, and may begin a sentence (for example, '**As** it's hot, you may go now', 'Buy fish **and** chips', 'The book is short **but** contains everything').

Conjunctions (such as 'and', 'but', 'next', 'then', 'yet') may link ideas that could stand alone (for example, these two sentences can be joined using 'but': 'The book is short. It contains everything').

Conjunctions can link a main idea and a dependent idea (for example, 'They bought a car, **although** it was costly').

Commonly used conjunctions include:

'when'	'because'	'whether'
'where'	'although'	'so that'
'why'	'though'	'in order that'
'what'	'even though'	'with the result that'
'as'	'if'	'after'
'since'	'unless'	'as soon as'

Paired sets of conjunctions include:

'either/or'	'neither/nor'	'both/and'	'not only/but also'

What is a preposition?

Prepositions are locating words coming in front of nouns or pronouns (for example, 'The box is **under** the bed'). They may form parts of verbs (for example, 'I must get **down** to finishing this book').

What is an interjection?

Interjections are words expressing feelings or emotions, used frequently in direct speech. For example:

◆ *'**Whew!** That was a close shave.'* (relief)

◆ *'**Oh!** What a beautiful dress.'* (delight)

Syntax

Syntax is the name given to the patterns in which sentences are constructed. A sentence is a group of words that conveys a complete meaning, with **subject** (noun or noun group) and **predicate** (finite verb, or finite verb + enlargers or object). The table shows some examples.

Subject	Predicate
I ...	... like chocolate
The tired, old lady ...	... went straight to bed
The last, weekday train ...	... is at 11.30 pm.

What is a subject?

Subjects are common or proper nouns, which are the 'doer' words or word groups governing the actions of finite verbs (for example, '**The report** *is finished*', '**Joan** *is away today*').

The subject may be a pronoun (for example, '**They** *are gorgeous!*'), and take the form of a phrase (for example, '**Rushing a three course lunch** *gave him an awful stomach ache*') or a clause (for example, '**That you were ignorant of the rules** *makes no difference*'). The terms 'phrase' and 'clause' are explained in the definitions at the start of this section.

Although subjects usually precede verbs, additional ideas about them can be inserted in between (for example, '*My student,* **a hard working member of the class**, *will do well in the examinations*').

What is a predicate?

A predicate may include not just the finite verb but words that enlarge the meaning (for example, 'I washed **thoroughly**') or provide additional information (for example, 'I washed **with hot water**').

Some predicates need an object (action receiver) to complete the meaning (for example, 'I washed **my jeans**'). Therefore, simple sentences may be constructed as follows:

◆ subject + finite verb

◆ subject + finite verb + enlargers

◆ subject + finite verb + object

What is a finite verb?

All sentences require finite verbs, carrying out the action of the 'doer' or subject word. They must meet three requirements:

◆ A number: singular or plural

◆ A person: first, second or third

◆ A tense: past, present, future or conditional

For example, 'I washed' (singular, first, past tense).

Simple and complex sentences

When sentences contain a single subject and a single finite verb (such as 'I washed') they are called **simple**. When more than one subject and finite verb are used in linked groups, the sentence is called **complex** (for example, 'I and my friend, Sue, washed our jeans before we went to the disco').

Many complex sentences are composed of two or more clauses with the following relationships:

◆ Main clause + main clause: *'She played tennis and she did not finish the game until dusk.'*

◆ Main clause + dependent clause: *'She wanted to go early because she had a bad headache.'*

Main and dependent clauses can be combined in a number of ways. For example, *'Although it wasn't convenient (dependent), she played tennis until dusk (main) because she wanted to finish the game (dependent)'.*

Ideas are linked in this way to provide variety and show the relationship between ideas. All clauses must have a subject and finite verb. Dependent clauses cannot stand alone and need to be accompanied by a main clause.

It is easy to loose control in complex sentences. For example:

◆   *'The new teacher, who wanted to make a good impression on the first day in her new class, although she was feeling nervous because the place was unfamiliar, despite the friendly smiles of the pupils.'*

Here, we wait in vain for the main verb to follow *'The new teacher'*. To avoid this problem, it is wise to shorten the structure and create two sentences:

◆   *'The new teacher wanted to make a good impression on the first day in her new class. She received friendly smiles from the pupils but was feeling nervous because the place was unfamiliar.'*

Verb tenses

Infinitive:	*'to write'*
Present participle:	*'writing'*
Past participle:	*'written'*

Tenses		Active (He)	Passive (The book)
Present	simple	writes	is written
	continuous	is writing	is being written
Past	simple	wrote	was written
	continuous	was writing	was being written
Perfect	simple	has written	has been written
	continuous	has been writing	
Past perfect	simple	had written	had been written
	continuous	had been writing	
Future	simple	will write	will be written
	continuous	will be writing	
Future perfect	simple	will have written	will have been written
	continuous	will have been writing	
Conditional	simple	would have written	would have been written
	continuous	would have been writing	

Using verbs

Finite verbs are governed by subjects and possess a number, person and tense. When verbs literally convey ideas of action they are easily identifiable (for example, 'The teacher **cut** the paper', 'Jack **painted** his picture carefully').

Many verbs, however, express abstract notions (for example, 'He **loves** his bed in the mornings').

Some verbs consist of more than one word (for example, 'I **shall have left** for work before the post comes').

A knowledge of tenses is necessary to recognise verbs successfully, as well as understanding their active and passive use.

Active and passive

Verbs that take objects, when used actively, convey the action of the subject or 'doer' on to an action receiver or object. For example, 'Rosie (subject) typed (finite verb) the report (object)'.

The same idea, however, may be expressed in a passive form. Here the object becomes the grammatical subject of the sentence and the active subject becomes an agent of the passive. For example, 'The report (subject) was typed (finite verb) by Rosie (agent)'.

The passive structures of verbs are formed by using the verb 'to be' and sometimes the verb 'to have' as well with the past participle of the verb (for example, 'It is being typed', 'It was typed', 'It has been typed').

Verb forms as adjectives and nouns

There are two parts of the verb that are used in sentences, not as verbs, but as nouns or adjectives.

Present participle as adjective:	'The **pouring** rain drenched my clothes.'
Past participle as adjective:	'The **typed** book is ready for the publisher.'
Present participle as noun:	'Her **going** was very sudden.'

What is an object?

Objects in sentences receive the action of the verb. Some verbs, which need objects to complete the sense, are called **transitive**. Verbs that do not need an object to convey the meaning are called **intransitive**. It is helpful to think of objects as answering the question 'What?'. For example, 'Mary (subject) made (finite verb) a cake (object)'. What did Mary make?

Some objects take the form of word groups (for example, *'Pat wrote **a long and interesting report**'*). Others take the form of clauses (for example, *'Ted hit **what appeared to be a sliced shot of the ball**'*). When transitive verbs are used in the passive form, the object of the active voice of the verb becomes the subject (for example, *'**A long and interesting report** was written by Pat'*, *'**What appeared to be a sliced shot of the ball** was hit by Ted'*).

Enlarging intransitive verbs

When verbs are used intransitively (not needing an object), adverbial words or expressions may be used to extend meaning (for example, *'The meal went on **for quite a while**'*).

◆ Punctuation

Punctuation is used to help convey meaning in writing and replaces some of the functions of voice and gestures in spoken language. It signals breathing spaces and sometimes the feelings of a writer. There are eleven major punctuation marks in use in English.

Mark	Name
.	full stop
,	comma
;	semi-colon
:	colon
'	apostrophe
( )	brackets
?	question mark
!	exclamation mark
-	hyphen
–	dash
" "	direct speech marks or inverted commas

Full stop

The full stop has two principle uses: to signal the end of a sentence, and to indicate abbreviations (as in Mr. Dr. Rev. e.g. and so on). Some current practices, such as business correspondence, embody 'open punctuation' in their format by omitting full stops (and commas) other than in the body of the text. The use of this must be consistent. Examples where full stops are omitted include OBE, Ltd, HMS, Dr, Mr, Mrs.

Messages sometimes contain abbreviations such as a.s.a.p. ('as soon as possible'), but these should be avoided in formal documents.

Comma

The comma is used within sentences to indicate pauses between sense groups (for example, *'Reaching the edge of the pavement, he stopped, looked both ways, then crossed'*).

Commas are also used:

◆ to separate lists. For example, *'He put the butter, cheese, ham and bread on the table'*).

◆ to separate enlargements from the main subject and verb. For example, *'The visit, which had been unexpected, took them by surprise'*. When the insertion defines a preceding noun, the comma is not used, as in *'The bread that you ordered hasn't arrived'*. Commas are not normally used before conjunctions ('and', 'or', 'but', 'then' and so on) linking main clauses (for example, *'He went and they all cheered'*).

◆ after narrative devices (such as 'lastly', 'it proved', 'nevertheless, 'moreover'). For example, *'Moreover, the mistake was very irritating'*.

◆ to indicate hesitancy in direct speech. For example, *'Oh, one more thing, don't forget the flowers'*.

In general, the comma should be used sparingly to assist rather than impede reading.

Semi-colon

The semi-colon indicates a pause that is longer than a comma but shorter than a full stop, and which separates main clauses. For example, *'The rain was a real disappointment; it caught us unprepared'*.

In such constructions the semi-colon is effective in securing a dramatic pause. The ideas, however, must be closely related. The semi-colon could be replaced by 'and' but this would lose the emphasis.

Colon

The colon is a stronger stop than the semi-colon. It is normally used to introduce an example or quotation, as below.

'As we are reminded in this quotation:

"Learning is a treasure that accompanies its owner everywhere."'

The colon can also be used to preface a list, as below.

'The book will include:

▼ *brain diagrams*

▼ *charts*

▼ *photographs*

▼ *a variety of case studies.'*

Apostrophe

The apostrophe has two major uses.

Possession

Used with the letter 's', the apostrophe denotes possession, as in *'The teacher's book'*. The apostrophe is placed after the 's' in the plural form: *'The students' books'*. If the noun has an irregular plural form the apostrophe goes before the 's', as in *'children's shoes'*. Where 'y' changes to 'ies' in the plural, the apostrophe comes after 's', as in *'ladies' clothes'*. A simple test is to re-arrange the sentence or phrase and insert 'of the' (for example, *'the clothes of the ladies'*) and if this makes sense the apostrophe is needed in the original form!

Remember: when *'its'* means *'of it'* the apostrophe is *not* used (for example, *'the dog wagged its tail'*).

Omission

The second use of the apostrophe is to indicate that one or more letters has been omitted. For example, *'do not'* becomes *'don't'*. These contractions are normal in speech but not in formal written documents.

Brackets

Brackets separate an additional idea from the rest of a sentence. The additional idea is often a source of reference or information (for example, *'The results (Appendix 2) indicate big differences between the research groups'*).

Question mark

Question marks are placed at the end of a sentence that is structured to form a direct question (as in *'What time is it?'*) and replace any other end-of-sentence mark (full stop or exclamation mark). Rhetorical questions (not expecting an answer) are used for effect but still require the question mark (for example, *'New learning strategies are needed. Who would deny these are long overdue?'*).

Exclamation mark

Exclamation marks are often used to indicate feelings of surprise, as in *'Wow! I can't believe that's true!'*

Hyphen

A hyphen links words or word parts that have such a close connection they are almost one word: *'turn-table'*, *'leap-frog'*. Some words have been used together for so long that they are now written as one word: *'timetable'*, *'racecourse'*, *'turnover'*.

The other use of the hyphen is to join word parts that are pronounced separately (such as *'co-operative'*, *'co-existence'*) although many writers now drop these. In text, the hyphen is also used to indicate the continuation of a word that starts on one line and finishes on the next.

Dash

The dash is used in a similar way to brackets and signifies an insertion. For example, *'The number of students – over all courses, in fact – has been high this year'*.

Direct speech marks or inverted commas

These are used to show the exact words spoken by a speaker. For example, *'"I'm not sure," she said, "but I'll go and check"'*. When a second speaker is introduced, the spoken words begin a new paragraph.

Similar-looking double inverted commas are sometimes used to indicate a quotation or title. For example, *'Have you read "Class talk"?'*

◆ Spelling guides

The 100% rules

There aren't many!

> **1** No English word ends in 'v' or 'j'.
> **2** 'Q' is always followed by 'u'.

Plurals

Most plurals are formed by adding 's' to the singular form (for example, *'book'* becomes *'books'*). The following are exceptions.

- ◆ *'brushes'*, *'buzzes'*, *'fuzzes'*, *'potatoes'*, and so on

- ◆ foreign words now used in English, such as *'aquaria'*, *'bases'*, *'bureaux'*, *'formulae'*, *'stadia'*, *'stimuli'*

- ◆ irregular forms, such as *'child/children'*, *'woman/women'*, *'ox/oxen'*

- ◆ y-ending words that drop the 'y' and add 'ies'; for example, *'berry/berries'*, *'hobby/hobbies'*, *'lady/ladies'* (NB if 'y' is preceded by a vowel, the plural simply takes an 's', as in *'journey/journeys'*)

- ◆ for words ending in 's', 'x', 'z', 'sh', 'ch' or 'ss', add 'es' to form the plural; for example, *'batches'*, *'crosses'*, *'fixes'*

- ◆ some words ending in 'f' use 'ves' in the plural; for example, *'leaf/leaves'*, *'loaf/loaves'*

Prefixes

Adding a prefix to a word does not alter the basic spelling. For example, *'did'* becomes *'undid'*, *'appear'* becomes *'disappear'*.

Some prefixes use the hyphen, such as *'co-edition'* and *'pre-emptive'*.

Suffixes

The suffix 'ly' is added in a straightforward way to most words. For example, *'free'* becomes *'freely'*, *'live'* becomes *'lively'*, and *'critical'* becomes *'critically'*.

When adding 'ing' to a word that ends in 'e', the 'e' is dropped (for example, *'move'* becomes *'moving'*). When adding to a word ending in a consonant, this is doubled (for example, *'tip'* becomes *'tipping'*).

When adding 'er', 'ed' or 'est' endings, follow the same rules. For example, *'fast'* becomes *'faster'* or *'fastest'*, *'big'* becomes *'bigger'* or *'biggest'*.

In verbs ending in 't', the 't' is replaced with 's' before adding the ending 'ion' (for example, *'convert'* becomes *'conversion'*).

In base words ending in 'y', the 'y' is often replaced by 'i' before adding a suffix (for example, *'happy'* becomes *'happiness'*).

NB The spellings of certain words with Latin roots simply have to be learned. For example, with respect to 'able' or 'ible' endings, the following words follow no constant rule: *'commendable'*, *'divisible'*, *'incomprehensible'*, *'infallible'*, *'avoidable'*.

Homophones

Homophones are words that *sound* the same but which are *spelled differently*. Some examples include:

air, heir	rose, rows
course, coarse	their, there
thrown, throne	watt, what

These must be learned by heart.

Rules of thumb

◆ The soft 'g' is usually followed by 'e', 'i' or 'y' (for example, *'dingy'*, *'intelligent'*, *'impinge'*).

◆ The letter 'i' comes before 'e' except after 'c' (for example, *'height'* but *'receive'*).

◆ The letter 'l' doubles before a suffix, if preceded by a single vowel (for example, *'actual'* becomes *'actually'*, *'typical'* becomes *'typically'*).

◆ The letter 't' doubles in multi-syllable words with stress on the final syllable (for example, *'permit'* becomes *'permitting'*, *'submit'* becomes *'submitting'*).

◆ 'Ph' is used for 'f' in Greek words, such as *'photograph'*, *'physics'*, *'philosophy'*.

◆ Short vowels usually precede double consonants, as in *'hammer'* and *'tunnel'*.

◆ Long vowels usually precede single consonants, as in *'dining'* and *'draping'*.

◆ A 'sh' sound is usually spelled as 'ti', 'ci', 'si' (rather than 'sh') when it appears after the first syllable, as in *'confusion'*, *'notion'* and *'specious'*.

Spelling 'B'

Can you spell these words?

Sports person:	a _ _ _ _ _ e	(7 letters)
Act of looking down on people:	c _ _ _ _ _ _ _ _ _ _ n	(13 letters)
One who owes money:	d _ _ _ _ r	(6 letters)
To bubble:	e _ _ _ _ _ _ _ e	(10 letters)
Luminous:	f _ _ _ _ _ _ _ _ t	(11 letters)
Graded organisation:	h _ _ _ _ _ _ y	(9 letters)
Payment in parts:	i _ _ _ _ _ _ _ t	(10 letters)
Senior University lecturer:	p _ _ _ _ _ _ r	(9 letters)
Special given right:	p _ _ _ _ _ _ e	(9 letters)
Artificial:	s _ _ _ _ _ _ c	(9 letters)

Answers: athlete, condescension, debtor, effervesce, fluorescent, hierarchy, instalment, professor, privilege, synthetic.

How did you score?

8–10 correct – excellent

5–7 correct – good

2–4 correct – encouraging

below 2 – stick at it!

Weasel words

Problem pack

Below are the most commonly misspelled words. The parts underlined are where most people go wrong!

accessible	accessory	accommodation	acquiesce
acquire	address	aggressive	analysis
appalling	argument	beneficial	benefited
changeable	chargeable	committed	committee
commitment	conscious	contemptible	deceive
deferment	deferred	definite	develop
disappear	disseminate	embarrass	equipped
exaggerate	existence	foreign	fulfil
gauge	government	grateful	honorary
humorous	illegible	immovable	inconsistent
insistent	intelligible	irresponsible	maintenance
manoeuvre	miscellaneous	mischievous	necessary
negligible	noticeable	occasion	occurred
omission	omitted	parallel	precede
procedure	profess	psychology	receive
recommend	referred	regrettable	resistant
secede	separate	sincerely	skilful
succeed	supersede	technicality	temporary
tragedy	unnecessary	untouchable	woollen
wreath			

Double troubles

advice/advise	affect/effect	appal/appeal	canvas/canvass
complement/ compliment	council/counsel	confidant/confident	continuous/continual
dependant/ dependent	decent/descent	draft/draught	faint/feint
forward/foreword	farther/father	licence/license	to lie/to lay
lightening/lightning	lose/loose	passed/past	precede/proceed
principal/principle	practice/practise	rose/rows	throne/thrown
stationary/stationery	straight/strait	their/there	to/too
waver/waiver	watt/what	witch/which	yew/you

◆ English consonants: voiced/voiceless

Distinctive features of sound

There are ten contrasting features of sounds:

1. **consonantal**: obstruction in the vocal tract
2. **vocalic**: free passage of air
3. **diffuse**: Dispersed air ejection
4. **compact**: low vowel
5. **grave**: front and back sounds
6. **flat**: rounded vowel/semi-vowel
7. **voice**: with sound
8. **continuant**: air partially stopped
9. **strident**: high frequency sound
10. **nasal**: air emitted through nose rather than mouth

Voiced and voiceless sounds

These eight pairs are made in the same way, but one is whispered (voiceless) and the other is sounded (voiced).

Voiceless sound	Voiced sound
p	b
t	d
k	g
f	v
th	th
s	z
ch	dg
sh	su
	m, n, ng
	l, r
	w, j
h	

CLASS TALK — successful learning through effective communication

	1	2	3	4	5	6	7	8	9
A									
plosive	p, **b**			t, **d**				k, **g**	
affricate					tr, **dr**	ch, **dg**			
fricative		f, **v**	th, **th**	s, **z**		sh, **su**			h
B									
nasal	**m**			**n**				**ing**	
lateral				**l**					
fritionless continuant	**w**				**r**		**j**		

Key to table: Consonants are normally paired; *voiceless* consonants (no sound) are in normal type, while *voiced* consonants (sound) are marked in bold.

1 bilabial	made with lips together: p, **b**, **m**, **w**
2 labio-dental	made with top lip biting bottom one: f, **v**
3 dental	made with tongue tip between teeth: th as in teeth; **th** as in mother.
4 alveolar	tongue tip on ridge behind top teeth: t, **d**, s, **z**, **n**, **l**
5 post-alveolar	tongue tip on ridge behind top teeth and released: tr, **dr, r**
6 palato-alveolar	tongue tip on ridge behind top teeth and moving to the palate: ch, **dg**, sh, **su**
7 palatal	tongue towards the palate: **j**
8 velar	made with the back of the tongue: k, **g, ing**
9 glottal	air expelled strongly when the glottis is open: h

A – total closure or stricture of the air stream:

plosive	air stopped completely: p, **b**, t, **d**, k, **g**
affricate	air stop with slow release: tr, **dr**
fricative	air stream modified by lip/tongue/glottal movements: f, **v**, th, **th**, s, **z**, sh, **su**, h

B – partial closure or unimpeded oral or nasal escape:

nasal	air release through nose and not mouth: **m**, **n**, **ing**
lateral	air released from the side of the tongue: **l**
frictionless continuant	continuing sounds similar to vowels: **w**, **r**, **l**

Vowels made in the front, centre or back of the mouth

These are the common vowels in standard formation.

Mouth position	Front			Centre	Back
close	h<u>ee</u>d				h<u>oo</u>t
		h<u>i</u>d			h<u>oo</u>d
half close		h<u>ea</u>d		h<u>ea</u>rd	h<u>oa</u>rd
half open			h<u>a</u>d		h<u>o</u>d
open				h<u>u</u>t	h<u>ar</u>d

Appendix 4

 # COGS Assessment, goals 1 and 10

◆ Communication, goal 1: 6 minutes

Name: _____ Date: _____ Assessor: _____

Clarity — aspects of performance (1 min)

Learn a short verse. Use the right voice pitch, pace, pause and power to make the meaning clear.

Specific skills expected: 1 – Accurate recall; 2 – Ability to put over the mood of the poem.

Report

core skills   _____ [10 maximum]

specific skills   _____ [10 maximum]

Total   _____ [20 maximum]

Content — ideas presented [record level] (2 min)

Express a number of ideas about a topic (for example, yourself, your family or one of your interests).

Specific skills expected: 1 – Presentation of a range of ideas about the topic; 2 – Fluent delivery.

Report

core skills   _____ [10 maximum]

specific skills   _____ [10 maximum]

Total   _____ [20 maximum]

Convention — rules for organising messages [request for clarification] (1 min)

The assessor invites you to ask someone in the audience to give you their views on your poem and talk.

Specific skills expected: 1 – Ability to form a polite request; 2 – Ability to listen and accept the views of others.

Report

core skills   _____ [10 maximum]

specific skills   _____ [10 maximum]

Total   _____ [20 maximum]

Conduct — personal responses that give an impression of yourself to others (2 min)

The assessor invites the audience to ask questions on your programme. You choose who asks the questions and then give answers.

Specific skills expected: 1 – Careful listening; 2 – Answers that fit the questions; 3 – A pleasant manner.

Report

core skills   _____ [10 maximum]

specific skills   _____ [10 maximum]

Total   _____ [20 maximum]

Creative writing — recording ideas in handwriting or typed print [a personal profile]

Design a personal profile. Include name, address, interests and achievements. Use illustrations.

Specific skills expected: 1 – Accurate content; 2 – Appropriate range of information.

Report

core skills   _____ [10 maximum]

specific skills   _____ [10 maximum]

Total   _____ [20 maximum]

Final comment

Strengths and areas for development:

Total   _____ [100 maximum]

◆ Communication, goal 10: 15 minutes

Name: _____ Date: _____ Assessor: _____

Clarity — aspects of performance (3 min)

Select a report from a paper or magazine. Summarise it and state its interest. Introduce and read a section chosen by the assessor.

Specific skills expected: 1 – Effective summary; 2 – Clear reasons for the interest of the report; 3 – Appropriate interpretation.

Report

core skills _____ [10 maximum]

specific skills _____ [10 maximum]

Total _____ [20 maximum]

Content — ideas presented in order [teaching a skill to a partner] (5 min)

Teach a partner a simple skill (for example, tying a fancy knot), showing knowledge of the sequence of events. 1 – demonstrate whole task. 2 – model steps, learner repeats. 3 – learner carries out task with support. 4 – review and repeat.

Specific skills expected: 1 – Pre-teaching of relevant information; 2 –Analysis of task into steps; 3 – Clear demonstration.

Report

core skills _____ [10 maximum]

specific skills _____ [10 maximum]

Total _____ [20 maximum]

Convention — rules for organising messages [an announcement] (2 min)

The assessor presents written information to be announced to the audience. Ensure listener attention. State facts clearly. Repeat and conclude.

Specific skills expected: 1 – Control of audience; 2 – Concise presentation; 3 – Reinforcement of important facts.

Report

core skills _____ [10 maximum]

specific skills _____ [10 maximum]

Total _____ [20 maximum]

187

Conduct – personal responses that give an impression of yourself to others (5 min)

The assessor asks **specific** questions on issues to do with teaching and learning and invites **general** questions from the audience.

Specific skills expected: 1 – Listening and appropriate response; 2 – Knowledge of teaching and learning issues.

Report

core skills _____ [10 maximum]

specific skills _____ [10 maximum]

Total _____ [20 maximum]

Creative writing – recording ideas in handwriting or typed print (a 1000-word essay on learning)

Discuss what helps and hinders learning using your own experiences as illustration. Give **introduction**, defining the subject, **develop** ideas with some illustrations and conclude with your own views on the matter.

Specific skills expected: 1 – Balanced structure; 2 – Relevant illustrations; 3 – Reflective comment.

Report

core skills _____ [10 maximum]

specific skills _____ [10 maximum]

Total _____ [20 maximum]

Final comment

Strengths and areas for development:

Total score _____ [100 maximum]

Communication skills rating

Name: _____ **Date of Birth:** _____ **Assessor:** _____

Mark each skill according to the code below:

1 = high competence

2 = competence

3 = adequate competence (some lapses)

4 = Some evidence of skill

5 = No evidence of skill

General skills	Description	code
Attention	Attends throughout a task	
Informal talk	Chats to others	
Informal reading	Reads for pleasure 3 or more times weekly	
Group activity	Attends formal/informal group/s outside school hours	
Feeling/space	Demonstrates physical awareness in activities	
Vision	Interprets visual information	
Hearing	Notices sounds in environment	
Emotion	Expresses feelings appropriately	

Formal conversations	Description	code
Listens and responds	Attends to what is said and makes a suitable response (may be non-verbal)	
Initiates topic	Introduces new information into conversation	
Requests	Asks questions to clarify information/situation	
Directs	Directs others appropriately in collaborative activity	
Contributory comment	Makes an appropriate remark without adding new information	
Maintenance comment	Signals and wish for conversation to continue (nod, smile, *'mmm'*)	

Formal presentation (speech/writing)	Description	code
Record	Expresses a number of ideas without order	
Recite	Expresses ideas with some order	
Replay	Retells ideas with some order	
Recount	Makes explanation e.g. giving instructions	
Report	Reports event: summarising, discussing and evaluating	
Relate	Narrates with setting, event, action, result, reaction	

Non-verbal communication	Description	code
Eye reference	Makes eye contact with person/objects involved in conversation for 50% of the time	
Voice: pitch	Uses a variety of speech tones	
Voice: pace	Uses a rate if speech that can be followed	
Voice: Pause	Uses pause in speech so that ideas can be followed	
Voice: power	Uses volume appropriate for space	
Voice: pronunciation	Uses intelligible speech	
Gesture	Uses movements to support ideas	
Posture/breathing	Uses a stable posture that supports speech production	
Movement	Controls physical movements to maintain confidence (i.e. does not fidget)	
Facial expression	Uses facial expressions to reflect content (e.g. smiles on hearing happy news)	

Appendix 6

The Sage assessment of language and thinking (SALT)

◆ Level 1, 4—10 years

Content and convention

Name: Tom   **Date of birth**: 12.3.92   **Date of Test**: 16.5.99

	Questions	Content	Score		Convention:	Score	
1	Who lives with you? Mum and Pete	1+ ideas [people or animals]	[1]	1	proper names [e.g. Tom]	[1]	1
2	What do you like doing? Playing	2+ activities	[2]	1	actions/verbs	[2]	1
3	Where do people keep food? Cupboards	3+ ideas	[3]	1	articles prepositions [in, on, under and so on]	[3] [3]	0 0
4	What do people wear on their feet? Shoes and socks	4 ideas	[4]	2	plurals	[4]	2
5	Tell me a drink you like, and one you don't like. Sprite and Cola	2 ideas	[2]	2	connective [but] negative	[1] [1]	0 0
6	What did you do yesterday? Went football	4 events appropriate vocabulary	[4] [2]	1 0	past tenses link words [then, after and so on] relative clause noun/verb phrase	[4] [2] [1] [1]	1 0 0 1

	Questions	Content	Score		Convention:	Score	
7	Tell me some things you might do next weekend. *See my mates*	4 events appropriate vocabulary	[4] [2]	1 0	future tense link words [then, after and so on] relative clause noun/verb phrase	[4] [2] [1] [1]	0 0 0 1
8	Think of a loaf of bread, a pencil and your bed. Which is the lightest, and which is the heaviest? *Pen and bed*	2 ideas lightest/ heaviest	[2]	0	articles comparative end [use of 'est']	[1] [1] [1]	0 0
9	What do you do when you cross the road? *Look and listen*	6 actions appropriate vocabulary	[6] [2]	2 0	link words correct sequence	[2] [2]	1 1
10	Tell me a story that would make me laugh. *Spiff (family dog) drank beer. He sleep and sleep.*	7 ideas	[7]	2	Adjectives/ adverbs coherence	[2] [1]	0 0
		test total	[40]	13	test total	[40]	8

Clarity and conduct

Name: Tom   **Date of birth**: 12.3.92   **Date of Test**: 16.5.99

Code:
8 = high competence in the skill
7 = competence in the skill
6 = generally competent (some lapses)
5 = adequate competence
4 = inconsistency in skill
3 = some evidence of the skill
2 = little evidence of the skill
1 or 0 = no evidence of the skill

Clarity	Score	Conduct	Score
Appropriate use of:		Appropriate use of:	
Pitch	4	Creativity	0
Pace	4	Eye contact	3
Pause	3	Facial expressions/ gestures	3
Power (word emphasis)	2	Posture	3
Pronunciation	4	Manner (pleasant/polite)	3
Total	**17**	**Total**	**12**

Total score

Clarity	17
Conduct	12
Content	13
Convention	8
Grand total	**50**

◆ General notes about assessment and scoring

Explain to the students that you are going to ask some questions as someone might do in a TV interview. The students should answer as fully as possible.

For example, you might ask *'When were you born?'* An answer such as *'August'* would score 1 mark. A full answer such as *'17th August, 1971'*, would score 3 marks. Write down the students' responses, or record them on tape for later transcription.

Scoring for the content and convention sections is self-evident. Some subjective judgements have to be made, though, in the clarity and conduct sections.

Notes:

◆ The numbers in square brackets in the 'score' column are the maximum number of points that can be awarded, one for each idea/event/action described, even if more than this number of ideas are expressed. The ideas must be different, and not an expansion of one already stated. For example, *'swimming, breaststroke'* does not express two separate notions.

◆ **Link words** are those that bridge ideas across sentences, such as *'then'*, *'after'*, *'meanwhile'* and so on.

◆ **Connectives** are words within sentences, which bring together ideas, such as *'and'*, *'but'*, *'so'*, *'because'* and so on.

◆ **Relative clauses** are groups of words, with a verb, that expand on the main ideas (for example, in *'The girl, **who was sitting on the wall**, seemed very happy'*, the clause in bold expands on the noun phrase *'the girl'*).

◆ **Phrases** are groups of words that extend a noun or verb (for example, *'I went to school **with my dad'**, or 'I was writing **with a new pen'**).

◆ **Structure** refers to the organisation of ideas. A report or story must demonstrate a beginning, middle and end, and show a logical development of ideas.

◆ **Comparatives** are words used to compare one thing with another, such as *'lighter'*, *'lightest'*, *'heavier'* and *'heaviest'*.

◆ **Coherence** refers to the logical flow of ideas.

◆ **Creativity** refers to the originality of ideas and words expressed in the answers to questions.

◆ If a student uses the *entirely* the correct sequence in answering question 9, award 2 marks. If part of the sequence is right, award 1 mark. Appropriate vocabulary earns a maximum of 2 marks. Award 2 if the choice of words used is very good, and 1 mark if the words are adequate for meaning but not very expressive.

Overall scores may be compared with standard scores but interpretation should be cautious because these represent a pilot version. Those with effective communication have even scores across areas, which are not significantly different. A lack of balance in scores may point up areas for specific development.

Appendix 7

 # Communication Opportunity Group Scheme (COGS)

◆ Setting up session 1

About eight participants sitting in a circle.

1   **Welcome** from the course leader.

2   **Letter** in the middle of the circle addressed to COGS members. This gives brief details about the group. Someone opens and reads.

3   **Introduction: Bean bag game** – the bean bag is thrown to someone who says their name clearly and mimes something they like to eat. This focuses on the non-verbal aspects of communication. Continue until all participants have had a turn.

4   **Musical objects**: Play music – hand a box round filled with small objects. When the music stops, the one who has the box takes an object out and says three things about it. The game continues.

5   **Kim's game**: Use the objects from the previous game. Place them on a tray and give one minute to view. In secret, remove one object and get participants to draw or write down the name of the missing object. This helps to improve memory.

6   **Take a check**: What have we been doing? Get participants to recall.

7   **Sending messages**: Carry out the Persian megaphone activity. Four students each stand in a corner of the room. They pass round a message *'Meet me in the Tick Tock Club at 6.15'*. After this get the group to say what happened. (For example, the speaker looks at the listener, the speaker uses a louder voice to carry over a longer distance, words are slower and clearer and so on). This focuses on using words in space and understanding how to vary them.

8   **Clear sounds**: Give each student a sound – p, b, t, d, k, g. Call out two sounds and the respective students have to change places. Make sure the voiceless sounds p, t, k are said without the vowel sound 'er' on the end.

9 **Silly sentences**: Use the sounds in the previous game to make up silly sentences (for example, *'Big Ben bought baked beans'*). Get a leader to beat out the rhythm on his knees with his hands. Start slowly and softly and increase volume and speed over six repetitions. This helps to establish awareness of voice dynamics.

10 **Musical poems**: Pass round a small box, to music, which contains slips of paper with small poems written on them. When the music stops – the one who has the box takes out a poem from inside and reads it alone or chooses someone to do it with them. Then the group repeats the poem line by line. Continue until all have had a go.

11 **Recap**: Ask participants to think of some things we need to do to make our poems clear. (For example, hold the head straight to produce the voice well, use louder and slower voice on important words, pause before and after main ideas, make sounds by opening the mouth.)

12 **End** by recalling the activities and bringing out the importance of clear, interesting messages. Explain that at the end of 8–10 sessions, everyone will have the opportunity to present the activities that have been worked on and to gain a certificate of communication. This session has looked at the way we put words across to make them clear and interesting for others to listen to. Next time we will look at the *information* we put into messages.

◆ Games for COGS

Contact games (greetings, icebreakers and warm-ups)

1 Throw a bean bag to a participant. They say their name and mime something to eat. Continue until all have had a turn. This activity focuses on non-verbal messages.

2 Throw a bean bag to someone. They respond with their name and how they feel (for example, *'My name is Rosie Sage and I feel happy'*). Continue until all have responded.

3 Throw the bean bag to someone. They respond with their name and an adjective that describes them, beginning with same sound or letter (for example, *'I am Rosie and I am ridiculous'*). The process continues.

4 Throw the bean bag to someone. They respond with their name and a reason why they like it (for example, *'I am Rosie and I like my name because it sounds friendly'*). Continue the process round the group.

5   Throw the bean bag, calling out either *'air'*, *'land'* or *'sea'*. The catcher must reply with something associated with the label. General categories, such as 'car', 'fish' or 'bird', are not allowed – the name link must be specific (for example, 'land – Ford Escort', or 'air – robin').

6   **Colour ball**: Throw the bean bag and call a colour. The catcher says something that is that colour (for example, 'brown – mud') and throws to someone else. No repetitions of objects are allowed, although colours may be called again.

7   **Name verb**: Each person introduces themselves with a verb (for example, *'I am Rosie, rollicking Rosie'*). Choose words with the same sound or letter.

8   **Introductions**: The facilitator starts by introducing herself: *'My name is Rosie Sage'*. The first person to the right says *'My name is Luke Fox and this is Rosie Sage'*. The process continues until all have said their name and introduced the person on their left.

9   **Name call**: Everyone sits in a circle and when their name is called they stand up and sit down straight away. Vary by including other activities (for example, stand up–turn round–touch toes–sit down).

10   **Name left and right**: The facilitator says the name of the person on his right, his own name, then the name of the person on the left. The next person repeats the pattern.

11   **Name chain**: One person calls another's name, and moves to that place. For exampl, Rosie calls Luke and moves to his place. Luke calls Helen and moves to her place. Continue until all the group have moved.

12   **Copy and add**: The first person mimes one action, such as clapping hands. The second person copies the mime and does one of his own, such as clapping hands and clicking fingers. Continue, with each person carrying out two actions – the previous action, plus her own.

13   **Indian teepee**: Each person chooses an Indian name and a non-verbal sign to go with it (for example, Falling Rain – ripple fingers downwards; Sleeping Papoose – close eyes and rock a baby). A person starts by making their sign and that of someone else. Whoever has the sign must respond with this and another sign from the group. If the response is not immediate, the person owning the sign made is out. The aim is to eliminate others quickly!

14   **Dates**: Divide into pairs and discuss between themselves an important date in each of their lives. Each participant then takes a turn to introduce his partner to the group with information about her important date.

15   **Play buzz**: Choose any number (for example, 5) and count round the group. Any number that contains 5 or is a multiple of it (51, 15, 25 and so on) is replaced by *'Buzz'*. Make it harder by introducing two numbers (for example, 5 and 7) with 5 as *'Buzz'* and 7 as *'Bizz'*. Remember, 35 is *'Buzz-Bizz'*!

16 **Kim's game**: Put a number of objects on a tray. Give participants time to view. Cover and ask them to recall within a time limit. As a variation, remove an item without participants seeing, and ask the group to guess what is missing.

17 **Remove**: Choose a person to be 'It', who leaves the room. All of the remaining participants remove something they are wearing. The 'It' person returns and has to guess what is missing from each person.

18 **Talk numbers**: One participant calls a name and asks that person to say a number. That person then calls a second name, who has to double the number. The third person adds four, the fourth divides the number in half and the fifth subtracts two. The whole process is then repeated with another number. You can put the instructions on cards in a box in the middle of the circle, and the 'named' person has to take one before calling another participant and telling that person what to do with the number.

19 **The pea and the spoon**: Each participant needs a spoon and a pea or marble. Everyone sits in a circle with their hands behind their backs. They all hold the spoons between their teeth and the object is to pass the pea or marble from spoon to spoon without handling it. Anyone who drops it pays a forfeit.

20 **Eye for eye**: Divide the group into two teams. One team leaves the room, while the other selects one of its members to sit on a chair, completely covered with a sheet with only the eyes exposed. The second team comes back and each guesses who is under the sheet and writes the name down. The winner is the team who gets the most correct answers.

Games for clarity

1 **Posture and relaxation**: Play musical statues. When the music stops the facilitator calls out an activity for participants to mime (for example, a road digger, or traffic policeman).

2 **Musical walks**: Instruct the group how to walk while the music is playing (for example, in straight lines, in curved lines, or hopping on one foot). When the music stops everyone freezes.

3 **Breathing and vocal**: The facilitator teaches participants three signs – finger to lips for '*silence*', thumb and first finger a little apart for '*small noise*' and hands wide apart for 'large noise'. Participants are then instructed to yawn silently, with a little noise or with a large noise according to the sign given.

4 Teach breathing in through the nose to a count of three, holding the breath for three, and breathing out to a count of three. Play a circle game: number 1 breathes, holds and breathes out to count of one; number 2 breathes, holds and breathes out to count of two, and so on. When the last person in the circle has completed, reverse the process so each gets a chance to change the counting sequence.

5   Vary the breathing game, using sounds on the outward breath: 'ah', 'ay', 'ee', 'oh', and so on. Go round the circle with each person choosing a different sound to breathe out on.

6   Breathe in and hum quietly and then loudly. Hum up and down the scale. Hum with a partner – forehead to forehead, and cheek to cheek, to feel the vibration.

7   **Optimum pitch**: Ask each person to count to five, starting on the lowest note that can be managed, and pitching the note higher each time. Note which number is each person's comfortable note (optimum pitch). Do this round the circle and discover the differences between each person's optimum pitch.

8   **Tongue twisters**: Introduce a tongue twister (for example, 'red leather, yellow leather'). Get all participants standing and beating out the rhythm on their knees. Start chanting very quietly and slowly, repeating until everyone is saying the tongue twister quickly and loudly. (This is great fun.) Encourage everyone to make up their own silly sentences with a particular sound (for example, 'Silly Susie sold salmon soup', *'Unique New York'*, *'Peggy Babcock'*, *'Mr Mick's mixed biscuits'*, *'Six thick thistle sticks'*, *'Good blood, bad blood'*).

9   Take three of the exploding sounds ('p', 'b', 't', 'd', 'k', 'g') and go round the circle saying them forwards or backwards in groups of three (for example, 'p-t-k', 'p-t-k', 'p-t-k'). Make sure that the voiceless sounds ('p', 't', 'k') are whispered without the vowel sound 'er', which often happens. The facilitator uses a hand signal to indicate the movement of the sequence: right for forwards ('p-t-k', 'p-t-k', 'p-t-k'), left for backwards ('k-t-p', 'k-t-p', 'k-t-p').

10 Throw the bean bag with a word (such as 'pen') and the recipient has to find another word that rhymes (such as 'ten'). He then chooses a word (such as 'car') and throws the bean bag to another person who finds a rhyming word (such as 'tar'). Continue until all participants have had a go.

11 **Betty Brown**: In turn around the circle, students have to come up with an adjective and a noun that begin with the same sound as a chosen name. For example, the facilitator might start with *'Betty Brown likes beautiful books'*. The next person adds *'baked beans'*, the next says 'blue bats', and so on. Another example might be *'Sid Smith likes salmon soup … silk socks … sizzling sausages …'*, and so on.

12 **Letter words**: Put some words into a hat. Play music and when it stops, whoever has the hat takes out a word and makes a sentence in which the words begin with the letters in that word. For example, if the word chosen is 'pass', the sentence might be 'peas are so sweet'; if the word is 'soap', you could say 'she opens a parcel'. If the participants are small people, use small words; for big people, use big words!

13 **Chair challenge**: Each participant takes the chair and is given a category (for example, 'flowers'). In one minute, they must name as many items in this category as they can, clearly and accurately. Any mistakes in fluency or pronunciation mean 'time's up'. The winner is the one to say the most in a minute.

14 **America**: One player starts by saying *'I packed my bag for America and put in an apple'*. The next repeats the statement and then adds something beginning with 'b' (for example, 'blanket'). The game continues until the end of the alphabet.

15 **Aunt Agatha's cat**: A letter is chosen (for example, 's'). The first player says 'Aunt Agatha's cat is a super cat'. The game continues, each person choosing an adjective beginning with the selected sound (for example, *'sleek'*, *'slender'*, *'soppy'*, *'sage'*, *'sly'*, and so on). Anyone repeating a word is out, so this is a good activity to encourage careful listening as well as clear speaking.

16 **Seasons**: The 'caller' says the name of something seasonal (for example, a kind of fruit, flowers or clothing, a specific holiday, an event). The others call out the season associated with it. For example, *'roses – summer'*, *'camping – summer'* (ideally!), *'harvest – autumn'*, *'valentine – winter'*, 'Halloween – autumn', 'snow – winter', and so on). Points may be awarded to the first to call. Arguments may arise about the item and season. Encourage discussion.

17 **Ghosts**: One participant thinks of a word and calls out or writes the first letter. The next person provides another letter and so on until a word is made (probably not the word the first participant originally thought of). Participants should try not to complete the word, but keep it going – the person that completes a word is the 'ghost' and is out of the game.

18 **Six letters**: Supply six letters. Each person must make up an e-mail message using the six letters in order, as the first letters of each word (for example, 'S M A G J P' could become *'Send Me A Good Joke Please'*). The first to complete is the winner, and must read out the message clearly.

19 **Chinese whispers**: One person makes up a sentence and whispers this to the person on her left, who then passes it on. The last person says the message out loud to check any differences in the first and last transmission.

20 **Silent songs**: Each person chooses a section of a well known song. In turn, each person mouths the chosen song without voice or whispers it to the whole group – everyone has to try to guess what the song is. Points may be awarded for correct answers if so wished.

Games for content

1 **To develop ideas**: Throw the bean bag to a person with a word (such as 'cold') and that person finds a word that links (such as 'snow'). The process continues until people have had enough.

2 Pass round an interesting but unfamiliar object that could have many possible functions (such as a hologram disc). Each person contributes an idea about what the object could be used for. Get one person to keep a tally record of the number of ideas produced. The facilitator should try to be creative to encourage lateral thinking. For example, the hologram disc could make a stunning earring or an eye-catching mug mat!

3   On a separate piece if paper, each person writes the name of, or draws, an object (for example, 'button'). Put all the folded papers in a box. Pass the box round to music. When the music stops the person has to take a paper slip out and speak for one minute on the topic. Choose a person to be time keeper.

4   **Just a minute**: Choose a topic and decide rules for speaking – for example, no hesitations, no repetitions, no deviations. Elect a chairperson and a time keeper. A person starts to speak on the topic but can be challenged, accordingly to the rules. If the chairperson upholds the challenge, the challenger continues with the topic until further challenged or until the minute is up. Points are awarded for the speaker who has the topic when the minute is up. (The time keeper could use a bell or a whistle to show that time is up.)

5   **Scavenger hunt**: Divide the group into two teams. Ask each team to prepare a list of 20 objects for the other team to find, such as 'book', 'paper clip', 'pencil case' and so on (inside) or 'leaf', 'twig', 'stone' and so on (outside). Each team has a large bag and the first one to collect all the items correctly is the winner.

6   **The hat game**: Give each person ten slips of paper. Everyone then writes the name of a well-known person on each slip, folds it up, and puts it into a hat. Two teams compete. One member of one team starts and has a minute to take one slip at a time from the hat, and describe the person on it to his team-mates, without saying the person's name (for example, *'The Queen's youngest son'* – Prince Edward). If the team guesses correctly, another slip is taken from the hat, and so on, until time is up. The team counts the slips they have guessed successfully, and passes the hat to the other team. The game continues until all the slips are used. The winning team is the ones that has the most.

7   **Choosy Jane**: Choose a vowel letter that 'Jane' does not like, such as 'e'. What can we give Jane for her birthday? A 'pair of socks' (no 'e's) but *not* a 'packet of sweets', a 'cat' but not an 'elephant'. Younger groups may find it easier to choose words excluding consonants. For example, if Jane cannot stand 'd', we could give her a *'pink jumper'* but not a *'red dress'*.

8   **Word chains**: Throw the bean bag to a person, with a word (such as *'tin'*). The person has to respond, saying a word beginning with the last letter of the previous word (such as 'no'). Encourage participants to speak fluently and pass the bean bag quickly.

9   **Bean bag stories**: Start a story holding a bean bag. After a couple of sentences, stop and throw it to someone else, who must continue the story.

10 **Detection**: Draw a plan of a room on a large sheet of paper. Explain that there has been a break-in, and this is what was found: the door was off its hinges, a picture was missing, a hat was left under the window, there was a bloodstain on the mantelpiece, a bus ticket on the floor and a pair of gloves on a chair. Draw these on the plan. Split the group into twos or threes. Tell them they are to imagine that they are the police, and their task is to consider the evidence and work out what has happened. After ten minutes they have to make a brief report to the large group.

11 **Pass the buck**: The leader holds the 'buck' (any chosen object) and tells the rest that no-one can speak unless they are holding it. Pass it to anyone in the circle who must speak a sentence before giving it to someone else.

12 **What If?** Participants each compose a 'What if' question: *'What if cars had not been invented?'*, *'What if we did not have to go to school?'* Choose one to discuss.

13 **£1000**: Choose a player who describes what they would buy if they had £1000, without naming the object. For example, 'If I had a £1000, I would buy something that moves along the road without wheels'. Others have to ask questions to help them identify the object, to which only a 'yes' or 'no' response is allowed.

14 **Six questions**: A reporter asks six questions when covering the news – *'What ...?'*, *'who ...?'*, *'when ...?'*, *'where ...?'*, *'how ...?'*, *'why ...?'*. Choose a *'reporter'*, who leaves the room, while the others decide on something to guess (for example, a pencil). The reporter asks the six questions and then must make a guess.

15 **Desert island**: Divide into groups. Everyone should imagine they are going to spend a year on a desert island and they can take five books, three videos, four songs, four musical instruments, three games, six tools, four medicines, and a year's supply of food and drink. Each group should discuss what they would take, and make a list to compare with other groups.

16 **Soap box**: Each participant has one minute to talk about something she feels strongly about. The group then chooses the one who speaks with the most feeling.

17 **Compliments and insults**: Why do you like or dislike an object or person? Choose the subject and then go round the group, each taking a turn to give an adjective to describe the object or person. The first letters of the words must follow the sequence of the alphabet. For example, *'I like Tom because he's ... ambitious ... bright ... clever ...'*, and so on.

18 **Wishes**: Decide on some possible wishes – for example, visiting a particular place in the world, talking with a pop star, or choosing a birthday treat. Decide on one wish. Everyone then writes their specific wish along those lines on a slip of paper and puts it in a box. For example, if 'visiting a particular place' was chosen, one person might wish to visit the Pyramids of Egypt, while another might wish to go to a theme park. The box is shaken, each person in turn takes out a wish and guesses who made it.

19 **Choosing**: Divide into groups. A rich benefactor has decided to donate a car (or any other suitable present). However, the groups have to agree on five important features that they want (for example, bright colour, soft top, large luggage space, power steering, electric windows). Also, they have to decide on a basis for sharing the present. Bring the groups together and ask how everyone feels about the decisions made.

20 **Dictionary dilemma**: Choose a word that is outside the group's vocabulary. In pairs, participants think about what the word could mean, and write their definition down on a slip of paper. These are added to others in a box, one of which is the correct definition. Each student takes a turn to read out a definition from the box. After this, the group votes for the correct one.

Games for convention (understanding rules)

1 **Stop when I do**: Sit on the floor in a large circle. One person starts to beat out a simple rhythm of claps, using floor, hands and knees. The others copy and stop when the leader stops. Repeat, but build to a climax/de-climax. After this, one person chooses a beat and the next adds a sound to fit. Continue round the circle.

2 **Killer**: Every one sits in a circle. One person goes out of the room. While she is away, the others choose a 'killer' who slays her victims by winking at them. The person returns and tries to guess the 'killer'. When a person is winked at by the 'killer', they have to fall dead into the middle of the circle.

3 **Rounds**: Work in a circle. The second person begins when the first person has finished the first line, and so on! Some examples are given below.

Jelly on a plate,
Jelly on a plate,
Wibble wobble,
Wibble wobble,
Jelly on a plate.

Chop chop, choppity chop,
Chop off the bottom and chop off the top,
What we have left we will pop in the pot,
Chop chop choppity chop.

4 Ask a student to draw, on paper or on the board, a picture of a man looking at a tall tree – a black cat is stuck on the highest branch. Write the following sentence:

Bob Brown came down the stairs and out through his front door when suddenly he looked up and saw a tiny, black cat in a frightened state crawling along the top branch of the tree opposite but he was just in time to catch him as he fell.

The aim is to reduce the sentence, each person taking out a word at a time but still preserving the sense and reading out the sentence after the deletion.

5 **Word order**: Ask a student to draw Eve, Adam, a tree and an apple on the board. Get someone to write a minimal sentence about the picture (for example, *'She gives him an apple'*). Each participant has to add a word to expand the sentence, and read the new sentence out to the rest of the group.

6 **Reason**: Get the group to sit in a circle. The facilitator starts by saying something like *'Mark, I'd like you to sit next to me because you are younger than me'*. The student crosses the circle to occupy the space. The student on the left of the empty space continues in the same way. The game can be varied so that the person opposite the empty space says to the person next to it *'I'd like to sit next to you because I want a change'*.

7 **Conversation**: One person starts a conversation, holding the end of a ball of string. The next person to speak has the string ball thrown to them, and so on until a complex 'spider's web' is constructed around the circle. Identify those who have made the most contributions and the least (i.e. the ones holding the most and least loops of string). Encourage the reverse of this pattern on the next game.

8 **Role play**: Divide the large group into smaller ones and give each of them three objects. The participants have five minutes to act out a scene containing the three objects.

9 **Adverts**: Put participants in pairs and ask them to prepare a 30 second advertisement for a new drink or sweet, to perform to the rest of the group.

10 **Scene stealers**: Put participants in pairs and give each pair a prepared first line, such as *'Promise you wont tell anyone'*, *'Right, I've caught you now'*, or *'It's disgusting'*. Each pair should use the line as the starting point for a two minute scene, to prepare and perform to the rest of the group.

11 **Status**: Divide the group into two teams. Number the members of one team consecutively. For example, in a team of five, the participants would be numbered 1 to 5. Tell the group that the numbers represent their status (1 is highest status, 5 is lowest status). The numbered people are instructed to walk round the room in their status role. The other team (who do not know who has which number) then arranges the numbered group from 1 downwards, checking afterwards if they were right. They take turns to greet each of the status people, and afterwards discuss the rules for greeting people in different status roles.

12 **Directions**: Either draw a diagram of the place you are in, or use a map. In pairs, participants use the drawing or map to give each other directions on how to get to a particular spot. Discuss the problems of giving and receiving directions.

13 **Telephoning**: The group is divided into two teams, A and B. Each person in team A receives a copy of an 'A-role' card (for example, ringing up to renew a library book). Each person in team B has a copy of a 'B-role' card (for example, ringing up to find out about a football match). The participants of each group discuss what needs to be said during the telephone conversation. Then one person from each team pair up and role play their telephone conversations in front of the others. Each pair has a turn. De-brief and discuss what makes an effective telephone call.

14 **Presenting a person**: Participants work in pairs and decide roles for each other (for example, a pop singer, a famous sports person, a nurse, and so on). They discuss details of themselves and their lives 'in role' and then present each other in role to the rest of the group. De-brief on the important information that you need to give in such circumstances.

15 **Word change**: Explain to the group how they can change the meaning of a sentence by adding one word only. Write up their suggestions. For example, 'I am a hotel', 'I am *not* a hotel', 'I am a hotel *manager*', 'I am a hotel *porter*', 'I am *running* a hotel', 'I am *selling* a hotel', and so on.

16 **Circle shout (focusing on word functions)**: Form the group into a standing circle. Pick someone for the centre, who has to tell the others the daily routine of someone he knows well. For example, '*My dad gets up at 7 o'clock …*' Every time the teller says an agreed word, the whole group must shout it out (for example, 'gets'). This can be used to highlight any word form and make people aware of sentence structure, if this needs attention.

17 **Controversy**: Take an issue, such as pollution, celebrations, morning-only schools, junk food, and so on. Divide the group into smaller ones, each of which prepares arguments about the issue from a particular point of view – for example, the viewpoint of parents, teachers, students, press, employers, and so on. The final step is a panel discussion with a representative from each group presenting their arguments.

18 **Consequences**: Divide into small groups. Each group has an 'action card' with a statement written on it – for example, '*A 20 hour working week is introduced*', '*A lorry driver empties poisonous waste into a river*', '*People have been avoiding payment on the buses*', '*Robots can now do housework*', '*Men can get paternity leave*', and so on. Each group has to explain the consequences of the action on their card.

19 **Awards**: Divide into small groups. The participants think up an award for something – for example, a 'Smile Award', 'Help Award', 'Listening Award', 'Public Speaking Award', 'Reading Award', and so on. The group decides on two categories for the award and the basis on which candidates could be considered. One person in each group takes notes on suggestions. Finally, the group has to agree on who to give the award to and report this to the large group.

20 **Brainstorms**: Divide into groups. Each group has a task – for example:

◆ Think of as many possible uses as you can for a paper clip/a plastic bag/a coat hanger/a tea cup/a piece of A4 paper/a matchbox, and so on.

◆ You have to make a phone call but have no change. Think of as many ways as you can to get money.

◆ Think of as many ways as you can to have a cheap holiday.

After making lists of ideas, the groups discuss their suggestions according to a common criterion – for example, practicability, cost, or danger.

Games for conduct (encouraging question-and-answer)

1 **Finishing a sentence**: The facilitator provides the start of a sentence, to which each participant has to provide an ending, going round the group. For example *'My favourite colour is …'*, *'I feel happy when …'*, or *'I would love to …'*

2 **Role play**: Start a music game with a box of props. Pass a bean bag round the circle to music, and when the music stops the person who has the bean bag chooses a prop from the box. When all participants have received a prop, encourage each to think of a character to go with the prop. In turn, each character then takes the 'hot seat' and is asked a question by everyone in the circle. The questions must be answered in role.

3 **Change the baton**: The group sits in a circle and is given a baton or stick to pass round. Each member uses the baton to represent an object (such as a wooden spoon, a cricket bat, and so on). The others guess what the object is.

4 **This is a hippopotamus**: Players sit in a circle and an object or a bean bag is passed round. A passes it to B, saying *'This is a hippopotamus'*. B asks, *'A what?'*, as he returns it to A. A passes it back, and repeats, *'A hippopotamus'*. B then turns to C and says *'This is a hippopotamus'*; C passes it back to B saying *'A what?'*; B passes it back to A saying *'A what?'*; A passes it to B repeating *'A hippopotamus'*; B passes it to C repeating *'A hippopotamus'*; C turns to D … and so on, round the circle, but always going back to A each time. The word can be anything (rhinoceros, lepidopterous and so on) as long as it is hard to say. Although it may seem a pointless game, if done fast enough it is like a tongue-twister and makes you respond quickly to another person.

5 **Can you listen?** Arrange the group in pairs. Ask one person in each pair to talk about something they know about. Ask the other partner to constantly interrupt with questions, irrelevancies, 'helpful' comments and so on. Discuss how easy or difficult it is. Change roles, with the listener reacting with inattention, boredom, indifference and so on. Discuss what makes a good listener.

6 **20 questions**: Each participant thinks of an object, and takes the 'hot seat' in turn while the others ask up to 20 questions to guess the answer. The responses must be 'yes' or 'no'.

7   **The street**: Take a piece of paper and make a grid with categories, such as 'name', 'any pets', 'favourite drink', 'favourite TV programme' and so on, written down the left hand side. In a large circle, get each person to fill in the details for the person to their left, by asking them questions about each category (for example, *'What is your name?'*, *'Do you have any pets?'* and so on). Discuss what the grids reveal.

8   **Master builder**: Choose a pair to complete a building task. The two sit back to back, each with an identical set of building bricks. One constructs a building and instructs the other (who cannot see it) how to make the same construction. The rest of the group, who are watching, compare the buildings at the end. Discuss any differences.

9   **Trademarks**: Each person in the group has paper and a pencil and is asked to draw a trademark that tells something about his own personality. In turn, each person explains this trademark to the others, who are encouraged to ask questions.

10 **Names**: Each participant writes her name on a piece of paper. All the papers are collected and re-distributed so that everyone receives a name that is not theirs. Everyone walks around the room and tries to find the person who holds her name. Questions such as *'Is your name …?'* and *'Are you …?'* are asked.

11 **Group interview**: One volunteer in the circle is the focus of the group. Anyone may question him, though he may respond *'I'd rather not answer that'*. The purpose is to get to know the person by asking about feelings, views and so on. The facilitator must prevent the group from criticising the focal person and encourage listening and accepting. Continue as long as there is interest.

12 **Guess who said it**: One person leaves the circle. Four others make positive statements about her, using information that not everyone might know, and write them down. When the person returns she has to guess who made the statements when they are read out.

13 **It's obvious**: Break into groups of three. Within each group, one person is A, one is B and the other is C. B and C focus on A and say in turn *'It's obvious that you …'* (*'like red'*, for example, if A is wearing a red sweater). The focus then shifts to B and then to C, with the same type of statement being used (*'It's obvious …'*). Then start again, with a different statement to A, then B, then C: *'I see that you have …'* (*'a scratch on your hand'*, for example). Participants should look closely to try to see details that are less-than-obvious. Start again with A with a new statement: *'I imagine that you …'* (*'would like to swim in the Olympics'*, for example). At this stage wild imaginings are allowed. Continue round the group as before. The groups then join, for a round of *'I discovered …'* among the large group. This builds awareness of others.

14 **Mental gifts**: Participants write their names on four pre-cut paper shapes – triangles, hearts, trees, eggs, and so on. These are put in a hat. Each person draws out four and writes out some mental 'gifts' for the people named (for example, success, happiness, good friends, and so on). These are then delivered to the people concerned. They can be shared aloud if wished.

15 **Partner conversations**: Participants choose a partner, and then find another pair. The two pairs hold a conversation, each pair speaking as one 'person' by saying single words alternately until a sentence is formed. This becomes an exercise in mind-reading and understanding how someone else thinks.

16 **Headbands**: Prepare enough headbands for the group. Each headband should have written on it a mood or attitude (for example, *'bad tempered', 'very funny', 'bully', 'depressed', 'friendly', 'leader', 'shy', 'caring', 'good sport', 'practical joker', 'reliable', 'boring', 'liar'*, and so on). The participants should all wear their headbands with the words facing forwards so each person should not know what his own word is. Ask them to pretend they are going on a weekend camping expedition and are to discuss arrangements. They must react to everyone according to their label. After 5–10 minutes, ask each person to guess what is on his own headband, from the reactions he has received, and comment particularly on the non-verbal reactions (gestures and movements).

17 **Blindfold**: One person has a blindfold on her and allows herself to be guided around by someone else, avoiding obstacles. Reverse the roles and discuss feelings.

18 **Problems**: Give the main group a problem, such as one of those listed below. Participants then split into smaller groups, and each group tries to find as many solutions to the problem as possible. One person in each group jots down the ideas to feed back to the main group later. Problem examples:

◆ A man has a house on a street corner, with a beautiful garden but no fence. Every day a neighbour takes a short cut across the garden instead of walking round on the path. What can the man do?

◆ The local playground is very boring. How could it be made more fun?

◆ Show the participants a large jar, bottle or box and ask them to imagine they have six of these. What could they do with them?

19 **Not the Yes/No game**: Choose a person. The rest of the group have to ask him questions and the reply must not contain 'yes' or 'no'. For example, if asked *'Do you like eating ice-cream?'*, the person should reply *'I do like eating ice-cream'*. Encourage quick questions for speedy replies. If 'yes' or 'no' is given in the answer, someone else takes the place of the 'victim'.

20 **Why/because**: Introduce the 'why/because' form, by group chanting:

Why can't a dog climb a tree?

Why, oh why, oh why?

Because, because, because, because,

Goodbye, goodbye, goodbye.

Prepare questions suitable for the learning level of the group (for example, *'Why are you wearing a jumper today?', 'Why can't a cat do a jigsaw?', 'Why do we go to school/work?'*, and so on). Write the questions on paper and place them in a box. The box may be passed around to music. The person who has the box when the music stops, takes out the question and answers it.

Games for creative writing

1   **Good things/bad things**: Participants divide into pairs. One writes or draws all the good things about school/college/work. The other writes all the bad things. Discuss the lists.

2   **Party list**: In pairs, participants decide on a party theme and how they would organise the event. They write a shopping list of items they will need.

3   **Identity cards**: In pairs, participants decide on the information required to complete an identity card. They make one up and share with the group.

4   **Word wizard**: Participants divide into pairs. The facilitator asks the pairs to imagine the following: *'A wizard has taken away all the words from the world. Everyone is allowed to keep only four words'*. Each pair to chooses and writes their four words. Each pair joins with another and communicates using only their four words. They then have eight words to share with another pair or pairs.

5   **Comments**: Each person writes her name at the top of a piece of paper. The papers are shuffled and re-distributed. Each person then writes a comment under the name – either a question or a statement. The papers are re-distributed and more comments are added, until the group have had enough. Then each person receives her named paper and shares the information.

6   **Chain story**: Each participant writes a word on a piece of paper and places it in a box. The facilitator starts off with a sentence such as *'It was a dark, stormy night in November'*. Participants then take turns choosing a word from the box and making up a sentence containing this word, which continues the story. Tape the chain story, and play it back so all can listen. Then ask everyone to write a summary, or draw two events in the story.

7   **News report**: Supply a number of pictures from old magazines. Divide into small groups giving each one five pictures. The aim is to choose three pictures and link these in a story, giving it a title. Write the story as a group each doing a small section.

8   **Picture stories**: Supply some cartoon strips with the words in the speech bubbles blanked out. In pairs, participants write the text for the pictures and then read to the group.

9   **Consequences**: The facilitator gives each person a piece of paper and delivers the following instructions: *'Write down a girl's name (fold this over and pass on to the person on your right). Write down a boy's name (fold and pass on). Write what the boy said to the girl (fold and pass on). Write what the girl said in reply (fold and pass on). Write down the consequences (fold and pass on).'* Each person then reads out their story.

10 **A day in the life**: Divide into small groups. One person from each group leaves the room. The remaining people draw up a schedule of the missing person's previous day – where he was, what he did and so on (not more than six things). The missing person returns and questions the others to find out what they have said. The group then questions the 'victim' to find out what really happened.

11 **Self-directed interviews**: Each person writes down 5–10 questions that she would like to be asked. Participants choose partners and exchange question sheets and interview one another using the questions.

12 **Letters and e-mails**: Each student receives a copy of a letter, which he reads out to a partner. The partner then has to prepare an e-mail to be sent as a reply.

13 **NASA Game**: Participants imagine they are the crew on board a spaceship that has to rendezvous with the mother ship on the lighted side of the Moon. They have had to crash land due to mechanical failure and only ten items remain:

◆ box of matches

◆ concentrated food

◆ 10 metres of nylon rope

◆ a case of dried milk

◆ two 50 kilogram tanks of oxygen

◆ magnetic compass

◆ silk parachute

◆ first-aid kit

◆ signal flares

◆ star map

The task is to rank these items in order of importance to the crew (1–10), in order to reach their rendezvous 200 kilometres away. Participants take the first ranked item and explain why they think it is the most important. They write their explanations at the bottom of the list.

14 **Advertising a new product**: In small groups, participants 'invent' a new product (for example, an everlasting sweet) and plan an advert for a magazine.

15 **The XY Society**: Participants invent a new society with a 'nonsense purpose' (for example, The Trouser Society, which aims to make trousers compulsory dress for everyone). They give the society a name and an aim and write some rules for the conduct of the group. Further activities could include designing a membership card and writing an agenda for a meeting.

16 **Selling**: In pairs, participants discuss something they want to sell that belongs to them (for example, a computer, football boots, books, and so on). They write an advertisement for a local paper.

17 **Treasure hunt**: Divide into two groups. Each group has to write six clues that end in finding 'treasure' (a bar of chocolate or something similar). Each team finds the treasure hidden by the other team by reading and working out their set of clues.

18 **One day out**: With a partner, participants decide on a place to visit. They then discuss a plan for the day and record this in a timetable. The day plans are discussed in the main group and similarities and differences in suggestions are considered.

19 **Magic shop**: The facilitator prepares slips of paper with positive human qualities written on them (for example, *'honesty'*, *'intelligence'*, *'kindness'*, *'gentleness'*, *'humility'*, *'health'*, *'beauty'*, *'curiosity'*, *'imagination'*, *'fairness'*, *'humour'*, *'optimism'*, *'politeness'*, *'perseverance'*, *'friendliness'*, *'adaptability'* and so on). The participants write three slips of their own and add them to the pile, which is then shuffled and four slips are dealt out to each person. The participants decide which qualities they would like to keep and which they would like to give away.

20 **Curriculum Vitae**: In pairs, participants decide what they would include in their curriculum vitae or personal profile. They write up this information and share it with the group.

If you start a group playing games on a regular basis they will suggest their own variations and bring new games to try. It is important to encourage this participation and give people a chance to explain and instruct others. Always try to encourage the group in the closing, feedback time to work out what the game teaches so they become aware of what it is they are learning. They will soon link the contact period with preparation for the goal activities. Above all, in your groups – have fun!

Useful books for games are:

Circle Time, by T. Bliss and J. Tetley (1993), Lame Duck Publishing

Look, Listen and Trust, by G. Rawlins and J. Rich (1985), Macmillan Education

100 Ideas for Drama, by A. Scher and C. Verrall (1987), Heinemann

Another 100 Ideas for Drama, by A. Scher and C. Verrall (1987), Heinemann

Keep Talking, by F. Klippel (1985), CUP

Games for Trainers (Vol. 1 and 2), by A. Kirby (1992), Gower

Reaching their Minds, by D. DiMattia and T. Ijzermans (1996), Institute for Rational-Emotive Therapy

Creative Drama in Group Work, by S. Jennings (1996), Winslow Press

Appendix 8

Speech and language

◆ Development of the sound system of English

First year	'First words' with much individual variation		
	Lip	Tongue (front)	Tongue (back)
1–2 years	p, b, m, w	t, d, n	
2–2.5 years	p, b, m, w	t, d, n	(k, g, ng) h
2.5–3.5 years	p, b, m, f w	t, d, n s y (l)	k, g, ng h
3.5–4.5 years	p, b, m, f, v w	t, d, n sz yl	k, g, ng sh, ch, j h
4.5+ years	p, b, m, t, v w	t, d, n s, z, (th) y, l, r	k, g, ng sh, ch, j h
5–6 years	th	r	
6–7 years	blends: tw, tr, dr, pl, str, shr, spl		

Development of syntax

Approximate age	Feature	Example
1–2 years	Two-word combinations, no sense of word order.	*'car nice'* *'biscuit want'*
2–3 years	Three-word combinations, talking about present only.	*'He lost shoe.'* *'Where lady go?'* *'Give Mummy cup.'*
3–4 years	Four-word combinations, use of questions, statements, comments. Starts to associate ideas e.g. knife and fork. Many words left out in sequence.	*'Luke kicking ball now.'*
4–5 years	Uses co-ordinating words ('and', 'but', 'so') and subsidiary connectives ('because', 'where'). Uses five attributes to describe.	*'I like chocs but I don't like spinach.'* *'baby, big (shape), red (colour)', etc.*
5–6 years	Uses language beyond the immediate situation. Orders ideas in some way.	*'If baby falls, what does Mummy do?'*
6–7 years	Tells back a sequence with about half of the details correct. Uses discourse features: *'then', 'after', 'before', 'however'.*	Replays events in past holiday weekend.

Checklist of language skills 1—8 years

with regard to listening, talking, writing and reading

Use of checklist

1   Select items for the child's chronological age.

2   Tick those things the child can do. Cross those that he or she can't do. Query unsure items.

3   If the child gets more than three crosses for the ten items for the appropriate age group, obtain specialist advice.

1–2 Years

1 Attends to any activity of own choice.

2 Responds to own name and 'no'.

3 Recognises names of objects familiar to her: e.g. *'Show me the cup/ball,'* etc.

4 Recognises parts of the body on self and others: e.g. *'Show me the doll's hair,'* etc.

5 Matches common shapes – circle/square/triangle/rectangle/diamond.

6 Recognises representations (such as toys or pictures) of common objects: e.g. car, bed, chair, dog, cup.

7 Marks with pencil/crayon – circling motion, up and down, side to side.

8 Understands relations of two objects in correct order: e.g. *'Put the spoon in the cup.'*

9 Uses two-word combinations spontaneously: e.g. *'Mummy gone.'*

10 Uses sounds – 'p', 'b', 'm', 'w', 't', 'd', 'n'.

2–3 Years

1 Attends to adult activity choice for short spells.

2 Recognises objects/pictures by function/action: e.g. *'Which one do we sleep in?'*, *'Which one is eating?'*

3 Groups objects/shapes/colours/sizes/thicknesses.

4 Copies 1 and 0 from imitation.

5 Repeats two numbers: e.g. 4–7, 6–3, 2–9.

6 Names primary colours – red, yellow, blue.

7 Names common actions and objects/toys/pictures – people, animals, objects that are handled (ball/brush), body parts, clothes, food, furniture, real world things (car/clock etc.).

8 Uses three or four words spontaneously in subject–object expansion, in a variety of sentence types. e.g. *'He lost* (his) *shoe'* (statement), *'Where* (that) *lady gone?'* (question), *'Give Mummy* (that) *cup'* (command).

9 Talks to self mostly about immediate present.

10 Uses sounds – 'p', 'b', 'm', 'w', 't', 'd', 'n', 'k', 'g', 'ng', 'h'.

3–4 Years

1   One-channel attention only (i.e. cannot carry on what he is doing and attend to something else at the same time).

2   Understands commands, including abstractions (e.g. colour): *'Give me the red brick,' 'Show me the little doll,' 'Give me the brick on the table'*. Understands negatives: e.g. *'Give me the doll that is not in the box'*.

3   Repeats three numbers: e.g. 5–2–5, 6–9–4, 8–2–6.

4   Claps out simple rhythm to song or rhyme: e.g. Baa, Baa, Black sheep.

5   Says full name.

6   Says at least one nursery rhyme.

7   Copies a cross.

8   Uses sentences of at least four words: e.g. *'Luke's kicking the ball now.'* Regular use of questions, statements, commands.

9   Carries out associations between objects/pictures: e.g. knife and fork, cup and saucer.

10 Uses sounds: 'p', 'b', 'm', 'w', 't', 'd', 'n', 'k', 'g', 'ng', 'h', 'j', 'i', 's', 'z', 'sh'.

4–5 Years

1   Integrated attention for a short spell: e.g. while playing with something, can take in short verbal instruction.

2   Carries out three commissions in the correct order: e.g. *'Put the pencil in the box, shut the door, and bring me the book on the table.'*

3   Repeats four numbers: e.g. 2–9–6–5, 1–3–2–7, 8–4–2–1.

4   Copies a square.

5   Draws two or more recognisable forms: e.g. man, house, cat, dog etc.

6   Repeats a 12-syllable sentence: e.g. *'Ann wants to build a big castle in the play house,'* and *'Luke has lots of fun playing ball with his brother.'*

7   Using an integrated picture, e.g. home/school scene, can abstract the central meaning: e.g. *'This is a picture of playtime at school.'* Uses language to explain, report, detail, predict, hypothesise and express feeling.

8   Uses at least five attributes to describe an object: e.g. name, colour, shape, size and function of a ball.

9   Uses co-ordinating (*'and'*, *'but'*, *'so'*) and subordinating connective devices (*'because'*, *'where'*) in speech.

10 Uses sounds: 'p', 'b', 'm', 'w', 't', 'd', 'n', 'k', 'g', 'ng', 'h', 'j', 'i', 's', 'sh', 'f', 'v', 'ch', 'dg'.

5–6 Years

1   Integrated attention sustained.

2   Assimilates a number of concepts in sentences requiring sequencing in some length: e.g. *'Put the white horses on the outside of the field'* (in a toy farm).

3   Understands beyond the immediate situation, and so can:

    ◆ Predict – e.g. *'If the baby falls down, what would Mum do?'* (use toy people/pictures)

    ◆ Order in time – e.g. construct a 4–6 card story sequence and tell the story.

4   Copies a diamond shape.

5   Writes own name and copies simple words of 3–4 letters.

6   Understands the concepts same/different, and verbalises groups of attributes: e.g. from apple, ball and pear, *'Apple and pear are the 'same' because they are both fruit and you can eat them'.*

7   Gives full name and address, and names family and friends.

8   Can distinguish words with minimum contrast, e.g. *'cap'/'cat', 'pea'/'bee', 'bitter'/'bidder',* when sounds are in initial, medial and final positions.

9   Deals with a book in the correct way: understands that it is read from beginning to end, from left to right, and from top to bottom. Knows concepts of letter and word.

10   Uses sounds: 'p', 'b', 'm', 'w', 't', 'd', 'n', 'k', 'g', 'ng', 'h', 'j', 'i', 's', 'sh', 'f', 'v', 'ch', 'dg', 'th' and 'r'.

6–7 Years

1   Integrated attention sustained and controlled: i.e. can cope with interruptions and return to task.

2   Recites numbers to 50+ and records numbers 20+.

3   Repeats 5 digits: e.g. 5–5–1–6–6, 6–8–8–7–2, 9–4–8–1–3.

4   Names common coins.

5   Recognises more that 20 words (use flash cards from reading scheme).

6   Tells back a familiar story, e.g. The Three Bears, with half the details correct, and using discourse features: e.g. *'then', 'after', 'before', 'however'* etc.

7   Recognises pictures from a small part revealed, and recognises words when some sounds are deleted: e.g. d a _ _ y = daddy.

8   Knows sound/symbol relations and can blend sounds to form words when given in isolation: e.g. c–a–t.

9   Can give a verbal plan of activity: e.g. going shopping. Solves a physical problem with words: e.g. how to get an object off a high shelf.

10 Uses all consonant sounds plus simple blends (e.g. 'tw', 'tr', 'dr', 'pi' etc.) and complex blends ('str', 'shr', 'spl' etc.).

References

Chapter 1

1 M Maclure, T Philips and A Wilkinson, *Oracy Matters* (Milton Keynes: Open University Press, 1988)

2 R Sage, *Communication Support for Students in Senior Schools* (Leicester: University of Leicester, 1998

3 R Schank and R Abelson, *Scripts, Plans, Goals and Understanding* (Hillsdale, New Jersey: Lawrence Erlbaum, 1977)

4 R Schank, *Dynamic Memory: A Theory of Remind and Learning in Computers and People* (Cambridge: Cambridge University Press, 1982)

5 M Saville-Troike, E McClure and M Fritz, *Communication Tactics in Children's Second Language Acquisition* (New York: Newbury House, 1984) pp. 60–70

6 B Hawkins, *Scaffolded Classroom Interactions* (University of California: unpublished PhD thesis, 1988)

7 M Dyer, *The role of TAUs in narratives*, Proceedings of the Third Annual Conference of the Cognitive Science Society (Hillsdale, New Jersey: Lawrence Erlbaum Associates, 1981) pp. 225–7

8 C Jordan, R G Tharp and L Vogt, *Compatibility of Classroom and Culture*, Working Paper No. 18 (Bishops Estate, Honolulu: Kamehameha Schools, 1985)

9 S Phillips, 'Participant structures and communicative competence', in C Cazden, D Hymes and V John (Eds), *The Function of Language in the Classroom* (New York: Teachers College Press, 1972) pp. 370–94

10 S Phillips, *The Invisible Culture: Communication in Classroom and Community on the Warm Springs Indian Reservation* (New York: Longman, 1983)

Chapter 2

1 P Grice, *Logic and Conversation: Studies in the Way of Words* (Massachusetts: HUP Cambridge, 1986)

2 R B Adler, L B Rosenfeld and N Towne, *Interplay 6th Edition* (London: Harcourt Brace, 1995)

3 C Westby, 'Development of narrative language abilities', in G P Wallach and K G Butler (Eds), *Language Learning Disabilities in School-age Children* (Baltimore, Maryland: Williams and Wilkins, 1984)

4   J Piaget, *The Origins of Intelligence in Children* (New York: Norton, 1963)

5   L S Vygotsky, *Thought and Language* (Cambridge, Massachussetts: MIT Press, 1962, originally published in 1934)

6   A Smith, *Accelerated Learning in Practice* (Stafford: Network Educational Press, 1998)

7   E L Boyer, *Ready to Learn: A Mandate for the Nation* (Princeton, New Jersey 08540: The Carnegie Foundation for the Advancement of Teaching, 1992)

Chapter 3

1   D Barnes, J Britton and H Rosen, *Language, the Learner and the School* (Harmonsworth, Middlesex: Penguin, 1969)

2   M Barr, P D'Arcy and M Healy, *What's going on? Language/Learning Episodes in British and American Classrooms* (Montclair, New Jersey: Boynton Cook, 1982)

3   M Galton and B Simon, *Progress and Performance in the Primary Classroom* (London: Routledge and Kegan Paul, 1980)

4   A D Edwards and D P G Westgate, *Investigating Classroom Talk* (Lewes: Falmer Press, 1987)

5   D Hayes, *Effective Verbal Communication* (London: Hodder and Stoughton, 1998)

6   N Flanders, *Analysing Teaching Behaviour* (Reading, Massachusetts: Addison-Wesley, 1970)

7   R Fox, 'Development and Learning', in C Desforges (Ed), *An Introduction to Teaching* (Oxford: Blackwell, 1995)

8   K R Wagner, 'How Much Do Children Say in A Day?', *Journal of Child Language*, Vol. 12 (1985) pp. 475–87

9   D Crystal, *The Cambridge Encyclopedia of Language* (Cambridge: Cambridge University Press, 1994)

10   R Sage, 'Communication in Learning', in M Hunter-Carsch and M Herrington (Eds), *Dyslexia and Effective Learning* (London: Whurr, 2000)

11   H J Eysenck and S B G Eysenck, *Manual of the Eysenck Personality Questionnaire* (London: Hodder and Stoughton, 1975)

12   R B Cattell, *The Scientific Analysis of Personality* (Harmonsworth, Middlesex: Penguin, 1965)

13   G A Kelly, *A Theory of Personality – the Psychology of Personal Constructs* (New York: Norton, 1955)

14   A Maslow, *Motivation and Personality* (New York: Harper and Row, 1954)

15   C R Rogers, *On Becoming a Person* (Boston: Houghton Mifflin, 1961)

16   A Adler, *The Practice and Theory of Individual Psychology* (New York: Harcourt Brace Jovanovich, 1927)

17   A Freud, *The Ego and the Mechanisms of Defence* (London: Chatto and Windus, 1936)

18   C G Jung (Ed), *Man and his Symbols* (London: Aldus-Jupiter Books, 1964)

19   E H Erikson, *Identity and the Life Cycle* (New York: Norton, 1980)

20   J Luft, *Of Human Interaction* (Palo Alto, California: National Press Books, 1969)

21   J C Pearce, *Evolution's End, Claiming the Potential of our Intelligence* (San Francisco: Harper, 1992)

22   J Biederman, S Fatoane, K Keenan, E Knee and M Twuang, 'Family Genetic and Psychosocial Risk Factors in DSM-III Attention Deficit Disorder', *The Journal of the American Academy of Child and Adolescent Psychiatry* Vol. 29 (1990)

23   A Paivio, 'Mental imagery in associative learning and memory', *Psychological Review* Vol. 76 (1969) pp. 241–63

Chapter 4

1   B Badger, 'Changing a Disruptive School', in *School Effectiveness: Research, Policy and Practice*, D Reynolds and P Cuttance (Eds) (London: Cassell, 1992)

2   R V Exline, 'Visual Interaction: The Glances of Power and Preference', *Nebraska Symposium on Motivation* (Lincoln USA: University of Lincoln Press, 1972) pp. 163–206

3   K Ryan, *Don't Smile 'til Christmas* (Chicago: Chicago Press, 1970)

4   A Mehrabian, *Non-verbal Communication* (New York: Aldine Atherton, 1972)

5   R L Birdwhistell, *Kinesics and Context: Essays on Body-Motion Communication* (Harmondsworth, Middlesex: Penguin, 1973)

6   D Lewis, *The Secret Language of Your Child* (Souvenir Press, 1978)

7   S R ST. J Neill, 'Non-verbal Communication – Implications for Teachers', in B G Martinsson (Ed), *On Communication*, 4 (SIC13) (Linköping, Sweden: University of Linköping, 1987)

8   C Caswell, 'Non-verbal Communication in the Classroom', Proceedings of the Conference: 'Getting the Message', in the *Journal of Human Communication International* Vol 1.1 (1998)

9   A Isen, 'The Influence of Positive Effect on Clinical Problem Solving', *Medical Decision Making* (July–Sept 1991)

10   E C Wragg, *Managing Behaviour*, BBC Video and Book (London: BBC Education, 1994)

11   J Robertson and N Webb, 'Rainbow Shades to Tone it Down', *Times Educational Supplement* (30 June 1995)

12   A Kendon, 'Some Functions of Gaze-Direction in Social Interaction', *Acta Psychologica*, Vol. 26 (1967) pp. 22–47

◆ REFERENCES

13   M Rutter, B Maughan, P Mortimore and J Ouston, *Fifteen Thousand Hours* (London: Open Books, 1979)

14   G Upton and P Cooper, 'A New Perspective on Behaviour Problems in Schools: The Ecosystem Approach', *Maladjustment and Therapeutic Education*, Vol. 8, No. 1 (1990) pp. 3–18

15   B Rogers, *Behaviour Recovery: A Programme for Behaviourally Disturbed Students in Mainstream Schools* (Camberwell, London: ACER, 1994)

16   R M Broden, 'The Effects of Self-Recording on the Classroom Behaviour of Two Eighth Grade Students', *Journal of Applied Behaviour Analysis*, Vol. 4 (1971) pp. 277–85

17   E McNamara and C Heard, 'Self Control Through Self-Recording', *Special Education: Forward Trends*, Vol. 3, No. 2 (1976) pp. 21–30

18   J S Kounin, *Discipline and Group Management in Classrooms* (New York: Holt, Rinehart and Winston, 1970)

19   T Gordon, *Teacher Effectiveness Training* (New York: Wyden, 1974)

20   A W Johnson and F P Johnson, *Joining Together, 2nd Edition* (Engelwood Cliffs, New Jersey: Prentice-Hall, 1982)

21   R Bandler and J Grinder, *The Structure of Magic 1* (Paulo Alto, California: Science and Behaviour Books, 1975)

22   E Susskind, 'The Role of Question Asking in the Elementary Classroom', in F Caplan and S Sarason (Eds), *The Psycho-Educational Clinic* (New Haven: Yale, 1969)

23   E Susskind, 'Encouraging Teachers to Encourage Children's Curiosity', in *Journal of Clinical Child Psychology*, Vol. 8 (1979) pp. 101–6

24   E C Wragg, *Class Management* (London: Routledge, 1993)

25   S Delamont, *Interaction in the Classroom* (London: Methuen, 1976)

26   F S Perls, *Gestalt Therapy Verbatim* (Utah: Moab, Real People Press, 1969)

27   C Turney, *Sydney Microskills* (Sydney: University of Sydney, 1973)

28   R T Pate and N H Bremer, 'Guiding Learning Through Skilful Questioning', *The Elementary School Journal*, Vol. 67 (1967) pp. 417–22

29   E Dunne and S N Bennett, *Talking and Learning in Groups* (London: Macmillan, 1990)

30   D Barnes, J Britton and H Rosen, *Language, the Learner and the School* (Harmonsworth, Middlesex: Penguin, 1969)

31   D Barnes, *From Communication to Curriculum* (Harmonsworth, Middlesex: Penguin, 1976)

32   A D Edwards and D P G Westgate, *Investigating Classroom Talk* (London: Falmer Press, 1987)

33   G Brown and E C Wragg, *Questioning* (London: Routledge, 1993)

34   J Kingman, *Report of the Committee of Inquiry into the Teaching of English Language* (London: HMSO, 1988)

35   G A Nuthall and P J Lawrence, *Thinking in the Classroom* (Wellington, New Zealand: New Zealand Council for Educational Research, 1965)

36   M Blank, *Instructional and Classroom Discourse* (Boston, Massachusetts: The Language Learning Disabilities Institute, Emerson College, 1985)

37   M Blank and A Marquis, *Teaching Discourse* (Tucson, Arizona: Communication Skill Builders, 1987)

38   O Caviglioli and I Harris, *Mapwise – accelerated learning through visible thinking* (Stafford: Network Educational Press, 2000)

39   D P Ausubel, J D Novak and H Hanesian, *Educational Psychology: A Cognitive View* (New York: Rinehart and Winston, 1978)

40   L Miller, 'Problem Solving, Hypothesis Testing and Language Disorders', in G P Wallach and K G Butler (Eds), *Language Learning Disabilities in School-Age Children* (Baltimore, Maryland: Williams and Wilkins, 1984)

41   A Smith, *Accelerated Learning in Practice* (Stafford: Network Educational Press, 1998)

42   R Watson and I Jones, 'The Harlow On-line Learning Initiative', in the proceedings of the conference: 'Communication in the Technological Age', *Journal of Human Communication International*, Vol 3.1 (2000)

43   H Taba, *Teaching Strategies and Cognitive Functioning in Elementary Schools*, USIOE Co-operative Research Project No. 1574 (California: San Francisco State College, 1966)

44   M J Dunkin and B J Biddle, *The Study of Teaching* (New York: Holt, Rinehart and Winston, 1974)

45   B S Bloom, *Taxonomy of Educational Objectives: Cognitive Domain* (New York: David McKay, 1956)

46   N L Gage, *Explorations of the Teacher's Effectiveness in Explaining* (Stanford USA:Stanford University, 1968)

Chapter 5

1   W Thourlby, *You are What you Wear* (New York: American Library, 1978)

2   J H Fortenberry, J Maclean, P Morris and O'Connell, 'Mode of Dress as a Perceptual Cue to Deference', *Journal of Social Psychology*, Vol. 104 (1978) pp. 131–39

3   P Ekman, E R Sorenson and W V Friesen, 'Pan Cultural Elements in the Facial Displays of Emotion', *Science*, Vol. 164 (1969) pp. 86–8

4   I Vine, 'Communication by Facial-Visual Signals', in J H Crook (Ed), *Social Behaviour in Animals and Man* (New York and London: Academic Press, 1971)

5   P Ekman and W V Friesen, 'Hand movements', *Journal of Communication*, Vol. 22 (1972) pp. 353–74

6   S Weitz, *Non-verbal Behaviour* (London: Academic Press, 1979)

7   N M Henley, *Body Politics* (Englewood Cliffs, New York: Prentice-Hall, 1977)

8   A Mehrabian, 'Communication Without Words', *Psychology Today* (Dec 1969)

9   K Wheldell, K Bevan and K Shortall, 'A Touch of Reinforcement: The Effects of Contingent Teacher Touch on the Classroom Behaviour of Young Children', *Educational Review*, Vol. 38, No. 3 (1986) pp. 207–16

10   A Mehrabian, *Silent Messages* (Belmont, California: Wadsworth, 1971)

11   J V Fenton, *Choice of Habit* (New York: Macdonald and Evans, 1973)

12   D Crystal, *Linguistics* (Harmondsworth, Middlesex: Penguin, 1971)

13   R Sage, *A Question of Language Disorder* (Sheffield: MRC Trent Research Report, 1986)

14   E Hall and C Hall, *Human Relations in Education* (London: Routledge, 1988)

15   E Hall and A Kirkland, 'Drawings of Trees and the Expression of Feelings in Early Adolescence', *British Journal of Guidance and Counselling*, Vol. 7.1 (1984)

16   J O Stevens, *Awareness: Exploring, Experimenting and Experiencing* (Lafayette, California: Real People Press, 1971)

17   C Hannaford, Smart Moves, *Why Learning Is Not All in Your Head* (Arlington, Virginia: Great Ocean Publishers, 1995)

18   P E Dennison and G E Dennison, *Brain Gym, Teachers Edition: Revised* (Ventura, California: Educ-Kinesthetics, Inc., 1994)

19   M Argyle, 'New Developments in The Analysis Of Social Skills', in L H Strickland (Ed), *Non-verbal Behaviour* (London: Academic Press, 1979)

Chapter 6

1   A A Tomatis, *Education and Dyslexia* (Fribourg, Switzerland: Association Internationale D'Audio-Psycho-Phonilogie, 1978)

2   A Stiller and R Wennekes, *Sensory Stimulation Important to Developmental Processes* (1992)

3   W J H Nauta and M Feirtag, 'The Organization of the Brain', in *The Brain, A Scientific American Book* (San Francisco: W H Freeman, 1979)

4   C F Stevens, 'The Neuron', *Scientific American* (Sept 1979)

5   D Chopra, *Quantum Healing, Exploring the Frontiers of Mind/Body Medicine* (New York: Bantam Books, 1989)

6   M Merzenich, 'Brain Plasticity Origins of Human Abilities and Disabilities', Sixth Symposium, Decade of the Brain Series, NIMH and the Library of Congress, Washington DC (7 Feb 1995)

7   D Kolb, *Experiential Learning, Experience as the Source of Learning and Development* (Englewood, New Jersey: Prentice-Hall, 1984)

8   A Thomas and S Chess, *Temperament and Development* (New York: Brunner/Mazel, 1977)

9   D Gelernter, *The Muse in the Machine, Computerizing the Poetry of Human Thought* (New York: Free Press, 1994)

10 A Harvey, *The Numbered Brain* (Louisville: Center for Music and Medicine, University of Louisville School of Medicine, 1985)

11 R J Haier, 'Images of Intellect, Brain Scans May Colorize Intelligence', *Science News*, Vol. 146 (8 October 1994) pp. 236–37

12 P E Dennison, *Whole Brain Learning for the Whole Person* (Ventura, California: Edu-Kinesthetics, Inc, 1995?)

13 C Hannaford, *Smart Moves, Why Learning Is Not All in Your Head* (Arlington, Virginia: Great Ocean Publishers, 1995)

14 H Gardner, *Frames of Mind: The Theory of Multiple Intelligences* (New York: Basic Books, 1983)

15 A Mattson, '40 Hertz EEG Activity in Learning Disabled and Normal Children', presentation at the International Neuropsychological Society, Vancouver, British Columbia (Feb 1989)

16 D Diorio, V Viau and M J Meaney, 'The Role of the Medial Prefrontal Cortex in the Regulation of Hypothalmic-Pituitary-Adrenal Responses to Stress', *Journal of Neuroscience*, Vol. 13.9 (1993) pp. 3839–47

17 D Shaffer, 'Attention Deficit Hyperactive Disorder in Adults', *American Journal of Psychiatry* (May 1994) pp. 633–8

18 M E Seligman, *Helplessness: On Depression, Development and Death* (San Francisco: W H Freeman, 1975)

19 H T Epstein, 'Growth Spurts During Brain Development: Implications for Educational Policy and Practice', in J Chall and A F Mirsky (Eds), *Education and the Brain* (Chicago: University of Chicago Press, 1979)

20 E L Boyer, *Ready to Learn: A Mandate for the Nation* (Princeton, New Jersey 08540: The Carnegie Foundation for the Advancement of Teaching, 1992)

21 A R Luria, *The Mind of a Menemonist* (New York: Basic Books, 1968)

22 J Healy, *Endangered Minds, Why Children Don't Think and What We Can Do About It* (New York: Simon and Schuster, 1990)

23 H N Levinson, 'The Cerebellar–Vestibular Basis of Learning Disabilities in Children, Adolescents and Adults: Hypothesis and Study', *Perceptual Motor Skills*, Vol. 67 (1988) pp. 983–1006

24 R Sage, *Teaching School Success Skills* (Leicester: University of Leicester, 2000)

25 D Wood, *How Children Think and Learn, 2nd Edition* (Oxford: Blackwell, 1999)

26 M Hunter-Carsch, *Report on the Leicester Summer Literacy Scheme* (Leicester: University of Leicester, 1999)

27 R Sage, *Communication in the Classroom* (Leicester: PhD, University of Leicester, 1992)

28 K Perera, *Children's Writing and Reading: Analysing Classroom Language* (London: Blackwell in asociation with André Deutsch, 1984)

225

29   K M Hart, *Children's Understanding of Mathematics*, 11–16 (London: John Murray, 1981)

30   L S Vygotsky, *Thought and Language* (Cambridge, Massachussetts: MIT Press, 1962 originally published in 1934)

31   L Frazier and K Rayner, 'Making and Correcting Errors During Sentence Comprehension', *Cognitive Psychology*, Vol. 14 (1982) pp. 178–210

32   G Underwood and V Batt, *Reading and Understanding* (Oxford: Blackwell, 1996)

33   A Walker, 'Applied Sociology of Language: Vernacular Languages and Education', in P Trudgill (Ed), *Applied Sociolinguistics* (London: Academic Press, 1984)

34   S Romaine, *The Language of Children and Adolescents: the Acquisition of Communicative Competence* (London: Blackwell, 1984)

35   A Karmiloff-Smith, *A Functional Approach to Child Language: A Study of Determiners and Reference* (Cambridge: Cambridge University Press, 1979)

36   Bullock Report, *A Language for Life* (London: Department of Education and Science/HMSO, 1975)

37   P Bryant, T Nunes and M Bindman, 'Children's Understanding of the Connection Between Grammar and Spelling', in B Blachman (Ed), *Linguistic Underpinnings of Language* (Hillsdale, New Jersey: Lawrence Erlbaum, 1999)

38   J Oakhill, N Yuill and A Parkin, 'On the Nature of the Difference Between Skilled and Less-Skilled Comprehenders', *Journal of Research in Reading*, Vol. 9 (1986) pp. 80–91

39   M Clark, Young Fluent Readers (London: Heinemann, 1976)

40   R Sage, *A Question of Language Disorder* (Sheffield: MRC Trent Research Report, 1968)

41   A S Palinscsar and A L Brown, *Reciprocal Teaching of Comprehension Fostering and Monitoring Activities: Cognition and Instruction* (Hillsdale, New Jersey: Lawrence Erlbaum, 1984)

42   A L Brown and J C Campione, 'Communities of Learning and Thinking, Or a Context By Any Other Name', in D Kuhn (Ed), *Developmental Perspectives on Teaching and Learning Thinking Skills*, in *Contributions to Human Development* Vol. 21 (Karger, Basle: 1990)

43   C F Feldman, 'The New Theory of Mind', *Human Development*, Vol. 35 (1992) pp. 107–17

44   P T Rankin 'The Importance of Listening Ability', *English Journal*, Vol. 2 (1981) pp. 623–30

45   E K Werner, *A Study in Communication Time*, Masters Thesis (unpub) (Maryland: College Park, University of Maryland, 1975)

46   Arbor A, *Americans' Use of Time Project* (Inter-University Consortium for Political Research, 1993)

47   N Bennett, C Desforges, A Cockburn and B Wilkinson, *The Quality of Pupil Learning Experiences* (London: Lawrence Erlbaum, 1984)

48   M Galton and J Williamson, *Group Work in the Classroom* (London: Routledge, 1992)

49   L Harvey, 'Communication Skills – He Could Do Better! Information from the Quality in Higher Education survey of employers', *QHE Newsletter* (November 1993)

Chapter 7

1   E L Boyer, *Ready to Learn: A Mandate for the Nation* (Princeton, New Jersey 08540: The Carnegie Foundation for the Advancement of Teaching, 1992)

2   P Piaget, *Six Psychological Studies* (London: London University Press, 1967)

3   J S Bruner, *Toward a Theory of Instruction* (New York: Norton, 1966)

4   W P Robinson, 'Language Development in Young Children', in D Fontana (Ed), *Psychology for Teachers* (London: British Psychological Society and Macmillan, 1981)

5   G Brown, A Anderson, R Shillcock and G Yule, *Teaching Talk: Strategies for Production and Assessment* (Cambridge: Cambridge University Press, 1984)

6   R Wardhaugh, *How Conversation Works* (Oxford and New York: Blackwell in association with André Deutsch, 1985)

7   C G Wells, 'The Centrality of Talk in Education', in K Norman (Ed), *Thinking Voices* (London: Hodder and Stoughton, 1992)

8   M B Rowe, 'Wait Time and Rewards as Instructional Variables, Their Influence on Language, Logic and Fate Control, I: Wait Time', *Journal of Research in Science Teaching*, Vol. 11 (1974) pp. 81–94

9   J N Swift and C T Gooding, 'Interactive Wait Time, Feedback and Questioning Instruction in Middle School Science Teaching', *Journal of Research in Science Teaching*, Vol. 20 (1983) pp. 721–30

10   R Sage, *Teaching School Success Skills* (Leicester: University of Leicester, 2000)

11   H Klein, A Constable, N Goulandris, J Stackhouse and C Tarlee, *The Clinical Evaluation of Language Fundamentals – Revised*, The Psychological Corporation (London and New York: Harcourt Brace and Company, 1994)

12   N Bell, *Visualizing and Verbalizing* (Paso Robles, California: Academy of Reading Publications, 1991)

13   J M Clark and A Paivio, 'Dual Coding Theory and Education', *Educational Psychology Review* (September 1991)

14   G H Wheatley and R H Frankland, *Hemispheric Specialization and Cognitive Development* (USA: Purdue University, 1976)

15   G Brigman, D Lane and D Switzer, 'Teaching children success skills', *The Journal of Educational Research*, Vol. 92, No. 6 (1999) pp. 323–329.

16   M C Wang, G D Haertel and H J Walberg, 'What Helps Students Learn?', *Educational Leadership*, Vol. 51, No. 4 (1994) pp. 74–9

17   R Sage, *Communication in the Classroom*, PhD (Leicester: University of Leicester, 1992)

18   R Sage and P Shaw, *Collaborative Teaching and Learning* (London: CSSD, 1992)

19   R Sage and J Whittingham, *Using the COGS in Senior Schools* (Warwick: Warwickshire AHA/LEA, 1997)

20   D Nelson and K Burchell, *Evaluation of the Communication Opportunity Group Scheme* (Warwick: South Warwickshire Combined Health Trust, 1998) pp. 1–31

21   C Black and W Butzkamm, 'Sprachbezogene und Mitteilungsbezogene Kommunikation im Englishunterricht', *Praxis des Neusprachlichen Unterrichts*. Vol. 24, No. 2. (1977) pp. 115–24

22   J Newsom, *Half Our Future*, Report for the Central Advisory Council for Education (England) on Average or Less Than Average Ability Children in Secondary Schools (London: HMSO, 1963)

Also available from Network Educational Press

The Literacy Collection

Class talk is the second book in NEP's Literacy Collection.

Helping With Reading by Anne Butterworth and Angela White
ISBN 1-85539-044-2

◆ Includes sections on 'Hearing Children Read', Word Recognition' and 'Phonics'.

◆ Provides precisely focused, easily implemented follow-up activities for pupils who need extra reinforcement of basic reading skills.

◆ Provides clear, practical and easily implemented activities that directly relate to the National Curriculum and 'Literacy Hour' group work. Ideas and activities can also be incorporated into Individual Education Plans.

◆ Aims to address current concerns about reading standards and to provide support for classroom assistants and parents helping with the teaching of reading.

Accelerated Learning Series
General Editor: **Alistair Smith**

Accelerated Learning in Practice by Alistair Smith
ISBN 1-85539-048-5

◆ The author's second book, which takes Nobel Prize winning brain research into the classroom.

◆ Structured to help readers access and retain the information necessary to begin to accelerate their own learning and that of the students they teach.

◆ Contains over 100 learning tools, case studies from 36 schools and an up-to-the-minute section

◆ Includes nine principles of learning based on brain research and the author's seven-stage Accelerated Learning Cycle.

The ALPS Approach: Accelerated Learning in Primary Schools
by Alistair Smith and Nicola Call
ISBN 1-85539-056-6

◆ Shows how research on how we learn, collected by Alistair Smith, can be used to great effect in the primary classroom.

◆ Provides practical and accessible examples of strategies used by highly experienced primary teacher Nicola Call, at a school where the SATs results shot up as a consequence.

◆ Professional, practical and exhilarating resource that gives readers the opportunity to develop the ALPS approach for themselves and for the children in their care.

◆ The ALPS approach includes: Exceeding expectation, 'Can-do' learning, Positive performance, Target-setting that works, Using review for recall, Preparing for tests … and much more.

MapWise by Oliver Caviglioli and Ian Harris
ISBN 1-85539-059-0
- ◆ Provides informed access to the most powerful accelerated learning technique around – Model Mapping.
- ◆ Shows how mapping can be used to address National Curriculum thinking skills requirements for students of any preferred learning style by infusing thinking into subject teaching.
- ◆ Describes how mapping can be used to measure and develop intelligence.
- ◆ Explains how mapping supports teacher explanation and student understanding.
- ◆ Demonstrates how mapping makes planning, teaching and reviewing easier and more effective.
- ◆ Written and illustrated to be lively and engaging, practical and supportive.

School Effectiveness Series

Series Editor: **Professor Tim Brighouse**

The School Effectiveness Series focuses on practical and useful ideas for individual schools and teachers. The series addresses the issues of whole school improvement along with new knowledge about teaching and learning, and offers straightforward solutions that teachers can use to make life more rewarding for themselves and those they teach.

Book 1: Accelerated Learning in the Classroom by Alistair Smith
ISBN 1-85539-034-5
- ◆ The first book in the UK to apply new knowledge about the brain to classroom practice.
- ◆ Contains practical methods so teachers can apply accelerated learning theories to their own classrooms.
- ◆ Aims to increase the pace of learning and deepen understanding.
- ◆ Includes advice on how to create the ideal environment for learning and how to help learners fulfil their potential.
- ◆ Offers practical solutions on improving performance, motivation and understanding.

Book 2: Effective Learning Activities by Chris Dickinson
ISBN 1-85539-035-3
- ◆ An essential teaching guide, which focuses on practical activities to improve learning.
- ◆ Aims to improve results through effective learning, which will raise achievement, deepen understanding, promote self-esteem and improve motivation.
- ◆ Includes activities that are designed to promote differentiation and understanding.
- ◆ Includes activities suitable for GCSE, National Curriculum, Highers, GSVQ and GNVQ.

Book 3: Effective Heads of Department by Phil Jones and Nick Sparks
ISBN 1-85539-036-1
- ◆ Contains a range of practical systems and approaches; each of the eight sections ends with a 'checklist for action'.
- ◆ Designed to develop practice in line with OFSTED expectations and DfEE thinking by monitoring and improving quality.
- ◆ Addresses issues such as managing resources, leadership, learning, departmental planning and making assessment valuable.
- ◆ Includes useful information for senior managers in schools who are looking to enhance the effectiveness of their Heads of Department.

Book 4: Lessons are for Learning by Mike Hughes

ISBN 1-85539-038-8

◆ Brings together the theory of learning with the realities of the classroom environment.

◆ Encourages teachers to reflect on their own classroom practice and challenges them to think about why they teach in the way they do.

◆ Offers practical suggestions for activities that bridge the gap between recent developments in the theory of learning and the constraints in classroom teaching.

◆ Ideal for stimulating thought and generating discussion.

Book 5: Effective Learning in Science by Paul Denley and Keith Bishop

ISBN 1-85539-039-6

◆ Encourages discussion about the aims and purposes in teaching science and the role of subject knowledge in effective teaching.

◆ Tackles issues such as planning for effective learning, the use of resources and other relevant management issues.

◆ Offers help in the development of a departmental plan to revise schemes of work, resources, classroom strategies, in order to make learning and teaching more effective.

◆ Recommended for any science department aiming to increase performance and improve results.

Book 6: Raising Boys' Achievement by Jon Pickering

ISBN 1-85539-040-X

◆ Addresses the causes of boys' under-achievement and offers possible solutions.

◆ Focuses the search for causes and solutions on teachers working in the classroom.

◆ Looks at examples of good practice in schools to help guide the planning and implementation of strategies to raise achievement.

◆ Offers practical, 'real' solutions, along with tried-and-tested training suggestions.

◆ Recommended as a basis for INSET or as a guide to practical activities for classroom teachers.

Book 7: Effective Provision for Able and Talented Children by Barry Teare

ISBN 1-85539-041-8

◆ Describes methods of identifying the able and talented.

◆ Addresses concerns about achievement and appropriate strategies to raise achievement.

◆ Discusses the role of the classroom teacher in provision for the able and talented, and of monitoring and evaluation techniques.

◆ Outlines the theory, and procedures for turning theory into practice.

◆ Suggests practical enrichment activities and appropriate resources.

Book 8: Effective Careers Education and Guidance by Andrew Edwards and Anthony Barnes

ISBN 1-85539-045-0

◆ Discusses the strategic planning of the careers programme as part of the wider curriculum.

◆ Takes practical consideration of the management careers education and guidance.

◆ Provides practical activities for reflection and personal learning, and case studies where such activities have been used.

◆ Discusses aspects of guidance and counselling involved in helping students to understand their own capabilities and form career plans.

◆ Suggests strategies for reviewing and developing existing practice.

Book 9: Best behaviour by Peter Relf, Rod Hirst, Jan Richardson and Georgina Youdell
ISBN 1-85539-046-9
- ◆ Provides support for teachers and managers who seek starting points for effective behaviour management.
- ◆ Focuses on practical and useful ideas for individual schools and teachers.

Best behaviour FIRST AID (pack of 5 booklets) by Peter Relf, Rod Hirst, Jan Richardson and Georgina Youdell
ISBN 1-85539-047-7
- ◆ Provides strategies to cope with aggression, defiance and disturbance
- ◆ Suggests straightforward action points for self-esteem.

Book 10: The Effective School Governor *(including audio tape)* by David Marriott
ISBN 1-85539-042-6
- ◆ Straightforward guidance on how to fulfil a governor's role and responsibilities.
- ◆ Develops your personal effectiveness as an individual governor.
- ◆ Practical support on how to be an effective member of the governing team.
- ◆ Audio tape for use in car or at home.

Book 11: Improving Personal Effectiveness for Managers in Schools by James Johnson
ISBN 1-85539-049-3
- ◆ An invaluable resource for new and experienced teachers, in both primary and secondary schools.
- ◆ Contains practical strategies for improving leadership and management skills.
- ◆ Focuses on self-management skills, managing difficult situations, working under pressure, developing confidence, creating a team ethos and communicating effectively.

Book 12: Making Pupil Data Powerful by Maggie Pringle and Tony Cobb
ISBN 1-85539-052-3
- ◆ Shows teachers in primary, middle and secondary schools how to interpret pupils' performance data and how to use it to enhance teaching and learning.
- ◆ Provides practical advice on analysing performance and learning behaviours, measuring progress, predicting future attainment, setting targets and ensuring continuity and progression.
- ◆ Explains how to interpret national initiatives on data-analysis, benchmarking and target-setting, and to ensure that these have value in the classroom.

Book 13: Closing the Learning Gap by Mike Hughes
ISBN 1-85539-051-5
- ◆ Helps teachers, departments and schools to close the Learning Gap between what we know about effective learning and what actually goes on in the classroom.
- ◆ Encourages teachers to reflect on the ways in which they teach, and to identify and implement strategies for improving their practice.
- ◆ Helps teachers to apply recent research findings about the brain and learning.
- ◆ Full of practical advice and real, tested strategies for improvement.
- ◆ Written by a teacher, for teachers, to stimulate thought and interest 'at a glance'.

Book 14: Getting Started by Henry Leibling
ISBN 1-85539-054-X
- Provides invaluable advice for Newly Qualified Teachers (NQTs) during the three-term induction period that comprises their first year of teaching.
- Advice includes strategies on how to get to know the school and the new pupils, how to work with induction tutors, and when to ask for help.

Book 15: Leading the Learning School by Colin Weatherley
ISBN 1-85539-070-1
- Shows how effective leadership of true 'learning schools' involves applying the principles of learning to all levels of educational management and development planning.
- Describes thirteen key principles of learning, derived from up-to-the-minute research on how our brains learn.
- Explains how these principles can be used improve teachers' professional knowledge and skills, make the learning environment more supportive and improve the design of learning activities.
- Describes how the American Critical Skills Programme has incorporated these key principles into a comprehensive, practical and outstandingly effective teaching programme.

Education Personnel Management Series

These new Education Personnel management handbooks will help headteachers, senior managers and governors to manage a broad range of personnel issues.

The Well Teacher – management strategies for beating stress, promoting staff health and reducing absence by Maureen Cooper
ISBN 1-85539-058-2
- Provides straightforward, practical advice on how to deal strategically with staff absenteeism, which can be so expensive in terms of sick pay and supply cover, through proactively promoting staff health.
- Includes suggestions for reducing stress levels in schools.
- Outlines ways in which to deal with individual cases of staff absence.

Managing Challenging People – dealing with staff conduct by Bev Curtis and Maureen Cooper
ISBN 1-85539-057-4
- Deals with managing staff whose conduct gives cause for concern.
- Summarises the employment relationship in schools, as well as those areas of education and employment law relevant to staff discipline.
- Looks at the differences between conduct and capability, and between misconduct and gross misconduct.
- Describes disciplinary and dismissal procedures relating to teaching and non-teaching staff, including headteachers.
- Describes case studies and model procedures, and provides pro-forma letters to help schools with these difficult issues.

Managing Poor Performance – handling staff capability issues by Bev Curtis and Maureen Cooper
ISBN 1-85539-062-0

- ◆ Explains clearly why capability is important in providing an effective and high quality education for pupils.
- ◆ Gives advice on how to identify staff with poor performance, and how to help them improve.
- ◆ Outlines the legal position and the role of governors in dealing with the difficult issues surrounding poor performance.
- ◆ Details the various stages of formal capability procedures and dismissal hearings.
- ◆ Describes case studies and model procedures, and provides pro-forma letters.

Managing Allegations Against Staff – personnel and child protection issues in schools
by Maureen Cooper
ISBN 1-85539-069-8

- ◆ Provides invaluable advice to headteachers, senior managers and personnel staff on how to deal with the difficult issues arising from accusations made against school employees.
- ◆ Shows what schools can do to protect students, while safeguarding employees from the potentially devastating consequences of false allegations.
- ◆ Describes real-life case studies.
- ◆ Provides a clear outline of the legal background plus a moral code of conduct for staff.

Vision of Education Series

The Unfinished Revolution by John Abbott and Terry Ryan
ISBN 1-85539-064-7

- ◆ Draws on evidence from the past to show how shifting attitudes in society and politics have shaped Western education systems.
- ◆ Argues that what is now needed is a completely fresh approach, designed around evidence about how children actually learn.
- ◆ Describes a vision of an education system based on current research into how our brains work, and designed to encourage the autonomous and inventive thinkers and learners that the 21st century demands.
- ◆ Essential reading for anyone involved in education and policy making.

Other Titles from NEP

Effective Resources for Able and Talented Children by Barry Teare
ISBN 1-85539-050-7

- ◆ A practical sequel to Barry Teare's Effective Provision for Able and Talented Children (see above), which can nevertheless be used entirely independently.
- ◆ Contains a wealth of photocopiable resources for able and talented pupils in both the primary and secondary sectors.
- ◆ Provides activities designed to inspire, motivate, challenge and stretch able children, encouraging them to enjoy their true potential.
- ◆ Resources are organised into National Curriculum areas, such as Literacy, Science and Humanities, each preceded by a commentary outlining key principles and giving general guidance for teachers.

Imagine That... by Stephen Bowkett

ISBN 1-85539-043-4

- ◆ Hands-on, user-friendly manual for stimulating creative thinking, talking and writing in the classroom.
- ◆ Provides over 100 practical and immediately useable classroom activities and games that can be used in isolation, or in combination, to help meet the requirements and standards of the National Curriculum.
- ◆ Explores the nature of creative thinking and how this can be effectively driven through an ethos of positive encouragement, mutual support and celebration of success and achievement.
- ◆ Empowers children to learn how to learn.

Self-Intelligence by Stephen Bowkett

ISBN 1-85539-055-8

- ◆ Helps explore and develop emotional resourcefulness in teachers and their pupils.
- ◆ Aims to help teachers and pupils develop the high-esteem that underpins success in education.

◆ Index

concentration 32, 44–5
cones (eyes) 127
construct theory 40
contextual learning 22, 24
contracts, behaviour 57
conversation
  at home 132–3, 142
    skills 32–4, 125, 135–6
  role play 33
  between students 23, 26–7, 29, 135, 138–9
    practical tasks 31
  with teachers 12–13, 25–26, 28, 29–30, 142
cooking lesson, example 12–18
corpus callosum (brain) 108, 118
cortex 111, 123, 134
cortisol 117
counselling 61
'crackles' (sociable) 39
cross-lateral 114
Crystal, D: voice intonation 91
curriculum requirements 36, 118–19

Delamont, S: questions 64
dendrites (nerves) 104
Denmark, literacy 118–19
Dennison, P E: dominance profiles 114
dialogues 36
Diorio, D: hormones and learning 117
disclosure 42
discussion groups 23, 37
dominance profiles 114–22
Donne, John: quotation on eye contact 84
drama, learning model 12
dress 81–82
Dunne, E: questions 65
Dyer, M: emotional response 20

ears, in babies 104, 124
Edwards, A D: teacher's monologues 36
Einstein, Albert
  as global thinker 116
Ekman, P: hand gestures 84
Emerson, Ralph Waldo
  quotation on eyes 81
  quotation on power 159
emotional response
  children 110
  expression of 60, 62, 118
  towards learning 35–6, 38, 41–2, 47
endorphins 52
epilepsy, and learning 105
Epstein, H T: reasoning skills 120
Erikson, E H: personality disturbance 40
Eustachian tubes (ears) 124
events
  comparisons 20
  links 32
exercises, learning aid 98–100
Exline, R V: control orientation 51
experiential learning see kinaesthetic learning
explanations 72
extroverts 40
  dress sense 81
eye contact 50–51, 78
  quotation on 81, 84
eyes
  reading skills 127
  tracking 121
Eysenck, H J: personality classification 40

face (interpersonal behaviour) 25, 28, 29
facial expressions 134
failure, quotation 25
feelings see emotional response
foetus, sound responses 104
Fortenberry, J H: power dressing 82
fovea centralis (eyes) 127, 136
Frazier, L: punctuation 126
Freud, S: personality disturbance 40–41
Friesen, W V: hand gestures 84
frontal lobe (brain) 108, 109, 110, 112, 123

Gage, Nate: explaining 77
Galton, M
  teacher's monologues 36
  conversation 135
games 156
  clarity 198–200
  conduct 206–8
  contact 196–8
  content 200–203
  convention 203–6
  creative writing 209–11
ganglia (brain) 110, 134
Gelernter, D: emotions 110
gender 15
general event memory 20–21
gestalt imagery 144–5
global hemisphere (brain) 113, 116
glucose, in the brain 111
goals
  actions 17
  learning process 11, 23
  time management 16
Grice, P: communication principles 25
Grinder, J: limitations 62
groups
  communication exercises 153–7
  discussions 23, 37
  games 156
  mixed ability 21, 30–31
  roles within 15
  size and participation 29, 154
  space 15, 88
guilt 40
gustatory area (brain) 112

hand gestures 84, 86
'hands on' experience 31
Hannaford, C
  dominance profiles survey 116, 122
  energising exercises 99
  intelligences 120–21
  stress 117
Hall, E: visualisation techniques 98
Hayes, D: teacher's monologues 36
hemispheres (brain) 108, 112–13
Henley, N M: body movements 86
hierarchy of needs 40
hippocampus 110
holistic approaches 144, 153
homo-lateral 114
hormones, and learning 117
humour 52
Hunter-Carsch, M: literacy summer schools 125
hypothalamus 110

CLASS TALK — successful learning through effective communication

sight 112, 121
  exercises 128
sign language 86
Simon, B: teacher's monologues 36
smells 104
smiling 51–2, 78
Smith, A: learning preferences 31, 73
'snaps' (high achievers) 39
socialisation 138–9
somesthetic area (brain) 112
sounds
  babies 104, 123
  brain 112
  children 213
  consonants 181–3
spatial awareness 129
speech
  calf muscles 117
  intonation 91
    exercises 92–6
Sperry, Roger: quotation on the brain 103
stage (classroom scenario) 15
status 15, 86
Stevens, J O: imagery 98
Stiller, A: smells 104
stories 133
storytelling 43
Strachey, Lytton: quotation on language 49
stress, and learning 117
students (see also behavioural problems; learning
  difficulties)
  communication with each other 139, 140–41
  communication with teachers 11, 78, 141
  confidence 78
  perception of teacher 37–8, 41
  support for 58–60
  surveys 11, 125
styles
  verbal messages 42
support 58–60
Susskind, E: questions 64
synapses (brain) 105

Taba, H: thinking levels 75
tactile learning 31
talk circles 33, 34
talking see verbal expression
tasks
  holistic approach 16
teachers
  annoyance 20
  breathing exercises 93–4
  consistency 56
  left brain dominant 121
  personal qualities 38
  position in classroom 15–16
  positive contact with students 50–53, 78
  posture exercises 93–4
  role in the classroom 17–18, 49
    controlling 50–64, 79
    explaining 72–7, 79, 141
    questioning 64–71, 79, 141
  speech therapy 92–6
  style 42–3
  support for 58–60
television 43–5, 123, 132, 134, 135
temporal lobe (brain) 112
tests
  COGS 185–8

thalamus (brain) 110
thematic response unit 20
thinking skills 120
Thomas, A: early learning 109
Thorlby, W: personal appearance 82
time
  allocation for tasks 16
Tomatis, A A: babies and sounds 104
tools see props
top-down processes 33, 73
touch 104
traffic lights, use in classroom 55
trust 26, 28, 29, 77
truth 26, 28, 29
Turney, C: questions 64
type and trait theories 40

understanding levels 76, 79, 144–5
Underwood, G: reading skills 127
utensils see props

verbal dynamics 91–2
verbal expression 125–7, 134–6 (see also
  language; communication; conversation)
  articulation 140
  chatting 139
  exercises 140
verbal learning 31
vestibulo (brain) 112
visual association 112
visual learning 31, 45, 47, 109–10, 120–21
visualisation 96–8, 107
vocabulary 36, 42–3
voice
  box 123
  tone 91–6, 126–7
Vygotsky, L S
  abstract thinking 27
  literacy 126

Wagner, K R: children's vocabulary 36
water, benefits of drinking 100
Watson, R: information technology 73
Watson, Thomas: quotation 25
weasel words 180
Webb, N: noise levels 55
Wennekes, R: smells 104
Wernicke's area (brain) 112, 124
Westby, C: narrative 27
Westgate, D P G: teacher's monologues 36
Wheldell, K: touch 88
Williamson, J: conversation 135
withdrawal strategies 25, 28, 29, 31–2
Wood, D: literacy 125, 126, 130
working parents 132
World Laughter Day 52
Wragg, E C: questions 64, 68
writing skills 24, 27, 118–19
  children 125, 130–1
  exercises 128

young children see infants
Yuill, N: comprehension 131